CHILD TRAINING AND PERSONALITY

Child Training and Personality:

A CROSS-CULTURAL STUDY

by John W. M. Whiting

GRADUATE SCHOOL OF EDUCATION, HARVARD UNIVERSITY

and Irvin L. Child

DEPARTMENT OF PSYCHOLOGY, YALE UNIVERSITY

New Haven and London: YALE UNIVERSITY PRESS

ACKNOWLEDGMENTS

THE STUDY to be reported here has its intellectual origins in several major currents of social science. That we have been greatly influenced by modern behavior theory, by psychoanalysis, and by cultural anthropology will be immediately apparent to all readers of the book. The pervasive conceptual influence of the functional approach to cultural anthropology and of the comparative approach to sociology may be less evident, since these two currents of thought are reflected in the basic orientation rather than in the specific content of the book. We wish, therefore, to record here our indebtedness to them, and to Malinowski and Sumner as their outstanding creators and exponents.

The opportunity to do this study was, in a more immediate sense, provided by the Institute of Human Relations at Yale University. Both of us were associated with the Institute, first as graduate students and later as staff members. The Institute provided the financial support for this research; more crucial, however, is the fact that the Institute provided an intellectual setting in which such research, fusing ideas and techniques from several disciplines, could be conceived and carried out. For this intellectual setting we are greatly indebted to the members of the Institute staff and to its director, Mark A. May.

We are particularly indebted to those members of the Institute staff who were our teachers in the various disciplines. In learning and behavior theory, Clark L. Hull had a profound influence on the thinking of both of us. The younger psychologists who have most strongly influenced us are Leonard W. Doob, Neal E. Miller, O. Hobart Mowrer, and Robert R. Sears. John Dollard and Earl Zinn, our analysts, were important to us as interpreters of psychoanalytic theory. We learned from them much about the dynamics of personality development that we could not have learned from books. In anthropology and sociology we owe a great debt to G. P. Murdock, not only as our teacher but also for his role in developing the cross-cultural approach which is used in this study.

Of those who contributed more directly to this particular study, we owe a special debt to C. S. Ford. The basic concepts presented in Chapter 2 and used later in the book were in considerable part worked out in collaboration with him, though he should not be held responsible for the form in which they are presented here. Ruth Barcan Marcus was also an important contributor and critic of concepts in the initial planning of the research.

For their patience and fortitude in reading all the ethnographic material and making many thousands of judgments on it we are especially grateful to Dr. Marcus and to our other judges, Helen Glenn, Irma Z. Janoff, Herbert C. Kelman, and Claudine G. Wirths. In making use of judges to analyze data, we have brought together certain methodological skills developed in psychology and the long history of ethnographic field work which has provided the basic data for our study. These two methodological traditions were quite as essential to our work as were the theoretical traditions which we have already mentioned.

For permission to quote lengthy passages we are indebted to the following copyright holders: Michael Joseph, Ltd., McGraw-Hill Book Company, Inc., Margaret Mead through William Morrow & Company, Inc., W. W. Norton & Company, Inc., and Oxford University Press, Inc. Specific acknowledgment is made in the text in combination with the reference list following the last chapter, both for these passages and for various briefer passages. We are also greatly indebted to the various university presses which do not require specific permission for such quotations in scholarly publications.

CONTENTS

CHAPTER 1. *Introduction*

EVER SINCE Margaret Mead set out for Samoa to determine whether adolescent conflicts are inevitable, there has been an increasing interest in the relation between culture and personality. Her early field work was paralleled by the stimulating theoretical concern of Sapir with this problem. From the influence of these pioneers has grown a variety of scientific work, most of which has been centered on one or another of three general problems about culture and personality.

The first of these problems is that of the effect of culture upon personality. The culture of a group sets many of the most important conditions which influence what the individual member will learn and how he will learn it. At first anthropologists concentrated on various specific kinds of behavior which individuals learn from the culture of their group. Different groups of people have different technologies, different languages, different religions, as a result of their training in distinct cultures. In the late twenties and early thirties certain anthropologists became interested in the parallel influence of culture upon the general behavior tendencies of a person, which we call personality. The first problem, then, has to do with the extent to which personality characteristics differ from one society to another, the extent of uniformity in personality within each society, and the processes by which this difference in personality among members of different societies is brought about by the differences in their cultural traditions.

An example of work concerned with this first problem is provided by Margaret Mead's pioneer study in Samoa (1928). She began with the question, Are the storm and stress which characterize adolescent personality in our society a universal product of the biological changes which occur during and after puberty? By finding in Samoa a society in which adolescents have personalities no more troubled than in earlier or later periods of life, she was able to give a negative answer to her initial question. Adolescent disturbance, then, is a personality characteristic which does vary markedly from one society to another. Mead then presented evidence of contrasts between Samoan and American cultures which might plausibly explain the difference in the impact of adolescence upon members of the two societies.

The second of these general problems is that of the effect of personality upon culture. Members of a society are continually proposing and trying out minor changes and modifications in the customs by which they live. Thus, although culture is partly independent of the individual members of society, it is eventually and in the long run determined by them and represents an adjustment to their psychological and biological nature. Among the characteristics of members of a society which may in this way determine many aspects of the culture are those which are called personality. Differences in personality between members of different societies, then, may lead to differences in many details of the cultures of the societies. The problem is, what kinds of personality differences are important as having this sort of selective effect on culture, what are the effects in detail, and what are the processes by which they are brought about?

The best-known work which, as we see it, concentrates upon this second problem is Ruth Benedict's *Patterns of Culture* (1934). Benedict shows that many of the major aspects of a culture fit into a pattern or configuration which may be described in terms of motivational orientation or personality type. This basic orientation is held to have an important selective effect in the adoption, development, and modification of all sorts of specific aspects of the culture. The basic orientation, of course, Benedict believes to be culturally rather than biologically transmitted; in this book she is not concerned with the effect of culture on personality but with the selective effect on culture which this orientation has once it has been established.

The third general problem in culture and personality represents in effect a combination of the first two, dealing with personality as a connecting link between two aspects of culture. Thus if certain aspects of culture influence the personality of members of a society, and if these personality characteristics in turn influence other aspects of the culture, then the individual personalities become a link in a causal chain of indirect influences between different aspects of the same culture. The third problem, then, is that of the extent and ways in which personality processes in individual members of a society determine the integration of the culture. In order to deal with this one must be concerned with the reciprocal influence of culture and personality; thus the third problem encompasses the first two. Yet it leads to a sufficiently distinct emphasis so that it may well be considered as a separate general problem.

The chief study of this third general problem is the work of Kardiner with Linton and other anthropological collaborators in *The Individual and His Society* (1939) and *The Psychological Frontiers of Society* (1945). Kardiner distinguishes as *primary institutions* certain aspects of culture—especially child training practices—which he portrays as producing the basic personality structure of members of a society and as having an important influence on other aspects of culture, which are called *secondary institutions*. This general mode of analysis and interpretation is applied to several different cultures. In the interpretation of each culture the hypotheses about personality adapted from psychoanalysis are the link which establishes a theoretical connection between the primary institutions and the secondary ones that they indirectly influence.

The investigation which we will report in this volume is also concerned with the third of these general problems. We will deal with personality processes as mediating between certain aspects of culture which lead to them and others to which they in turn lead. Specifically we have taken child training practices and customary responses to illness as the two aspects of culture which are mediated by principles of personality development. As has already been implied in our statement of the third general problem, however, we will inevitably be concerned to some extent also with each of the first two problems: specifically, with the effect that child training practices have on child personality and the effect that adult personality has on customary responses to illness. Hypotheses about personality processes—that is, about the effects that personality characteristics established in childhood have upon the same people when they grow to adulthood—provide the final connecting link between the observed child training practices on the one hand and the observed reactions to illness on the other hand.

Our study differs somewhat from earlier studies of culture and personality in the specific character of the topics with which it deals. It differs more importantly, however, in the methods used and in the kind of conclusion which the use of those methods permits. To show what the differences are, we must consider some of the methodological problems which are confronted by those working on culture and personality.

Methodological problems in this field have to do, in part, with the data-gathering phase of the scientific task. Fieldworkers who have been interested in culture and personality have often felt that traditional ethnographic techniques need to be supplemented by special techniques for assessing the personality characteristics of members of primitive societies. The fieldworker cannot learn what he wishes about culture and personality unless the right data-gathering techniques are available, just as the physical anthropologist would be handicapped without his calipers and camera. Ideal data-gathering techniques in this field are far from being fully developed. But the quest for them has led to a surge of interest among anthropologists in the life-history technique and in projective tests of personality.[1] With this kind of methodological problem we are not concerned here. Since we are dealing with personality processes as a connecting link between different aspects of culture, our data are not about indi-

1. See, for example, publications by Dyk (1938), Ford (1941), Simmons (1942), Hallowell (1945), and Henry (1947).

vidual personality as such but cultural data suitably gathered by the traditional techniques of the ethnographic fieldworker.

The methodological questions which are of greater importance for understanding the relation of our study to previous work on culture and personality have to do with the explanatory phase of the scientific task. One problem has to do with the general orientation or aim of the research. A second has to do with the methods used in the effort to achieve that aim. A third has to do with the choice of basic concepts. We will discuss each of these problems in turn, indicating how our study is related to previous studies in culture and personality.

ORIENTATION TOWARD THE TESTING OF HYPOTHESES

Most previous work in culture and personality has been oriented primarily toward seeking concrete understanding of specific cases. Our work in contrast is oriented toward testing generalized hypotheses applicable to any case. The difference is not between interest and lack of interest in general hypotheses. The student who is primarily oriented toward full interpretation of the individual case inevitably makes use of general hypotheses as an interpretative device. But he is inclined to take their validity for granted and use them simply as tools which contribute to the understanding of the concrete case. We are not willing to take the validity of any hypothesis for granted until we see adequate evidence to support it, and we are willing to leave to the future the task of applying validated hypotheses to the interpretation of specific cases.

The orientation toward concrete understanding may be well illustrated by the work of those who might be called the National Character School in contemporary anthropology. The cultures of various modern nations have been interpreted—that is, certain aspects of those cultures have been made to seem reasonable—by considering them as consequences of child training practices followed in those nations. For example, both Gorer (1943) and LaBarre (1945) point to certain compulsive and ritualistic aspects of Japanese culture and attempt to account for them in terms of early and severe toilet training among the Japanese. We would like to stress here that neither Gorer nor LaBarre was primarily interested in testing the hypothesis that early toilet training produces a compulsive personality. They took this relationship for granted and used it as a conceptual tool in trying to construct a coherent interpretation of certain aspects of Japanese culture. This orientation is characteristic of various recent efforts to interpret the culture of modern nations through the use of hypotheses about personality development.[2]

We have of course no quarrel with the effort to achieve full understanding of specific cases. The psychiatrist in attempting therapy with disturbed patients obviously must have such an aim as a help in achieving his therapeutic objective. The anthropologist or administrator may have a similar practical objective which makes urgent the effort to understand as fully as possible the character of a people. In addition, the intrinsic interest of understanding specific *nations* provides for the anthropologist another and purely intellectual motive which may sometimes be lacking in the case of understanding specific *individuals*. But this effort at full and valid understanding of specific cases, whether societies or individuals, must necessarily depend upon valid general hypotheses. So far the hypotheses used in this interpretative task have not been at all adequately validated.

The testing of hypotheses has of course not been completely ignored in previous studies of culture and personality. Several studies have been concerned with testing what we may call a universal hypothesis of single causation. Thus Margaret Mead in her Samoan study may be said to have been testing the hypothesis that biological changes in adolescence lead to disturbances of personality so strongly and uniformly that no other factors working to the contrary could possibly conceal the effect in any single case. A single negative case is of course sufficient to disprove such a sweeping universal hypothesis, and Dr. Mead

2. See, for example, Mead (1942), Benedict (1946), Gorer (1948), Gorer and Rickman (1950).

provided the disproof, which is a useful achievement. We doubt, however, that studies of this sort could be accurately described as oriented primarily toward testing hypotheses. They seem rather to be oriented toward obtaining and organizing sound and persuasive evidence which will convince the layman of the falsity of an extreme statement already known to the anthropologist as an overstatement. In contrast, in embarking on the present research we were as much in doubt as anyone else could be about the outcome of the tests of our hypotheses. This was a natural consequence of the fact that we were not seeking to disprove an over-generalization which attributes an effect exclusively to a single cause, but were seeking to test more modest generalizations which suggest that a given condition is one (perhaps among many) of the antecedents that produce a given consequent. Such a hypothesis cannot be proved or disproved by a single case; systematic study is required to test its validity.

Some orientation toward the testing of this more modest sort of hypothesis is found in the work of those who have used psychoanalytic hypotheses to interpret cultural integration. Kardiner, for example, views his work as contributing to testing the hypotheses he uses (1939, p. 487). But in general, publications like his seem rather to use hypotheses, of whose validity the author has little doubt, as conceptual devices in the interpretation of specific case material.

In general orientation toward the testing of hypotheses, then, our study is by no means completely novel but does differ from previous work in relative emphasis on this objective.

METHOD OF TESTING HYPOTHESES

Where previous studies of culture and personality have been partially oriented toward testing general hypotheses (other than universal hypotheses of single causation), we feel that they have relied on inadequate methods.

The method on which these studies have relied may be described as a test of coherence in the interpretation of the specific case. Various relevant hypotheses are drawn upon to fit the detailed facts of the case into a meaningful interpretation. The test of the hypotheses is then provided by judging whether the interpretation forms a sensible coherent whole. Such a test on even a single case is often felt to have some value, but it is recognized that a hypothesis has greater validity if it has stood the test repeatedly, by forming an important part of a coherent interpretation of first one case and then another.

This test of coherence is of course a proper one to stress in seeking for understanding of a concrete case. But we feel that it never provides adequate evidence as to whether the hypotheses used are genuinely valid as general principles. This point is well illustrated by the status of psychoanalytic theory. Though it has now been used for many years by psychoanalysts, and continues its process of vital growth through its application to particular cases and subsequent modification, there is still little agreement about the validity of most of its component hypotheses. Those who are trained to use this theory in clinical practice are strongly convinced of the validity of these hypotheses, because they enter into coherent and useful accounts of the origins of the personalities they deal with. Those who are trained in other schools of psychiatric practice, for parallel reasons, feel equally convinced of the validity of other theories and of the errors of psychoanalysis. People who are not trained in any psychiatric school are left to be skeptical of all such theories, or to choose among them on other grounds than those of scientifically acceptable evidence. For practitioners pressed by patients needing help do not as a rule devote themselves primarily to a quest for scientific evidence for or against the hypotheses they are using; and if they do, they are likely to find themselves untrained in the methods required.

We would like, then, to consider briefly what we believe is needed for an adequate test of a scientific hypothesis. A scientific hypothesis consists of a tentative statement of a relationship between two events. Most often, one of these events is considered as an antecedent and the other as a consequent. For evidence as to the validity of such a hypothesis, some means are needed for isolating this antecedent condition from other conditions and determining whether in fact this supposed consequent is observed with some consistency to follow or accompany it. In the study of the individual case no such means are available. If the antecedent and the consequent specified in the hypothesis are both present, for example, so are an infinity of other conditions, and there is no way of knowing whether the supposed antecedent and consequent are genuinely related to each other, or whether on the contrary each may be the consequent of some quite separate set of antecedents among the infinity of other conditions which are present.[3]

In our view the ideal way of isolating the antecedent and consequent conditions specified in a hypothesis, to determine if there is in fact a consistent relation between them, is provided by the method of experimental research. This method, when properly applied, has three great advantages over the effort to verify general hypotheses by the study of the individual case.

1. A suitable sample of cases are studied, rather than a single case, and statistical techniques may be applied to determine whether the apparent connection between antecedent and consequent is a true or dependable connection, rather than their association being due to accidental concomitance in one or a few individual cases.

2. Since the occurrence or nonoccurrence of the supposed antecedent is produced by the arbitrary action of the experimenter, rather than by previous characteristics of the cases studied, it is possible to insure that the connection between ante-

3. It is of course possible, as the work of Baldwin (1942) has shown so well, to break the individual case down into a population of incidents, episodes, or the like, and to make an adequate test of hypotheses about consistent relationships between variables in this population. See also Allport (1942). Such a procedure can increase the certainty of a specific interpretation of the individual case; but it does not provide any sounder basis for evaluating a general hypothesis on the basis of study of a single case.

cedent and consequent is genuinely that of antecedent and consequent.

3. Evidence for the connection between antecedent and consequent is obtained by objective procedures which can be described and repeated by other investigators with the same outcome, rather than being dependent upon an intuitive judgment of relevance and coherence with which other investigators may legitimately disagree.

Because of possessing all these advantages, the experimental method is the ideal method of testing those scientific hypotheses for which valid experimental procedures can be devised. Unfortunately, in the study of culture and personality the experimental method is in general either impossible or excessively difficult. We have made no attempt whatever to apply it. In this field it is for most purposes necessary to fall back on a somewhat less satisfactory method of testing hypotheses—the correlational method.

In the correlational testing method the supposed antecedent condition is looked for as it occurs or fails to occur in the natural course of events in a number of cases. Instances are collected of its presence and its absence, or of its presence in various degrees. The supposed consequent condition is also looked for in each of these cases and determined to be present or absent, or present in a given degree. It is then possible to determine whether there is a consistent relation between the two, and thus whether the hypothesis is confirmed or negated. This method, when properly used, shares the first and third of the advantages which we have enumerated for the experimental method. Statistical techniques may be applied to determine whether the apparent connection between antecedent and conseqent is a true or dependable connection, rather than being due to an accidental concomitance in one or a few individual cases. The evidence of connection may be based entirely on objective procedures which are repeatable.

The correlational method clearly lacks, however, the second of the three advantages we have listed for the experimental method. In the correlational method one has to rely on the natural occurrence of the antecedent condition. It is then possible that the processes in nature which are responsible for this antecedent condition are themselves directly responsible for the consequent condition as well; in this case the hypothesis is not really confirmed as it may seem at first to be, for the relation between the two conditions specified in the hypothesis is not one of antecedent and consequent but one of consequents of some other common antecedent. Or, it is possible that the condition one has expected to be a consequent may really be the antecedent, and vice versa. Various devices may be used to narrow the area of uncertainty that is created by use of a correlational method, rather than an experimental method, but uncertainty must always remain. None the less, the two advantages which the correlational method has over the method of individual case study are so great as to make it an enormously more powerful tool for the verification of scientific hypotheses than can be provided by case study alone.

Our study differs from most previous studies in using the correlational method to test general hypotheses about culture and personality, instead of depending upon the less adequate test of coherence in the interpretation of specific cases. For our material the correlational method takes the specific form of cross-cultural techniques which have recently proved so fruitful in the hands of Murdock (1949) in the study of social structure. The only previous application of cross-cultural technique to the study of culture and personality seems to be found in Horton's study of the functions of alcohol in primitive societies (1943), though a very similar technique has been applied by Cattell (1950) to the study of national characteristics.

This cross-cultural application of the correlational method involves taking the single culture as the unit. Ethnographic reports about this culture are studied for evidence about the presence or absence, or degree of presence, of the antecedent condition and of the consequent condition specified in a hypothesis. This is repeated for a number of cultures which may be taken as a sample of human cultures in general. Statistical techniques are then applied to testing whether these two conditions do in fact vary together among human cultures.

Two rather specialized procedures are made use of in applying this method. One is the procedure used in analyzing the ethnographic reports; this is specific to our particular subject matter, so it has been necessary to introduce it in some detail (in Chapter 3). The other is the set of standard statistical procedures used in testing hypotheses. For the sake of those readers who are not familiar with them we have tried to express the outcome of our tests in terms which will be meaningful even without a knowledge of the procedures.

THE CONCEPTS TO BE USED

For an explanation of the phenomena of culture and personality we feel that concepts are needed about which we already have, from allied fields of knowledge, general principles which can be tested on this slightly different subject matter. It is true that an occasional genius may attack a new field of scientific study, devise almost completely novel concepts, and put them together into general principles of great explanatory value. But the more usual course of scientific progress in a new field calls for the use of concepts which will permit the tentative application of generalized principles about related phenomena which have already been studied. As those principles are tested in the new setting, they and their concepts may need to be modified; but the initial appeal to those concepts, providing the means of analyzing the new phenomena, starts the process of scientific development.

It is this sort of fact about scientific progress, we believe, which is principally responsible for the great interest that students of culture and personality have taken in psychoanalytic theory. Psychoanalytic theory is a body of hypotheses—tentative general principles—about the development of personality among individuals in our society. Its concepts have been developed for and used in hypotheses of this sort. Obviously, then, these are concepts which have strong initial promise of usefulness in the study of personality and culture, for they have an established usefulness in the study of personality development under one set of cultural conditions and enter into a number of hypotheses which might be tested under a greater variety of cultural conditions.

Psychoanalytic theory is in fact the major existing body of hypotheses about personality development, and it is not surprising that it has been used in the development of generalized knowledge about culture and personality. In a negative sense it has stimulated the discovery of negative instances which show that if certain psychoanalytic concepts and hypotheses are to be applied outside our own culture, they may need to be radically modified. Examples are the outcomes of a search for the Oedipus conflict among the Trobrianders (Malinowski, 1927) and among the Hopi (Eggan, 1943), which suggest that the Oedipus conflict, as specifically defined by Freud, is a function of certain social conditions which are not necessarily universal. A more positive, but less critical, use of psychoanalytic concepts has been made by various students who have applied psychoanalytic concepts and hypotheses in analyzing and explaining the course of personality development in various cultural settings. Notable examples in the case of primitive cultures are provided by the works we have already mentioned by Kardiner and his anthropological collaborators, and the similar work of Erikson (1950). We have already cited, in the studies of the National Character School, examples of similar application of psychoanalytic concepts in the analysis of personality tendencies in modern civilized societies.

Most studies which have been concerned with general hypotheses about culture and personality, then, have tended to express those hypotheses in terms of the concepts of psychoanalytic theory. Here we differ sharply from our predecessors. We have preferred to use, to a much greater extent, concepts drawn from the general behavior theory that has been developed by academic and experimental psychologists.

This choice may seem somewhat strange, since the hypotheses

which we have attempted to test are certainly derived primarily from psychoanalytic theory about personality development in our society. We should make it clear that we are not concerned with the validity of psychoanalytic theory as such. We are interested in making progress toward a body of systematic general knowledge about personality development and about culture integration. We have felt that psychoanalytic theory has invaluable suggestions to make in this effort, and we have tried to make use of those suggestions to the best of our ability. But the use we have made of them doubtless involves much modification from the original statements by psychoanalysts; part of this modification is deliberate, and part may inevitably follow from our lack of a specialist's understanding of psychoanalytic theory.

The reasons for our choice of the concepts of general behavior theory over those of psychoanalytic theory have to do partly with objections to psychoanalytic concepts and partly with positive advantages of the concepts of general behavior theory.

The objections we have to psychoanalytic concepts have often been made by others, and we see no need for repeating them here, since we are not interested in controversy on this question so much as we are in making clear the concepts on which our study is based. We can only express here our judgment that psychoanalytic concepts on grounds of clarity and relevance to our task are less useful than those we have chosen.

Our positive grounds for choosing the concepts of general behavior theory have to do with the same facts about scientific progress to which we ascribed the general interest of students of culture and personality in psychoanalytic theory. The reinterpretation of psychoanalytic hypotheses in terms of general behavior concepts brings them into relation with a vast body of scientific knowledge about the determinants of behavior, and out of this new relationship may spring new principles which go far beyond and behind the original psychoanalytic hypotheses. Miller's redefinition of the Freudian mechanism of displacement (1948) and experimental test of hypotheses generated by the redefinition (Miller and Kraeling, 1952; Murray and Miller, 1952) is an excellent example of what we mean. Another whole set of examples could be provided by the fruitful results of Dollard and Miller's efforts at extensive restatement of Freudian principles in terms of general behavior theory (1950). Our application of behavior concepts and principles to hypotheses originally suggested by psychoanalytic theory represents a part of this same general effort, and is motivated by a similar expectation of fruitful results for a science of human behavior.

The reasons for our positive preference for the concepts of general behavior theory, however, go beyond the special province of personality development, or of culture and personality, and have to do in part with more general questions of the relation between anthropology and psychology. We have decided, therefore, to devote a separate chapter to our basic concepts, and this we have done in Chapter 2.

SUMMARY

In summary of what we have said in this chapter we would describe the research to be reported in this book as having these four broad characteristics:

First, it is concerned with the problem of how culture is integrated through the medium of personality processes. This concern leads us inevitably to be interested in the influence both of culture upon personality and of personality upon culture.

Second, it is oriented toward testing general hypotheses about human behavior in any and all societies rather than toward achieving a detailed understanding of any one society.

Third, it uses the correlational method for testing hypotheses. The particular form this takes in our study is the cross-cultural method, in which each culture is considered as a unit.

Fourth, while it draws upon psychoanalytic theory as an important source of hypotheses, the concepts of general behavior theory are used in formulating hypotheses.

CHAPTER 2. *Basic Concepts*

THE DATA with which our study deals are cultural data. They are accounts given by anthropologists of the customary behavior of members of various primitive societies. These accounts are based partly upon their observations of the behavior of individual members and partly upon statements by informants about how people in their society typically behave or ought to behave. Whatever the source of the information, the accounts generally refer to the typical behavior customarily expected, rather than to the actual behavior of specific individuals. The concepts referring to such data are generally those of culture trait, culture pattern, custom, folkway, and mores.

While we are thus using data appropriately described by concepts on the cultural level, we propose to interpret them by reference to concepts having to do with individual behavior and its determinants, concepts derived from general behavior theory. A preliminary question, then, is how we propose to make the two sets of concepts relevant to each other. By what reasoning do we claim that a hypothesis about the determinants of a habit in a single individual can be relevant to understanding the occurrence of a culture trait which characterizes the customary expectations of behavior in a society as a whole?

A first step toward establishing a relationship between the two sets of concepts can be taken by providing a definition which will serve as a bridge between the two. By defining a unit at the cultural level in terms of some unit of individual behavior we may hope that principles about the latter can then be applied to understanding the former. The particular step we have taken in this direction is to define custom (a unit of culture) in terms of habit (a unit of individual behavior).

The Concept of Custom

We have chosen "custom" to refer to the cultural unit we propose to define in behavior terms, because it is more appropriate for our use than any other. Custom has been generally used with rather direct reference to behavior. Gillin, indeed, has already offered a definition of custom in terms of habit (1948, p. 18). The definition we propose, as somewhat more useful than his for theoretical development, we will postpone until after we indicate what we mean by "habit." We believe that the definition we will suggest does not do violence to established usage of the term custom by anthropologists.

We have preferred custom over the terms "culture trait" and "culture pattern" because the latter have been used to include non-behavior items of culture. The term culture trait is generally understood to include cultural artifacts, that is, the material apparatus produced and used by the members of a society. This meaning is a very useful one, since culture trait has been widely used in studies of the diffusion of culture and in the establishment of culture areas. In such studies it is as useful to note that two cultures have the same kind of canoe as that they use the same technique of paddling, and hence a cultural unit which is defined to refer to either kind of fact may be highly appropriate. For our purpose a canoe and a technique of paddling are events of quite different order. The building of a canoe and the technique of paddling are both behavior phenomena, but the canoe itself is not, and we need a cultural concept which will clearly exclude artifacts from its meaning.

The same objection holds true to some extent for the term culture pattern. Although culture pattern has not generally been used to refer to an artifact itself, it has sometimes been used to refer to the form of an artifact. For example, Kluckhohn (1943, p. 214) says, "Thus Navaho bows used in shooting and the miniature replicas (of varying sizes and materials) used in several Navaho chants are distinct culture traits. But all conform to the same general pattern. The problem of pattern is the problem of symmetry, of constancies of form irrespective of wide variations in concrete actualization." A constancy of form which makes a hunting bow perceptually similar to a miniature replica must be a product of human behavior, but it is not itself an item of behavior.

A second and more serious defect, for our purposes, of the term culture pattern is that it has been used, as both Kluckhohn (1943, p. 220) and Kroeber (1948, pp. 311ff.) point out, in numerous quite different senses. It has been equated with ethos, with orientation, with universal trait lists, with ideal (as distinguished from actual) elements of culture. The numerous attempts which have been made to give the term precise and uniform meaning have not been notably successful.

The Concepts of Habit and Habit Potential

The reason for our choice of habit as the psychological unit lies simply in the fact that it is the psychological concept which lends itself to use in a definition of custom.

As we are using the term, a habit is a relationship between a set of stimuli and a response (or series of responses) such that there is a probability that when the stimulus is perceived by a given organism the response will be evoked. Habit thus refers to a potentiality or disposition. Such a potentiality may vary in degree or strength; the probability of evocation of the response may be great or small. It may indeed even be zero as is the case when it is said that an organism does not have or has not learned a given habit. We will use the term "habit potential" for this quantitative aspect of habit.[1]

There are various measures that might be used to gauge habit potential. The most basic measure, perhaps, is that of probability of evocation. The habit whose response is almost always evoked by its stimulus has a much higher potential than the habit whose

1. Our term habit potential corresponds essentially to what Hull (1943) in a more technical context calls "effective reaction potential."

response is rarely evoked by its stimulus. Thus, for example, a series of mothers may be observed to respond differently to the crying of their children. One mother may be observed always to pick the child up, another to pick it up sometimes, and another to systematically "let the child cry it out." These mothers have a decreasingly strong tendency or disposition to pick up their crying child. We would say habit potential for this response in the first mother is very strong and in the last mother very weak. A habit with high potential will in general also have its response evoked more rapidly upon occurrence of the stimulus than will a habit of low potential. Hence latency or delay of response is another possible measure of habit potential. Thus the first mother in our example would be likely to pick up her child immediately, but the second mother only after some delay. Also the habit with high potential will in general lead to a larger or more vigorous response than will a habit of lower potential, so that amplitude or intensity of response provides a third measure of habit potential. Again, a habit of higher potential will in general be more resistant to unlearning or extinction than will a habit of lower potential, and this provides still another possible measure of habit potential. In precise laboratory studies of behavior it may be important to decide which of these measures is more basic, and to study the interrelations among them in detail. For our purposes, in applying the concept of habit to cultural data where our measures are very crude, we will simply go on the tentative assumption that for this application these various measures are approximately equivalent in the results they will yield.

Habit and habit potential, as we are using them, are thus constructs rather than descriptive terms, similar to such constructs as a recessive gene or an atom. They are the kind of constructs that have in recent years been called intervening variables (Tolman, 1935), constructs useful in dealing theoretically with relationships between observable variables but which do not necessarily have any physical referents themselves. For those who are more literal-minded, however, it might be assumed that a habit and its potential are determined by some organization of the neural structure of the organism. Whichever way one chooses to think of this concept, the observed events are the same. One cannot feel or see a probability, nor can one peer into the brain and see the neural organization which may be assumed to determine the probability. The observable events from which both a habit and its potential are inferred are regularities in the concurrence of a set of stimuli and a response.

As we are conceiving a habit, it is a potentiality or disposition which may be said to be present even when its response is not occurring; that is, an organism may be said to have a habit when it is not performing it. For example, a person who has learned to skate has the habits which go to make up the skill of skating in the summer when there is no ice just as much as he does in the winter when he is actually gliding over the smooth surface of a frozen lake. The event of skating is the performance of the habit, or of its response.

If one defines a custom in terms of a habit, there are a number of principles about determinants of habit potential which have been carefully formulated and experimentally tested which will be relevant to the scientific understanding of culture. A detailed presentation of such principles will be found in the works of various psychologists who have been interested in the development of general behavior theory, e.g., Tolman (1932), Guthrie (1935), Skinner (1938), Miller and Dollard (1941), and Hull (1943, 1951). There are a number of differences among the theories of these various authors. These differences are important in connection with the precise formulation and testing of behavior theory, but are unimportant for our purposes here. Our formulation of these principles is based primarily on the work of Hull and of Miller and Dollard; but, for the use that we make of them, an equally satisfactory formulation could probably be derived from the systems of any of the other authors we have mentioned.

Where later in this book we make use of particular principles drawn from behavior theory, they will be described in detail, but it is useful here to sketch the general nature of these principles. One group of principles in behavior theory has to do with the role of past experience of the organism with the stimuli and responses of a given habit. Thus if we wish to predict whether a child will pet a dog when he sees one, we should know what his past experiences with petting dogs have been. Past performances of the habit which have been followed by reward (drive reduction) increase the habit potential, those which have been followed by no reward or by punishment generally decrease the habit potential. These influences on habit potential have been expressed systematically as the principles of reinforcement and extinction. These are the sorts of principles that constitute most directly a theory of learning.

Since precisely the same set of stimuli seldom, if ever, present themselves to an organism, another group of principles which must be combined with this first group have to do with the effect on habit potential of the degree of similarity between the set of stimuli present now and those present on previous occasions. For example, the greater the similarity between present stimuli and those which have entered into rewarded performances of a similar habit, the greater will be the habit potential of the present habit. Thus a child who has learned to pet a pekinese will have some tendency, but a weaker one, to pet a great dane when he first sees one. Functional similarity for this purpose may be mediated by words as well as by perceptual similarity; if two sets of stimuli which are quite different from one another are given the same label, the habit potential associated with one set may be readily generalized to the other. Thus, in the above example, if the child calls both the pekinese and the great dane "dogs," the probability that he will pet the great dane will be increased.

Another group of principles has to do with the present motivation or drive state of the organism as a determinant of habit potential. For example, if one wishes to predict whether or not a child will eat an apple, one must not only know the history of the child's apple eating, but also how hungry he is at the moment. Drives may be either the innate biological drives, such as hunger, thirst, or pain, or learned drives such as fear, dependence, prestige, or a specific appetite. The role of drives and of drive reduction is so crucial that other principles are concerned with the conditions under which drives and drive reduction may themselves be acquired or modified through the learning process. In the following chapter it will be seen that our study is particularly dependent upon principles of this sort.

RELATION BETWEEN CUSTOM AND HABIT

Having indicated our reasons for choosing custom and habit as key concepts of culture and individual behavior, and having explained what we mean by habit, we may now present the bridge definition by which we make a connection between the two realms of discourse:

A custom is a characteristic habit of a typical member of a cultural category of persons.

Each of the major phrases in this definition needs elucidation.

CULTURAL CATEGORY OF PERSONS

By a cultural category of persons we mean any group or class of persons which is distinguished by the members of a society. In our society man, woman, child, husband, wife, farmer, priest, mechanic, and president are examples of cultural categories of persons.[2]

The broadest cultural category within a society is simply that of member of that society. Many customs are indeed characteristic of a typical adult member of the society as a whole, and many of the customs with which we deal in this book are of this character. For the specific purposes of our study, therefore, it would be suitable to define a custom as a characteristic habit of a typical adult member of a society. With the broader purpose

2. This term is thus given a meaning closely akin to one meaning of the term "status" (Linton, 1936).

in mind of establishing a connection between cultural and psychological concepts which would be useful in other studies as well, we have instead given the definition in a form which will make it correspond more closely with general usage of the term custom. For many customs do not characterize a society as a whole, but only some narrower cultural category within the society.

TYPICAL MEMBER

We have deliberately chosen the term "typical" rather than "modal," "median," or some other term expressing a precise measure of central tendency, because ethnological data do not really permit precision here, and because for most purposes the choice of a particular measure of central tendency would not matter greatly. We have chosen typical, then, just because it is not mathematically precise. Only some of the data gathered by social psychologists and sociologists, who often use precise sampling techniques, would be available if the definition referred to the modal or median member of a cultural category. The data with which we deal, and with which cross-cultural studies in general must deal at present, have been gathered by anthropologists who, using their judgment rather than precise procedures, report on how most of the people in a society behave or how the average person behaves. By typical, then, we mean a central tendency such as the mode or the median but arrived at by the ethnologist's judgment.

There are two important reasons for our choosing to define customs as habits of a typical person, rather than as habits shared by a category of persons. One reason is that while customs are usually shared they are not necessarily shared. The response of giving the annual presidential message to Congress is shared by the President with no one. Yet the tendency to give the presidential message is typical of the cultural category of President of the United States and would clearly be a custom by our definition.

The behavior of the President gives us a good opportunity to elucidate the difference we mean to imply between custom and habit in general. As we have said, the tendency for the President to give an annual message to Congress is clearly a custom. A given President's habit of taking a constitutional before breakfast is in our terms simply a habit—not because he may not share this with others but because the behavior is referred to him as an individual and not as a member of a cultural category. Were it the case that he takes his morning constitutional as a typical member of the ABC health cult, then this habit would be a custom (though not of the President as such).

The second reason for not defining custom by reference to shared habits is that this phraseology would suggest that the custom is uniform in all those individuals who share it. The phrase "characteristic habit of a *typical member*" suggests more adequately the point that culture does not mean precise uniformity but merely restriction of the range of variation in behavior.

CHARACTERISTIC HABIT

In speaking of a *characteristic habit* of a typical member of a cultural category we mean to imply that the habit must in some way be relevant to the person's membership in the cultural category. In the initial stage of anthropological inquiry the criterion for this relevance is likely to be distinctiveness. If the habits of one cultural category or of one society differ from those of another, those habits are judged to be customs. At a later stage of anthropological inquiry systematic knowledge may permit one to judge that certain habits grow out of the life of a society or of a smaller cultural category, and are thus characteristic of membership in it, even though they are not distinctive. This is the present interpretation of the habit in all societies of forbidding incest, and of living in family groups; these are considered to be customs, rather than instincts or simply products of some sort of purely individual learning in each person (Murdock, 1945).

In inquiries which deal with the customs of smaller cultural categories within a society this term "characteristic" would be highly important. The customs of the presidency, for example, include only those habits of a typical President which are characteristic of the category of Presidents, and not those habits which are characteristic of other cultural categories of which he may simultaneously be a typical member. This sort of problem does not appear in our study, however, because of the fact that we deal primarily with very broad cultural categories such as parent or child.

We have defined custom, then, as a particular kind of habit—, a characteristic habit of a typical member of a cultural category of persons.

CUSTOM POTENTIAL

If a custom may be defined as a particular kind of habit, and if any habit may be said to have a potential, then it follows that a custom may be said to have a potential. The potential of a custom is simply the potential of the habit in a typical member of the relevant cultural category. We prefer to use in this case the specific term "custom potential" rather than the more general term "habit potential." In predicting the potential of customs we intend to apply principles which have been formulated for dealing with the potential of habits in general.

It may appear that there is a grave difficulty here in that concepts of habit are ordinarily applied to some real, specific identifiable individual; whereas information about customs is information about some vaguely defined "typical" person who is not really known as any one specific individual. Actually this difficulty is not nearly so grave as may appear at first glance. Principles about determinants of habit potential have in fact themselves been tested by reference to information about a typical person who is not any one real person. They have been tested in experiments in which the results which are used have to do with average performance of a number of individuals (i.e., the mean performance of an experimental group), where the individuals vary from each other and no one of them conforms precisely to the principle as formulated quantitatively. The typical member of a cultural category does not differ in any fundamental logical way from the typical subject in a psychological experiment. There may be difficulties, indeed, in applying principles of individual behavior in a fully satisfactory way to the explanation of culture, but we believe that this is not one of them.

As we have already foreshadowed in discussing habit potential, the way in which we will seek to measure custom potential is varied. Sometimes we may rely on information about the probability that the given stimulus will evoke the given response in a typical member of the society. Often we are able to use information about the intensity or amplitude of the response when it is made. On occasion we may be able to make use of hints about the latency of the response, or about the resistance of the customs to extinction or unlearning. For our purposes we will be assuming that custom potential as measured in any of these ways may be considered as the same measure. Indeed, our study could hardly have been conducted without this assumption, as no one kind of information is available with sufficient consistency.

A special case of the use of probability of evocation as a measure of custom potential is to be found where societies in which a given custom is reported to occur are compared with societies in which it is not reported to occur. Here custom potential is measured only on a two-point scale, the points on which can be called "present" and "absent." Because of advantages of using more points on a scale, we have tried to make more refined measurements wherever possible. This problem will be discussed in more detail in Chapter 3.

THE CUSTOM COMPLEX

We have pointed out that a definition of a unit of culture (custom) in terms of a unit of individual behavior (habit) permits the use of psychological principles in the formulation of hypotheses about customs. It should not be lost sight of, however, that a custom is a particular kind of habit—it is a habit which is also a unit of culture. This fact sets certain special conditions which determine, and to some extent limit, the application of these psychological principles.

First of all, whereas a habit viewed under controlled experimental conditions may on occasion be fully understood without reference to other habits, this is not the case with customs. Each custom is imbedded in a complex of related customs which have an important determining effect on its potential. Symbolic processes, social interaction, and the many categories that a member of a society belongs to, have their effect in determining the potential of any given custom. The first two of these sociocultural factors give rise to what we would like to call the "custom complex." A custom complex typically consists of a customary practice and of beliefs, values, sanctions, rules, motives and satisfactions associated with it. We will define each type of custom in turn and show how it relates to the other types. For the sake of simplicity of exposition we will start with a practice and use this type of custom as a focal concept. We do not mean to imply that any other type of custom might not have been chosen for this purpose.

A *practice* may be defined as *a custom whose response directly effects a change in the environment, the performer, or the relationship between the two.* The fisherman catching a fish, his wife cooking it, and the two eating it are all instances of the performance of a practice. Similarly a mother nursing a child, a father scolding his son, or a man courting a woman is performing a practice. Practices are the most basic type of custom in that they are most directly related to living. They are the customs whose responses are immediately instrumental in getting food and shelter, mating, fighting, bringing up children, and gaining reassurance in the face of supernatural dangers.

Practices are always related to *beliefs*. The fisherman casts his net where he sees gulls fluttering because he believes that the gulls are after bait which is being chased by the larger fish which he wishes to catch. His wife puts the fish on a grill over the fire because she believes this will make the flesh more tender and tasty. The couple eat the fish not only because they are hungry but because they believe it is a food which will satisfy their hunger and not poison them. *A belief is a custom whose response symbolizes some relationship between events.* Thus it may be said that one or more beliefs contribute to the stimulus pattern of any practice. These beliefs may be either explicit or implicit. That is, the performer of a practice does not necessarily consciously rehearse the belief to himself at each performance. If asked, however, he will generally be able to report immediately at least some of the associated beliefs; in this case one may surmise that rehearsal of the belief was not a part of the stimulus pattern for the present performance of the custom but rather a significant part of the stimulus pattern earlier in the development of the custom. In some instances, beliefs may be repressed and alternative beliefs or rationalizations stated in their place. If Freud's hypothesis concerning repression is correct, however, even a repressed belief may be said to be part of the stimulus pattern of the relevant practice.

Practices are not only integrally related to beliefs but also to *values*. One parent may whip his child because he believes this will make him obedient and because he values obedience; another parent may refrain from punishing his child under similar circumstances because he believes this would make the child hate him and he values the child's love. We would define value as *a custom whose response attributes goodness or badness to some event*. If the event is evaluated as being good, such an event will be a goal to be sought; if it is bad, the need implied is that of avoidance. Like beliefs, values are symbolic customs. Although they differ in that the former symbolize what is felt to be true whereas the latter symbolize what is felt to be good, they both depend upon language or, to a limited extent, other symbolic responses. To make our definition even more mundane, it should be pointed out that gossip in many if not all societies provides one of the chief methods by which consensus with respect to values is achieved. In fact the very essence of gossip is the statement of values. The shaking of the head and the clucking of the tongue in a gossip session between two neighbors are among the most important of the overt customary expressions of value. In some religions, also, values are overtly expressed by some functionary in a ceremony as, for example, by the minister in his sermon.

As is the case with beliefs, however, the values related to a practice are by no means always expressed overtly at each occurrence. They may be implicit or they may even be repressed, but this does not imply that they fail to influence the custom potential of the relevant practice.

Even though practices are integrated with customary and commonly held beliefs and values, this does not insure that no members of a society will deviate from them and behave in an individualistic and unpredictable manner. The probability of deviation is lowered through the fact that two other types of custom are integrally related in the social setting to practices. These are *sanctions* and *rules*.

Most practices, particularly those which involve social interaction, lead to some kind of reward by other members of the society if properly performed, or to some type of punishment if improperly performed. The rewards may take the form of reciprocal practices performed by others leading to a common goal, or they may be more direct rewards such as praise, signs of acceptance, or material benefits. The punishments may be nonreciprocity, ostracism, fines, retaliation, or even execution. *The customary rewarding and punishing behavior of others following the performance of a practice* (or the failure to perform it when occasion demands) may be called respectively *positive* and *negative* sanctions.

Positive and negative sanctions, following as they do the performance or nonperformance of customs, have an important influence on the potential of a custom. Each time a practice is properly performed and followed by a positive sanction, the potential of the practice should increase. Furthermore, the positive sanction should gain acquired reward value and become one of the satisfactions following performance. Negative sanctions following an improper or deviant performance of a practice should create anxiety or fear associated with deviation and be a motive for the proper performance of the practice. Thus the practice of choosing a mate who is not interdicted by incest taboos is in part motivated by fear of negative sanctions should an improper choice be made, and the expectation of positive sanctions if the proper choice is made.

Sanctions are generally either stated or implied in *rules* which *specify the details of proper or improper performance of the practice*. These details include the stimulus conditions, e.g. time and place, a specification of the limits of permissible variations in the response, the sanctions, and the sanctioning agents. Rules, then, like beliefs and values are symbolic customs and form part of the stimulus pattern and of the motivation of the practice.

The two final types of customs which will complete our list are motives and satisfactions. A *motive* is *a custom which is responsible for acquired drive in its performer;* a *satisfaction* is *a custom which is responsible for acquired reward in its performer*. The response involved, in the case of a motive, may be thought of roughly as a state of tension. In the case of a satisfaction, the response may be thought of as a relaxation of tension.[3] Since these responses are for the most part internal

3. Consideration of acquired drive and acquired reward as having the functional characteristics of response, even though there may be no observable response, is a useful theoretical device. For further treatment of this question see Hull (1951) and Miller (1951).

and not accessible to ordinary observation, both motives and satisfactions are examples of what Gillin has called "mental customs" (1948, p. 183). In our society the tendency to be worried about achieving high status would be a motive, and the tendency to be gratified upon achievement of symbols of status would be a satisfaction. We have already dealt by implication with other examples of both of these kinds of custom as influencing the custom potential of a practice. For anticipations of negative sanctions are an example of motive, and the reward value of positive sanctions will often be an instance of satisfaction.

We have shown, then, in a general way that the custom potential of a practice may be influenced very significantly by the associated beliefs, values, sanctions, rules, motives, and satisfactions. But each of these itself is a custom, and the same thing may be said of it: that its custom potential may be influenced by the associated customs of other kinds in this list. For full understanding of any one custom, then, it may well be necessary to take account of a number of related customs as well. For such a set of related customs concerned with essentially the same items of behavior we suggest the term "custom complex." It may be instructive to define a custom complex as consisting of a practice with its associated beliefs, values, rules, sanctions, motives, and satisfactions, since it is the practice which will most often define quite simply the items of behavior around which the complex centers. But such a definition should not cause one to lose sight of the fact that some complexes may equally well center around a belief, a value, etc., nor of the point that the influencing of one custom by other related customs holds just as true for the other kinds of custom as it does for practices.

Now such complicated interrelations among habits are not lacking at the level of individual behavior. Indeed, if customs may, as we believe, be usefully defined as a special instance of habits, then by showing that customs have this sort of complex determination we have shown that one class of habits has it. But parallel complications could also be stated for habits that are not customs. It does remain true, none the less, that some individual habits may be relatively isolated from the rest of the habit structure in the individual, whereas one may at least argue that customs are always imbedded in a custom complex.

This sort of complication about culture has doubtless contributed to the view of some anthropologists that culture is of very different nature from individual behavior. It may have helped lead White (1949) to take the position that the study of culture, which he calls "culturology," is and must be kept completely distinct and separate from the field of psychology. For our part we would draw no such conclusion. Recognition of the importance of the custom complex and of other complications, which it has not seemed pertinent to discuss here, suggests to us that the integration of cultural study with the study of individual behavior offers difficulties and may be complicated in character; but since this is no more than is generally true of such an endeavor in science, it offers no reason for discouragement. We place our faith in specific measures toward conceptual integration which can be tested out in empirical research, and we are now ready to indicate how we believe the concepts we have presented in this chapter can play such a role.

PERSONALITY INTEGRATION OF CULTURE

The problem of culture integration, as we see it, is the problem of arriving at a scientific understanding of the way that one custom influences the potential of another custom.

The simplest instance of the problem, in a sense, has to do with the integration of customs within a single custom complex. Most of the customs in a single custom complex may be seen as habits of a typical individual of a cultural category; it should be possible, then, to study the effect of one of these customs upon the potential of another as a problem in the interaction of habits in the single individual. Certain customs within the custom complex, however, must be seen as habits of another individual with whom the first one is interacting. This is true of sanctions and, to a considerable extent, of rules. To understand the effect of a sanction and a rule upon the potential of some other custom within the same complex (e.g. the practice) one must expect to have to deal theoretically not only with the habit structure of a single individual but also with simple processes of social interaction. However, with one minor exception, in this book we will not be dealing with this matter of the integration of customs within the single custom complex.

The broader problem with which our study is for the most part concerned is that of the influence of one custom or custom complex upon the potential of some custom quite outside of this complex. These influences are, at least potentially, far more numerous than the influences of customs within a complex upon each other. For, in the first place, the role of a member of a single cultural category ordinarily includes a large number of separate customs in distinct custom complexes; thus a farmer performs such distinct practices as plowing, harrowing, planting, cultivating, storing, constructing and maintaining buildings, making and repairing tools, prophesying the weather, and performing magic to ensure a good harvest. In the second place, in performing the role of one cultural category, a person is ordinarily brought into contact with other people whose performance of other roles may influence his behavior; the farmer's choice of what to plant, for example, is influenced by the customary wants of his customers or by the relative number of children and adults he has to feed, and his weather prophecies may be modified in response to those of magical specialists or of the Weather Bureau. Finally, a single person does not perform the customs of only a single cultural category; he performs the customs of the various cultural categories to which he belongs, and these customs may interact with each other. Thus, the customs of the farmer in an American rural community may be greatly influenced by the fact that he must also perform the customs of son, husband, father, citizen, and church member.

Here again, then, the influence of one custom upon another may be seen as partly a problem in the influence of one habit upon another in the same individual, and partly a problem in the influence of one person's responses upon the habits of another person.

An example drawn from the subject matter of our study should be useful at this point to illustrate more concretely what we mean by this way of stating the problem. We will state the example in simple form. We start with the fact that two customs are present in a particular culture. One is the practice of weaning children in an abrupt and harsh manner; the other is the belief that sickness is the result of some type of oral activity. What connection can be traced between these two customs? Certain hypotheses about personality development in the individual are suggestive of a connection. It has been asserted that a child who is abruptly and harshly weaned will learn to react to oral matters with anxiety, that this anxiety will tend to persist into adulthood, and that in adulthood this anxiety will be manifested in concern about oral activities in a wide variety of specific situations which induce anxiety. Applying this analysis to the presence in a single culture of the two customs we have mentioned, a possible connection can be traced between them as follows: the practice of severe weaning leads the typical child in this society to develop a motive of anxiety in response to oral activities. This motive persists into adulthood. The typical adult in this society will therefore tend to react to oral activities with a motive of anxiety, and this motive will be manifested in the specification of oral activity in his beliefs about the cause of illness. For the sake of simplicity we have here presented an interpretation of a single case, and later we will have to state the problem instead in terms suitable for testing of hypotheses; but this example will illustrate the general way in which we apply these concepts.

We have traced here a connection between a practice which forms part of one custom complex (concerned with the weaning of young children) and a belief which forms part of another custom complex (concerned with responses to illness). The connection is traced through a hypothetical motive (which is part of still another inferred complex) and the continuation of this motive from childhood into adulthood. Such a motive and its continuation may be appropriately labeled as examples of *personality processes*. Where a connection between various overt customs is traced through reference to such personality processes, it seems appropriate to speak of *personality integration of culture*.

Personality integration of culture is the subject matter of our research, and we have now indicated how we intend to apply our concepts to its study. We may now rephrase our general mode of thinking in a way better adapted to posing hypotheses for testing. We begin with certain hypotheses about personality processes, about how they are initiated by the way a child is treated by his parents and other adults, and about how they lead to certain kinds of overt responses in adulthood. We extend these hypotheses to refer, not just to a particular individual, but to the typical member of a society; the personality processes in this extension refer to inferred internal customs. By considering one set of overt customs as representing the way the typical child is treated, and another set of overt customs as representing certain overt behavior in the same person when he becomes a typical adult, these hypotheses may be used to predict that certain customs in the one set should be found to be associated with certain customs in the other set. The hypotheses which we use in this way are in considerable part drawn from psychoanalytic theory, but we have phrased them in terms of general behavior theory, largely with the purpose of facilitating this kind of analysis which we believe to be of great value for the study of culture integration.

In sketching this idea of the personality integration of culture we do not mean to imply any expectation that all of a culture will be found thus integrated. Some of the customs which are found together in a single culture may have no relation with each other which can be expressed in systematic terms; where there is a relation between two customs in a single culture, the basis of integration may be something quite different from what we have called personality integration. We do not intend to develop these other possibilities in detail here, for they are pertinent to our study only as limitations. To make clear the existence of these limitations, however, it may be well to indicate some of the conditions which would make the concept of personality integration inapplicable.

One important limitation to personality integration of culture is caused by outside influences exerting differential pressure upon two custom complexes which might otherwise be integrated through personality processes. The result, for some period of time, would be a lack of correspondence between customs in these two complexes—a case of what Ogburn (1922) has called *cultural lag*.

This limitation, applied specifically to our problem, implies that some external pressures may directly influence only the magical beliefs of a culture, whereas others may influence only its child training practices. Both of these events may occur. As an example of the former there are numerous instances where missionaries have introduced a set of religious beliefs, including a special theory of disease, into a culture without changing the child training practices. The spread of the ghost dance cult among Indians of the Western United States during the last century (Spier, 1927) is a specific example. Here an apocalyptic theory of death and resurrection often replaced or at least modified the indigenous beliefs which were, if our hypotheses are correct, more compatible with the child training practices of each society. The reason for the acceptance by any society of the new beliefs, according to evidence presented by Nash (1937), lay primarily in the degree to which its members had suffered frustrations at the hands of the whites. For the most frustrated societies a cult based on a day of judgment when all whites would disappear from the earth and all the old customs and liberties return had a strong enough appeal to outweigh a set of beliefs based upon other motives. Thus if our hypotheses, even though generally valid, were applied to societies at a time when the ghost dance and its associated beliefs were at a climax, they could not predict a relationship at that time between child training practices and religious beliefs.

Child training practices may also be influenced by external events which do not comparably affect magical beliefs about illness. There are instances where a large number of captive women have been brought into a tribe after a successful raid and as wives and mothers have had a considerable influence on the child training practices, but perhaps little immediate effect on the magical beliefs. As another example, visiting nurses have introduced rigidly scheduled infant feeding into American Indian cultures whose magical beliefs may be more compatible with indulgent nursing.

Despite the lack of personality integration which may be brought about by external forces such as these, it is our thesis that in the long run the new customs and the old will be slowly modified under the influence of the personality processes now typical of the society. Thus the ghost cult in most of the societies which adopted it was short lived. The new beliefs were either radically modified to become more coherent with the old customs, or they were dropped altogether and remembered only as an interesting and passing fad.

A second general type of limitation or countervailing influence which can reduce the effect of personality as an integrating force in culture lies in specialization rather than external influence. If beliefs about illness, for example, are imposed upon the society by a highly specialized group of medicine men or priests who have been brought up in a different manner from the other members of the society, this may interfere with personality integration of the general culture. In our own society, beliefs about sickness have been developed and expounded by professionals drawn largely from the middle and upper class. At points where they go beyond established scientific knowledge, they are likely to reflect middle-class rather than lower-class motives; an example may well be found in the exaggerated belief in the efficacy of cleanliness as a general preventative. Yet these beliefs are to a large extent accepted by members of the lower class who have had childhood experiences very different from those of the specialists.

In a similar way pediatricians and psychologists may influence child training practices in a manner which is not consonant with the belief system of the parents whom they influence. If these new child training practices persist, it may require several generations for other customs to be completely changed under the influence of the new personality characteristics which result from the new child training practices.

This potential influence of specialization upon the personality integration of culture seems likely to be of much greater importance in complex than in simple societies. Largely for this reason we decided to omit from our sample certain complex societies, such as Japan and China, which we had originally intended to include.

External influences and specialization, then, are two of the many other factors which may also influence cultural integration. In other words—and this we wish to emphasize—personality processes are only one among many of the determinants of custom potential. Even if the hypotheses which we wish to test are valid there should be many societies where their operation is not apparent, because these other factors were of greater importance at the time when our data were gathered. It is partly for this reason that we have chosen as large a sample of societies as was possible, and have used statistical procedures to aid us in detecting an influence which we assume to be but one among many.

CHAPTER 3. *Method of Research*

MAKING CROSS-CULTURAL comparisons is by no means new in the history of ethnological research. As early as the middle of the last century the evolutionary school of anthropology was coming into being, and for more than fifty years societies were placed on a scale running from savagery to civilization according to such factors as whether their economy was based on collecting, hunting, herding, or agriculture; whether they possessed writing; whether they practiced patrilineal or matrilineal descent; and other similar criteria.

The classification of cultures on the basis of their constituent customs has also been practiced by early anthropologists of the historical schools who attempted to establish culture areas. However, few of the early attempts at comparative judgments by either evolutionary or historical authors were quantitative, and methodological considerations were generally neglected both by them and by their critics.[1]

In the 1930's a somewhat more systematic approach to problems of cultural comparison began to develop. Quantitative methods and statistical procedures were used by a group in California led by Kroeber (Driver and Kroeber, 1932), and in the cross-cultural studies of Murdock (1937) and others.

For the most part even these more sophisticated comparisons between cultures were made on the basis of either the presence or absence of a given trait such as agriculture, mother-in-law avoidance, cross-cousin marriage, or the presence of one or another of alternative traits such as matrilineal and patrilineal descent. Only rarely were estimates made of the importance or

1. The first major study using quantitative methods was that of Hobhouse, Wheeler & Ginsberg (1915).

degree of development of a trait. A large scale attempt to quantify cultural variables was made by Leo Simmons (1937) who used a scale running from absence through incipient presence, presence without dominance, to dominance. Scaled judgments were also used by Beatrice Whiting (1950) who measured the degree of importance of sorcery in each of 50 societies, and by Donald Horton (1943) who estimated the degree of insobriety, the level of subsistence insecurity, and frequency of warfare in a similar sample.

Although for certain purposes categorical judgments are adequate, there are some distinct advantages in using a more sensitive measure, the degree of presence of a trait or, as we would put it, its custom potential. These advantages may be illustrated by some examples.

Ford (1945) estimated the gradualness of weaning for a sample of societies which overlap in eleven instances with societies on which we made the same judgment. Ford made a categorical judgment of presence or absence of gradual weaning, whereas we made a quantitative judgment on a scale running from most gradual to most abrupt. A comparison of the judgments obtained by the two methods is presented in Table 1. It will be seen that there is perfect agreement between the two methods; that is, both show the Kurtatchi to have gradual weaning and all the other societies to be (relative to the Kurtatchi, at least) not gradual. But in deciding in advance what the criteria for the presence or absence of gradual weaning would be, Ford happened to divide the cases at a point near the extreme end of the distribution. Although there is nothing invalid in this procedure, it is not very useful, since it leaves only a single society (in this sample) to be compared with all the others as a group. It might be more useful to compare two groups of societies more nearly equal in size. The possibility of doing this could be insured by making quantitative judgments and deciding on a point of dichotomy after the judgments were completed. Thus on the basis of our ratings of gradualness of weaning, the Masai, Lepcha, and Bena could be classified

TABLE 1. A Comparison Between Quantitative and Categorical Estimates of Gradualness of Weaning

		PRESENT	ABSENT
Abrupt	21		
	20		
	19		
	18		
	17		Thonga
	16		Maori
	15		Dobuans, Hopi
	14		Baiga
	13		Kwoma, Kwakiutl
	12		
	11		
GRADUALNESS	10		
OF	9		Masai
WEANING on	8		
our 21-point	7		
quantitative	6		Bena, Lepcha
scale:	5	Kurtatchi	
	4		
Gradual	3		

GRADUAL WEANING
according to Ford's categorical estimate

with the Kurtatchi as having relatively gradual weaning, and the remainder as having relatively abrupt. This would represent for most purposes a more useful dichotomy. Furthermore, the quantitative method would enable one to pick the Thonga as a single example of extremely abrupt weaning to contrast with the Kurtatchi, whereas after using the categorical method one might have been just as likely to pick the Bena to contrast with the Kurtatchi.

Gradualness of weaning may seem peculiarly suited for a quantitative judgment, but even customs which seem at first glance to be obviously categorical in nature turn out to raise questions that require quantitative judgment. As Murdock (1949, pp. 27–28) points out in his discussion of classifying societies with respect to presence or absence of polygyny, the occasional occurrence of bigamy in our society would require it to be classed as polygynous if a strict criterion of nonoccurrence were used. On the other hand, polygyny is never found in all families in a society and is rarely found in a majority of families, so that "an impartial observer employing the criterion of numerical preponderance (of polygyny over monogamy), consequently, would be compelled to characterize nearly every known human society as monogamous despite the preference for polygyny in the overwhelming majority." Murdock then goes on to establish more reasonable grounds for his dichotomy. He says, "We shall classify a society as polygynous whenever the culture permits, and public opinion encourages a man to have more than one wife at a time, whether such unions are common or comparatively rare, confined to men of outstanding prestige or allowed to anyone who can afford them." With this definition he concludes that 193 societies are polygynous and 43 monogamous. Although he may well have chosen the most useful single dividing line, its use does inevitably conceal sizable differences among societies which are grouped together. One side of the dichotomy includes both societies in which polygyny is highly preferred and societies in which it is hardly more than tolerated; the other side includes those in which it is mildly disapproved, and those in which it is a heinous crime. For certain purposes these distinctions would be important, and a technique which would retain them while still permitting a dichotomy to be made would have distinct advantages in permitting a more varied use to be made of the analysis.

We have thus far pointed out primarily advantages which have to do with the flexibility of the analysis, where quantitative judgments are in the end reduced to the form of categorical judgments. But often it may be useful to retain the actual quantitative value of the judgments in the final treatment of the data. The advantage here, at the present stage of scientific development, lies primarily in the greater sensitivity which may at times characterize quantitative data. This advantage of sensitivity will be found, in general, where position on one scale is consistently related to position on some other scale, and this relationship is the object of inquiry. Since quantitative treatment of cultural data is as yet rare, it will be clearest to cite an example from other subject matter. Suppose that one were seeking to determine whether brothers tend to resemble each other in height. It would be necessary to measure the height of a number of pairs of brothers and see whether there is more similarity within a pair than could occur by chance. Suppose, now, that the measurement consisted simply of a categorical judgment as to whether each man were tall or short—that is, above or below the average height in the community. In many instances brothers would be placed in opposite categories who were in fact very close together in height, just above and just below the average. On the other hand, many pairs of brothers would be placed in the same category who differed a great deal in height. Clearly such a procedure would render the data less sensitive than a method which would retain more precise measurements. One general effect of this decreased sensitivity is that many more cases are needed to reveal a relationship in the data than would be needed with a more sensitive technique. Where the less sensitive categorical judgment is very much easier to make, and additional cases can be added with very little trouble, it may be preferable to use the less sensitive method and accumulate many cases. Where, on the other hand, addition of more cases requires more trouble than the use of the more sensitive method of judging, then clearly the more sensitive method of judging should be used.

In cross-cultural studies the logical parallel to determining whether brothers resemble each other in height is determining whether the position of a society on one scale of cultural variation is correlated with its position on another scale of cultural variation. If either or both of these scales can suitably be treated quantitatively, then this potential advantage of sensitivity is there to be gained. Much of our study meets this criterion and illustrates, also, the great need in cross-cultural work to take advantage of any possible gain in sensitivity, for the number of societies available is often very small. Additional cases can be added only by exhaustive library work, at best, and often only by an amount of field work which would be quite prohibitive for a single group of research workers. Hence, in cross-cultural work there is a very strong reason for applying the most sensitive methods possible to the available data.

A further advantage which the method of quantitative judgment has over the method of categorical judgment is that it facilitates taking into account the whole cultural context of the single aspect which is being attended to. Where a cultural variable is rated or ranked on a many-point scale, it is relatively easy for the judge to shift the judgment slightly up or down according to his impression of the bearing upon his judgment of other related facts about the culture. This is not so easy in the case of categorical judgments where each case must be put at one or the other extreme; a secondary consideration would have to be of great weight, indeed, in order to lead properly to a shift of the judgment from one extreme to the other. This characteristic associated with quantitative judgments does in fact play so important a part in the judging process used in this study that there is a very marked difference between this process and the simple judgment of presence or absence of cultural traits.

We have felt so strongly the advantages for cross-cultural study of quantitative judgments over categorical judgments that we employed them throughout our analysis. In the case of some variables, in particular some which will be presented in later chapters dealing with customary responses to illness, the variable was completely absent in many cultures; here too we did none the less use the method of quantitative judgment for societies in which the variable was present, hoping to obtain a gain in sensitivity. Certain of those variables have finally been treated as though categorical judgments were used; we would have had no way of predicting in advance, however, for which variables this would be desirable.

DIMENSIONS OF CULTURAL VARIATION

Child training practices vary in many ways from one society to another. In fact there is such diversity that it seems at first glance that it would be an impossible task to discover any systematic way of comparing them. To do this some dimensions or variables must be chosen which are universal. That is, each dimension chosen must be such that every society in the sample could be assigned to a position along it, except where information was lacking.

In choosing such dimensions we first distinguished five systems of behavior [2]—oral, anal, sexual, dependence, and aggression—on the assumption that these systems would occur and be subject to socialization in all societies.

The first three of these, the oral, anal and sexual systems, we could expect to be universal on the basis of the fact that they could be presumed to be motivated by the primary or innate drives of hunger, elimination, and sex respectively. The fact that we were drawing many of our hypotheses from Freudian theory which holds that these three systems are in part expressions of developmental stages in the libido gave us another reason for our choice of these three.

Dependence and aggression have a somewhat different status. These systems we would suppose to be motivated primarily by acquired drives rather than by innate primary drives. Even if they are acquired, however, these drives are probably universal. Infants are born helpless and must be cared for and nurtured to maintain life; as a result of this experience the wish to be cared for and nurtured should be developed in every society. Similarly, no child can grow up completely without frustration, and aggression is very likely to occur as a response to frustration. Moreover, parents and others with whom a child interacts are very likely in any society to comply with a child's aggressive

2. A system of behavior is a set of habits or customs motivated by a common drive and leading to common satisfactions.

demands at least part of the time. Therefore we expect aggression to "pay off" to some extent in all societies and hence become learned as a drive.[3]

For two of these five systems we distinguish several subsystems. Sexual behavior was analyzed into four components— immodesty, masturbation,[4] heterosexual play, and homosexual play. Aggressive behavior was analyzed into five components— temper tantrums, physical aggression, verbal aggression, property damage, and disobedience. An analysis was made so far as possible of child training practices with respect to each of these components or subsystems, but it was followed by an overall analysis of practices with respect to sexual behavior as a whole and aggressive behavior as a whole.

Thus we assumed that infants in every society would initially develop habits in each of these five systems of behavior. This was not the only criterion for selecting systems of behavior for study. We also wished to choose systems which were subject to control and discipline during the process of child training, and which continued to be relevant in adult life. These five systems also fulfilled this criterion. It appears that in every society children must be weaned from breast to bottle and taught to eat food in an appropriate manner; that in every society children must be taught to defecate at the proper time and the proper place; that in every society children must be taught the rules of sexual propriety; that in every society children must be taught to be self-reliant and responsible; and that in every society children must be taught to curb their aggressive impulses and express them only when it is considered appropriate or tolerable by the rules of the society.

Each of these five systems of behavior tends to be character-

3. Theoretically, if aggression were never rewarded it might not develop as a behavior system. We felt such a state of affairs to be highly unlikely, and in fact the control of aggression appeared to be a socialization problem in every society in our sample on which there was data.

4. "Masturbation" is used in this book to mean any form of autoerotic behavior involving stimulation of the genitals.

ized by an initial period when certain habits motivated by each of these five drives are learned, and by a later period—that of socialization—during which these initial habits are replaced, generally under pressure from parents, by habits appropriate to older children and adults.

Furthermore, societies differ from one another in the degree to which children are indulged during the initial period and in the severity of the discipline imposed during the socialization period. Since, according to principles of learning, one of the consequences of indulgence should be the development of satisfactions, this enabled us to specify one of our basic variables—initial satisfaction. Secondly, since the severity of discipline should, by learning principles, be related to the development of anxiety, this yielded our second basic variable—socialization anxiety.

Initial satisfaction, as was stated in the last chapter, is a type of custom corresponding to an acquired reward at the individual level. It corresponds most closely to the concept of security in psychoanalytic terminology. Since a satisfaction then is defined as a custom, it can vary in amount and degree, and this variation we would call the custom potential of initial satisfaction or more simply the *initial satisfaction potential*. One set of basic judgments therefore is that of the initial satisfaction potential for each of the five systems of behavior described above.

Socialization anxiety is also a type of custom. At the cultural level it may be classed as a type of motive; at the individual level, as an acquired drive. Our second basic variable then is the amount of anxiety engendered by the socialization process—in our terminology, the *socialization anxiety potential*. The details of the method by which these judgments were made will be presented later in this chapter.

Several other estimates of child training were made in addition to those described above. The age at the onset of socialization for each of the five systems was estimated in a way which will also be amplified later in this chapter. The relative importance of various agents of socialization, e.g. parents, relatives, nonrelatives, and specialists, and the frequency and intensity of various techniques of socialization such as physical punishment, threats, ostracism, denial of love, and ridicule were also judged. Since these other judgments did not play a central role in our study, and since the method used was essentially similar to that used for our ten basic judgments, we will not discuss them in detail here.

THE PROCEDURE OF JUDGMENT

THE JUDGES

The judgments were made by research assistants who were employed for this purpose. Had the judgments been made only by one person there would have been no way of determining how dependable or consistent the judgments were. Hence it was necessary to have at least two judges. Of the first two assistants whose services we obtained, however, one had a fuller acquaintance with the general purposes of the research than we considered desirable in order to exclude the possibility of biased judgments. We therefore obtained a third judge as well. Of the three judges, one was a logician and the other two were graduate students in psychology.

THE GENERAL TASK AND SOURCE MATERIAL

The task with which the judge was confronted was that of reading certain published material and making, on the basis of the evidence contained in this material, the various judgments called for by his instructions. The source material consisted of extracts from ethnographic reports about the culture of 75 different primitive societies which were selected and used in our study simply as being the 75 for which the necessary material was available.

We began with looking through all the societies which had been indexed in the Cross-Cultural File at the Institute of

Human Relations,[5] to determine for which ones there was adequate information about the handling of at least one of the five systems of child behavior we were dealing with, and information about the general aspects of adult behavior we were exploring. For these societies the judge read extracts from published ethnographic reports which had been classified in the File under the headings of Infancy and Child Care; in a number of cases, however, these extracts were supplemented by the reading of accounts of child training in especially pertinent articles or monographs which had not yet been entered in the File.

In addition to the societies studied entirely or partly through use of the Cross-Cultural File we sought additional societies for which especially full information was available about child training practices. We were able to add 10 such societies to the 65 obtained from the File. For each of these societies the judge was given from one to four articles or monographs with instructions to locate the evidence pertinent to child training practices and then treat this material in the same way as he had treated the extracts for the other societies in the File.

The material available to the judge varied from about one printed page to several hundred. The judge might make tentative judgments as he went through the material, but was instructed to review and revise all of his judgments carefully after having read all of the material. The judgments were entered on a mimeographed form. The form had room for several hundred separate entries, most of which were preliminary to and a basis for the relatively few over-all judgments which were the ones generally used for testing hypotheses. Not all (or even most) of these judgments were possible for most societies because of insufficient information. The judge made in each case only those judgments which could be made from the evidence available.

The judgment that is called for in measuring the cultural

5. For information about the nature and uses of this file, now known as the Human Relations Area Files, see the Preface in G. P. Murdock *et al.* (1950).

dimensions which we have defined is a complicated and rather general one. The judge is not called upon to note simply, for example, whether physical punishment is used in weaning but to evaluate the general effect on the children in a given society of all types of punishment and reward used in weaning, as he can judge it from the entire context of description of child training procedures in that society.

Since the judgment is thus complex it is necessary to give the judge detailed instructions, based in part on theoretical considerations, in order to guide him in making the judgment. This was, of course, done separately for initial satisfaction, socialization anxiety, and each of the other judgments which were required.

JUDGMENTS OF INITIAL SATISFACTION

The instructions given to the judges in the case of initial satisfaction were based on four specific ideas about factors that would influence the satisfaction potential that would become attached to a given system of behavior. These ideas, which will be presented below, were derived from the treatment of acquired reward in general behavior theory. The four factors were the duration of the initial period, the amount of freedom given the child to perform his initial habits, the amount of encouragement of these habits, and the amount of concurrent anxiety.

First, we assumed that the longer the child is allowed to perform the initial habits in a system, the greater the satisfaction potential developed with respect to that system. That is, the longer a child nursed before weaning began, the stronger would be the security gained through nursing and, by generalization, through other oral behavior. This assumption was based on the theory that a satisfaction is a learned product of responses being made and followed by reward and that the longer this concurrence of responses and rewards continues, the greater is the satisfaction potential established.

Second, we assumed that the more freely the child is permitted to perform his initial habits, the greater will be the satisfaction potential. This assumption was based likewise on the view that the satisfaction is learned; the more ample the natural reward for the behavior because of lack of interference and restrictions, the greater the satisfaction potential. For example, the child who is looked on with disapproval and made to feel uncomfortable when he soils himself is assumed to develop less satisfaction potential as a response to defecation than the child who upon soiling himself is not made to feel any discomfort.

Third, we assumed that the greater the encouragement of the child's initial habits, the greater would be the satisfaction potential. This assumption is similarly based upon principles of learning. Encouragement may be viewed as an exaggeration of freedom and as the offering of rewards in addition to those naturally associated with the behavior. For example, those societies in which parents were reported to manipulate their children's genitals would, by this instruction, tend to be judged as having higher initial sex satisfaction potential than those societies where masturbation was simply permitted. One reason for this lies in the assumption that the former societies added extraneous social rewards of approval and attention to the "natural" rewards resulting from genital stimulation.

Fourth and last, we assumed that an anxious child establishes stronger satisfaction potential through performing a permitted habit than does a non-anxious child. A child, for example, who engages in pleasurable sucking at a time when he is undergoing considerable anxiety because of severe toilet training is assumed to acquire a stronger satisfaction potential for sucking than a child who sucks only at a period of life when in his society there is no such source of anxiety. This assumption is also based on an interpretation of satisfaction as a learned response with, of course, the additional assumption that any of the initial responses we are dealing with are capable of reducing to some extent any anxiety. The greater the anxiety, the greater the drive reduction or reward obtained through the performance of the specific responses we are concerned with.

The judge was instructed to make a rating on a seven-point scale for each of these four aspects of patterned treatment of a given system of behavior. He was then asked to use these ratings, weighting them as seemed to him appropriate in the light of the evidence for the particular society and combining them with any other pertinent information for the particular society, in order to arrive at an over-all judgment of the initial satisfaction potential of the particular system of behavior for children in this society.

The measure of initial satisfaction is thus a measure of the custom potential of an internal response in the children of a society, the response of deriving acquired reward from performing the responses of a particular system of behavior. The initial satisfaction of oral behavior is a measure, for example, of the extent to which oral responses in children of a given society are predicted to have an acquired reward value above and beyond their basic biological reward value.

Since this measure is based primarily on information about the behavior of parents toward their children, it may also be taken as a measure of an aspect of the parental behavior. It may be taken as an approximate measure of the custom potential of the parents' practice of indulging the child with respect to the particular system of behavior. When we use this measure with reference to the parental behavior rather than to its effect on the child, we will refer to it as a measure of *initial indulgence.* It should be remembered that its use is an approximate one, the measure having actually been based on consideration of the effect of the parental behavior on the internal responses of their children.

JUDGMENTS OF SOCIALIZATION ANXIETY

For the socialization anxiety developed in the course of imposing inhibitory control, similarly, four separate aspects of evidence were to be attended to in arriving at an over-all judgment. These considerations, also, were based on general behavior theory; they derive from the theoretical treatment of acquired drive as, for example, by Miller (1951). The four aspects of evidence to be attended to here were brevity, severity of punishment, frequency of punishment, and signs of emotional disturbance in the children.

The first of these was the brevity of the transition from freedom of indulgence of the initial habit to the requirement of complete acceptance of childhood or adult inhibitions. It was assumed that in general the briefer this transition, the stronger must be the anxiety required to achieve it. The transition in behavior was viewed as a process of learning in which an earlier habit must be replaced by a new habit. A long period of transition permits gradual extinction of the old habit and gradual building up of the potential of the new habit, without the necessary development of any anxiety as a means of preventing the response of the initial habit. A very rapid transition, on the other hand, does not permit this process of gradual extinction and gradual development of new secondary rewards. In general, it presumably can be achieved only by developing an internal response of anxiety which will interfere with and thus prevent the response of the initial habit, which would otherwise still be dominant

Second, it was assumed that the more severe the punishments used in imposing inhibitory control, the greater would be the strength of the subsequent anxiety. This assumption is based on the view that socialization anxiety is a learned effect of painful or unpleasant consequences following the initial behavior, and the greater the pain or discomfort the greater the learned anxiety. This particular judgment was very difficult because it required an evaluation of the severity of a given punishment not just for mankind in general but for the children of a given society. While this difficult judgment could certainly not be made without error, particularly in view of the fact that the judge had available to him only material pertinent to childhood training and not to other aspects of the culture, it seemed possible to make the judgment in a way that would be an improvement over an assumption that a particular kind of punishment would universally be more painful or discomforting than another type of punishment.

Third, it was assumed that the more frequently the child was punished for a given type of behavior, the greater would be the anxiety developed. This assumption follows from a view of anxiety as a product of learning; repeated occasions for learning should on the whole lead to stronger learning.

Fourth of the aspects of evidence to be considered was that of the severity of emotional conflict actually produced in children of a given society by socialization of a particular system of behavior. For example, if it was reported that children were extremely miserable during the period of weaning, this was taken as evidence that a high degree of oral anxiety was, in fact, being learned at that time.

As in the case of initial satisfaction, the judge was then asked to take all four of these ratings into account, weighting them as he thought fit and taking into account also any additional evidence which for this particular society appeared to be relevant, in order to make an over-all judgment of the severity of anxiety developed in connection with the particular system of behavior.

As with initial satisfaction, this judgment was intended primarily as a measure of the custom potential of certain internal responses in the children of a society but also may be used as an approximate measure of certain aspects of the overt behavior of the parents. As a measure of custom potential of internal responses in the children it is a measure of the strength of the kind of custom which we have defined as a motive; it measures the custom potential of the tendency for responses and impulses of a given system of behavior to arouse the drive of anxiety in the typical child of a society. As a measure of the behavior of the parents it may be called a measure of *severity of socialization,* for it reflects the extent to which the child training practices of the parents are severe in the sense of being likely to produce anxiety in their children.

These four aspects of evidence that have been described for each of the two dimensions of initial satisfaction and socialization anxiety do not represent a selection of the types of evidence that would have been ideal in view only of our theoretical notions about satisfaction and anxiety. They represent rather a compromise between our notions of what would have been theoretically ideal and what appeared feasible in view of the kind of evidence available in the ethnographic reports. It was frequently true, even so, that the judge was unable to find evidence relevant to all four of the aspects listed under either satisfaction or anxiety. In these cases he was asked to make the over-all judgment of strength of satisfaction or anxiety as best he could on the basis of all the evidence that was available.

JUDGMENTS OF AGE OF SOCIALIZATION

Judgments of the age at which socialization of a given kind of behavior is seriously begun in each society were made, not with an arbitrary rating scale, but by the use of actual age estimates. The judges were instructed to make use of all relevant information in order to arrive at these judgments. In many cases the ethnographer provided the estimate of age himself. In other cases it was possible to make an estimate in the absence of such an explicit statement by the ethnographer. If it was reported, for example, that in one society children are weaned about the time they begin to walk, it was possible to make a rough estimate on the basis of the approximate age at which children begin to walk. For this purpose the judges were instructed to use the norms provided by Gesell and Ilg (1943) simply to have a uniform basis for transforming developmental stages into ages. In view of the way in which the judgments of age of socialization were arrived at, it should be clear that their exact value should not be taken very seriously. Even though they are expressed in terms of age, they should be taken as only very rough estimates; despite this, they can be of real value for comparing various societies, for the differences among various societies are much greater than the range of inaccuracy of the estimates.

In general, judgments of age of socialization could be made for many fewer societies than could the judgments of initial satisfaction and of socialization anxiety. Pertinent information was much more often lacking in this case. There was a great difference among the five systems of behavior in this respect. For oral behavior, dependence, and toilet training, age of socialization could be estimated in a reasonable number of societies. For sexual behavior as a whole, estimates of age did not seem to be very meaningful, as ages might be quite different for the several forms of sexual behavior; for two of these specific forms of sexual behavior, immodesty and heterosexual play, estimates of age of socialization could be made for a moderate number of societies. In the case of aggression, both in general and for particular forms of aggressive behavior, the estimates could almost never be made, for the treatment of children's aggressive behavior tended to be rather constant from the time it first appeared (so far as could be judged from the information contained in most of the ethnographic reports).

We have now indicated the general instructions that were given to the judge in order to permit his making judgments from a complex body of material in a way that would be relevant to the hypotheses we intended to test. There remain several specific points in the procedure of judgment that must be made clear.

RATINGS VERSUS RANKINGS

So far we have spoken only vaguely of over-all satisfaction or anxiety in each system of behavior. To be more specific, the over-all judgment was made quite separately in two different forms. The first of these was a *rating* on a seven-point scale. On the basis of all the evidence available the judge was, for example, required to rate the degree of anxiety developed in weaning in a given society on a scale ranging from one (indicating an extremely low degree of anxiety) to seven (indicating a very high degree of anxiety). The making of these ratings required in effect that a given society be directly compared in this respect with the other societies that were being rated. It required a definite idea on the part of the judge of the degree of anxiety represented by each of the seven points on the scale and then an ability to recognize which of these seven degrees of anxiety was most closely approximated by the given society. Clearly each judge had to familiarize himself with the data on quite a number of societies before he could begin to make these ratings. It appeared to us and to the judges that it was possible to develop standards which made such ratings meaningful. There was, however, the risk that we might have been wrong in this belief.

Because of this risk we had essentially the same judgment made also by a method of *ranking*. Here the judge was not asked to compare a given society in any way with other societies. He was asked only to look, for example, at the socialization process in this society for each of the five systems of behavior separately. He was then asked to judge in which of these five systems the mode of socialization was such as to develop the highest degree of anxiety, in which it was such as to develop the next highest degree of anxiety and so on down to the system of behavior in connection with which socialization in this society was mildest or least likely to develop anxiety. Thus he was asked here to order the five systems of behavior for this one society alone, without a necessity for taking into account any information about child training in other societies. (The ranking technique was thus used only for each of the five systems of behavior as a whole, whereas the rating technique was also applied when possible to separate forms of sexual and aggressive behavior.)

One implication of this difference between the techniques of rating and ranking is that only for ratings could there be tied scores for a single society on two or more systems of behavior. For example, a given society might conceivably be rated 5 on the socialization anxiety scale for each of the five systems of behavior. This would mean that the judge felt that the society was moderately severe with respect to each system. For the rankings, however, the five systems would have to be ordered according to the relative severity of each system as compared to the others, each system being assigned a different rank order. In fact, however, although there were instances of tied scores on the ratings for a given society for two or sometimes three systems, in general the ratings as well as the rankings represented a fair distribution of values. The effect of this is that, while the rankings and ratings might in principle be very nearly independent of each other, they are in fact very closely related.[6]

The judgments of initial satisfaction and of socialization anxiety, then, are available in two entirely separate forms, ratings and rankings. In general, we have preferred to use the ratings for two reasons: (1) they appear to us to be more directly relevant to the hypotheses we are testing; (2) a rating could be made for a given society for one or two systems of behavior alone if there was good evidence on those systems and not on the others, whereas rankings could be made only by taking all five systems into account. We have, however, cited certain results obtained with the use of rankings that seem particularly pertinent because they support, or aid in interpreting, the results obtained with ratings.

CERTAINTY OF JUDGMENT

The judge was required to indicate the degree of confidence he felt in making the judgment. Only two degrees of confidence were used, which we will here call *confident* and *doubtful*. If the judge could not even make a doubtful judgment he, of course,

6. The closeness of relationship between ratings and rankings may be expressed by a correlation coefficient. The correlation coefficients for each system of behavior, first for initial satisfaction and then for socialization anxiety, are oral -0.65 and -0.82; anal -0.77 and -0.92; sexual -0.95 and -0.90; dependence -0.64 and -0.76; aggression -0.55 and -0.79. These correlation coefficients are negative because the meaning of a high rating corresponds to that of a low ranking. These coefficients are based only on the most confident judgments (as defined later in this chapter).

simply omitted the judgment. This device of calling for indications of degrees of confidence was adopted as a result of the following reasoning. We did not wish to have the judge make only those judgments which he could make with a high degree of confidence; the number of cases might then be reduced to a number too small for use, whereas the doubtful judgments might have enough evidence behind them to yield meaningful results with the larger number of cases that would then be available. On the other hand, had we instructed our judges to include even the doubtful judgments but without making any discrimination between them and the confident ones, we might have introduced so much random variation into the judgments that they would be of no use at all. Requiring this discrimination on the part of the judges left us with freedom of action. If for a particular hypothesis confident judgments were sufficient in number to permit an adequate test, they alone could be used. If for another hypothesis the number of judgments available was extremely small, then in that case the doubtful judgments could be included. It did, in fact, turn out this way; for some hypotheses dealt with in this report an adequate number of confident judgments are available, while other hypotheses could be tested satisfactorily only if doubtful judgments were included.

The problem of what judgments to include is complicated by the fact that there were three judges, and that they did not necessarily agree in the confidence they expressed in a particular judgment. For the pooled judgment of all three judges we have arbitrarily decided on a three-point scale of confidence. In later chapters, when we indicate which judgments are included for particular purposes, "confident judgments" will refer only to instances where all three judges made the particular judgment and were confident in doing so. "Judgments of an intermediate degree of confidence" will refer to instances where all three judges made the particular judgment but one or more of them considered it doubtful, and to instances where only two judges made the judgment but both of them were confident of the judgment. "Judgments of lowest confidence" will refer to the remaining instances (those where two judges made a judgment but were not both confident, and those where only one judge made a judgment).

CONSISTENCY AND VALIDITY OF JUDGMENTS

We come now to consider whether the judgments about satisfaction and socialization anxiety had the consistency and validity necessary for their scientific use. The three judges did their work entirely independently of each other, except that they were given the same instructions as to how to make their judgments and were given the same ethnographic reports on which to base their judgments. If each judge made his judgments in a consistent and meaningful manner as dictated by the nature of the evidence and the instructions, this should be revealed by agreement among the judges in the ratings and rankings they produced. The measurement of degree of consistency in a situation such as this is something for which suitable statistical techniques are available in the common statistical procedures used by psychologists. The measure that is used is the coefficient of correlation between the ratings of any two judges.

Coefficients of correlation were separately computed for the ratings on each of the ten cultural dimensions by each pair of judges,[7] and separately for cases in which both the judges were confident and for cases in which one or both judges were doubtful. For the confident judgments the median coefficient of correlation was 0.65, and for the doubtful judgments the median correlation was 0.34. For the confident judgments this appears to us to be a fairly satisfactory degree of consistency. For the doubtful judgments the consistency is regrettably low. It is therefore clearly desirable that, when there are enough cases, the confident judgments alone be used.

In relating these dimensions of childhood training to aspects of adult behavior we have of course not been using the judgment of a single judge but the pooled judgment of all three

7. I.e., for each of the three combinations of two out of the three judges.

judges. For this reason a correlation coefficient expressing the probable consistency of the average of the three judges' ratings is the appropriate measure to use in determining how consistent were the ratings in the form in which we actually used them. For the confident judgments the median coefficient thus corrected is 0.85; for the doubtful judgments it is 0.61.[8]

We were satisfied, then, with the degree of consistency or reliability characterizing the confident judgments made by our judges on dimensions of child training practices and found that there was some useful degree of consistency even in the doubtful judgments. The question might still be asked, of course, whether this consistency arises from some spurious source. Could it be that the judges agreed with each other because they all knew what we wanted or because they worked together? We had this issue very much in mind in planning the research. For this reason neither of us made judgments on which our results would be based, or in any way directly influenced them. As we very clearly knew what relationships we were looking for, we could not have been certain that our preconceptions would not influence our judgments. We felt it essential to have the judgments made by other persons, and by other persons whose working conditions were such that they could not have been influenced in the same way we might have been. We made only one exception; as already indicated, one of our three judges was a research assistant who did help us in the initial planning of the research and had some considerable knowledge of our purposes. We took care that she, in making these judgments, was instructed to make them altogether on the basis of information on child training in each given society. Comparison of her ratings with those of other judges led us to believe that this effort was successful. The other two judges had no very definite knowledge of the hypotheses we were testing and had no knowledge of the other aspects of the cultures with which we were going to compare these dimensions of child training. Moreover, they worked

8. This correction is made by the Spearman-Brown formula described in standard books on statistics, e.g. Garrett, 1947, pp. 387–391.

in complete independence of each other and, in fact, in different years. The other cultural dimensions with which these dimensions were to be correlated were, furthermore, rated by a completely different pair of judges who worked in complete independence from the judges of child training practices and in ignorance of the child training practices of the societies with which they were dealing. It was thus virtually impossible that the judgments could have been contaminated by the judges' wishes or preconceptions about the outcome of this research. By the exclusion of these possibilities of bias we may claim that to that extent the judgments on which our results are based are valid as well as consistent measures of those dimensions of cultural variation which they were intended to get at.

Some readers may feel that the measures we have taken to insure against contamination of the judgments are rather extreme. They are. They are justified by the fact that we had to deal with material on which judgments are difficult. With this sort of material the danger of biased judgment is great. Had more clear-cut evidence been available, or had we been dealing with topics where judgments are less difficult, many of our precautions could have been dispensed with.

CHAPTER 4. *Variations in*
Child Training Practices

IN THE preceding chapter we have described the main concepts
we have used in analyzing the child training practices of primitive societies. We have dealt with five systems of behavior—
oral, anal, sexual, dependence, and aggression. For each system
of behavior we have attempted to analyze the conditions which
should produce initial satisfaction of varying degrees, the age
at which socialization begins, and the techniques of child training which should produce varying degrees of socialization
anxiety.

From our effort to apply this sort of analysis to the data on
child training in many primitive societies we have arrived at
two main conclusions of a simple factual nature.

One of these conclusions is that child training the world over
is in certain important respects identical. It is identical in that
it is found always to be concerned with certain universal problems of behavior. Parents everywhere have similar problems to
solve in bringing up their children. In all societies the helpless
infant, getting his food by nursing at his mother's breast and,
having digested it, freely evacuating the waste products, exploring his genitals, biting and kicking at will, must be changed
into a responsible adult obeying the rules of his society. While
there are many societies in our sample for which data are lacking on some of these problems, there is no clear evidence in any
case that any of these basic problems are in fact absent from
the life of any people. Child training everywhere seems to be
in considerable part concerned with problems which arise from
universal characteristics of the human infant and from universal

characteristics of adult culture which are incompatible with the continuation of infantile behavior.

The other general conclusion of a factual nature is that even in these important respects child training also differs from one society to another. Societies differ from each other in the precise character of the rules to which the child must be taught to conform; no society, for example, permits its children the complete sexual freedom which they might spontaneously develop, but the extent and exact character of the restrictions placed on sexual freedom vary tremendously. Societies differ, moreover, in the techniques that are used in enforcing conformity, in the age at which conformity is demanded to each rule of adult life, in the extent to which, in particular respects, children are trained into a distinctive culture of their own rather than directly from infancy into adult culture, and in countless other details of the socialization process.

Each of these two general conclusions plays an essential role in the study we are reporting in this book. We are engaged in a quest for scientific generalizations. For these to become possible we must make use of concepts which are applicable to a wide body of diverse data. The fact that our concepts do turn out to be pertinent to the child training of all sorts of primitive societies indicates that we have met this prerequisite of scientific inquiry, although they are not necessarily the best for all purposes. The anthropological fieldworker, in order to give a full and realistic account of child training practices in a particular society, may need concepts which are more narrow and specific, more closely identified with the peculiarities of the one culture that provides the framework of his description. Similarly, the educator in our society may need such specific and culture-bound concepts as "attitude toward teachers" and "acceptance of school routines." Our concepts have been chosen for their utility in permitting generalization about human behavior in general. While we believe that concepts which permit such broad generalizations will also have value in the more specific descriptive and practical tasks of the fieldworker or the educator, they were not chosen with that aim in mind.

For the scientific generalization we intend to seek, on the other hand, it is essential that there be variation among societies with respect to these concepts. We are looking for the relationship between one variable and another—specifically, for relationships between customs of child training and other customs which will provide indices of the adult personality traits characteristic of the members of a society. But for such a relationship to be demonstrated, it is essential that the two variables each be in some cases present and in some cases absent, or that each vary in degree, being in some cases present in high degree and in other cases present in low degree. Only in this way is it possible to test whether presence, or high degree, of one variable tends to be accompanied by presence, or high degree, of the other variable.

Thus, these two findings of universal applicability of the concepts we have used in analyzing child training practices, and of variation among societies with respect to these concepts, are both essential for the main purposes of our research, that of testing generalizations about human behavior.

In this present chapter, however, we propose to make use of these same two findings in a different way, a way that is preliminary to our main purposes but also has some justification of its own. We propose here to give some account of the way and extent to which human societies differ from each other with respect to the variables of child training we are dealing with. The object of this descriptive survey in relation to the main purposes of our research is to give the reader a better notion of what these variables of child training practice mean. He will thus be better prepared to understand and to make his own interpretations of the findings we report later about relationships between these variables of child training practices and indices of adult personality characteristics. The other justification for this descriptive survey lies in the interest of comparative knowledge for its own sake. We are living in a period when the child training practices of our own society are a topic of great general interest. They are the subject of frequent comment and criticism. Psychiatrists, pediatricians, psychologists, anthropologists and other writers have urged upon members of our society various changes in these practices. For the reader who is interested in possibilities of change, or who wishes to consider the probable wisdom of any specific change that is suggested, one thing important to know is how our present practices compare with those of other societies. The survey of child training practices that we offer here in rather brief form can contribute to providing this background of comparative information.

Since interest in child training practices of other societies for purposes of simple comparison is likely to be focused on a comparison of our own society with others, we have felt it important, for purposes of this one chapter, to include specific reference to the child training practices of our own society. With this in mind we had our judges analyze the practices of our own society in exactly the same way they analyzed the practices of the primitive societies which constitute our main sample. It was necessary for this purpose to select some report or reports which could be used as the document to be analyzed in this case. There is, however, the complication of considerable variation in child training practices among different segments of our society. For this reason it was desirable to choose some one defined segment which had been adequately studied with respect to child training practices. The best document we could find for this purpose consisted of a study by Davis and Havighurst (1946, 1947). This study was made in Chicago in the early forties. Their information was drawn from interviews with and observations of 200 families, representing in equal numbers white middle and lower class and Negro middle and lower class. The scores which we will use in this chapter for comparative purposes will be those relevant to the white middle-class group only.

It should be pointed out that, at the time the study was made,

the recent trend toward more permissive child training practices was apparently pretty much restricted to professional
groups of the middle class. The group studied by Davis and
Havighurst therefore was undoubtedly less permissive than a
similar group would be today. Furthermore, there may be considerable regional differences in child training practices which a
report restricted to the Chicago area of course will not represent.
Our reference group then consists of 50 middle-class families
living in Chicago in the early forties.

In this chapter we will first consider each of the five systems
of child behavior in turn. In connection with each of the five
systems of behavior we will report on three major aspects of the
socialization process:

1. Initial indulgence of this system of behavior. Here the
ratings we will review are the same which we have described
in the preceding chapter under the label of "initial satisfaction."
The ratings were based on a theoretical analysis of factors which
would tend to make for high or low satisfaction in connection
with a given system of behavior, and it is this learned satisfaction
which is of interest in connection with our later tests of hypotheses about the relation of child training to adult personality. For
present purposes, however, where our attention is focused on
the child training per se, it is more useful to use a term which refers to the parental behavior itself rather than the effect on the
child. As indicated in the preceding chapter, the term used for
this purpose is "initial indulgence." This is an accurate term for
summarizing three of the factors which the judges took into account in judging initial security—the factors of duration of the
initial behavior, freedom in performing the initial behavior, and
degree of encouragement of the initial behavior. "Indulgence"
does not correctly describe the fourth factor which was taken
into account—the amount of concurrent anxiety—but we have
felt that no great inaccuracy is introduced by using the term
"indulgence" as an over-all description of our "initial satisfaction" scale when interpreted, for purposes of this descriptive review, as reflecting the behavior of the parents toward the child.

2. Age of socialization. The meaning of these judgments has already been described in the preceding chapter. We would like to repeat here the caution expressed there about taking these judgments as precise measurements of age. They should be taken instead as very rough estimates, based often on rather indirect evidence, but useful for purposes of comparison among societies.

3. Severity of socialization. Here the ratings we will review are those which we have described in the preceding chapter under the label of "socialization anxiety." Again, choice of this label was dictated by our main orientation toward studying the effects upon children of their treatment by adults, whereas a more appropriate label here is one which directs attention at that treatment itself. In this case, "severity of socialization" seems to us perfectly appropriate as a label for this variable when it is being considered as representative of the behavior of parents toward their children rather than from the point of view of inferences about the effect of that behavior on the children.

For the scales of initial indulgence and severity of socialization we have based our statements in this chapter solely on those societies for which a judgment on the scale was made with confidence by all three of our judges. For judgments on age of the beginning of socialization, which were intrinsically rather uncertain judgments, this procedure would leave us with too few cases to make much use of. Consequently, for judgments of age we have included societies for which the judgments are only of an intermediate degree of confidence; that is, we have included all cases for which two of the judges made a confident judgment (regardless of whether the third judge made any judgment at all), and all cases for which all three of the judges made a judgment (regardless of whether they were confident of the judgment).

After reviewing socialization of the five systems of behavior in turn, we will consider at the end of the chapter the average degree of indulgence and severity in various societies. In the following chapter we will consider the interrelations among these various aspects of child training practices.

Nursing and Weaning

INITIAL NURSING INDULGENCE

Our rating scale for initial indulgence of each system of behavior had a possible range from 3 to 21 (because it represented the sum of ratings by three judges, who each used a scale from 1 to 7). On this scale the ratings of initial indulgence of the infant's oral interests had an actual range, for various societies, from a low of 6 to a high of 18.

About one half of the 51 societies on which we have confident ratings of initial oral indulgence are closely crowded together at the upper end of the scale. The median (the point above which one half of the cases fall) is at 15, only 3 points below the highest case which actually is found. Among these many societies high on initial oral indulgence it is very hard to make discriminations. These societies are characterized by the mother's having few responsibilities during the nursing period which would interfere with child care, and by her assuming the duty of being continuously near her infant, feeding him whenever he is judged to be hungry, and in general using nursing as a means of pacifying the child whenever he has discomforts which cannot readily be removed in other ways. This general pattern of high oral indulgence is encountered over and over again in accounts of child care in primitive societies, and could accurately be said to be the most characteristic mode of treatment of young infants the world over.

The other half of the societies in our sample show gradually decreasing degrees of oral indulgence of infants. The lowest point of indulgence is reached by the Marquesans, of whom Linton says (1939, pp. 164–165),

> The Marquesans believe that nursing makes a child hard to raise and not properly submissive. There was probably

a certain amount of nursing, dependent upon the will of the mother, but in any event the nursing period was very short. Women took great pride in the firmness and beautiful shape of their breasts, which were important in sexual play. They believed that prolonged nursing spoiled the breasts and consequently were reluctant to do it. Feeding times were irregular and dependent on the convenience of the adult rather than the protests of the child.

The rating of oral indulgence in the child-rearing practices of Davis and Havighurst's American middle-class group was 8, 2 points higher than the Marquesans but lower than any other of the 51 societies in our sample. The lowness of this rating was influenced both by the short duration of the nursing period in the American middle-class group and by the extremely low degree of freedom in indulgence of oral interests permitted by them. The rigid scheduling of feeding, with respect to time and amount, is an interference with free indulgence of oral satisfaction which is unknown in this form among the societies in our sample, and rivaled there only by interference resulting from neglect or rejection, as among the Marquesans. There has been in recent years, of course, a widespread effort to change the practices of the American middle class in this respect. These efforts have, we may see, been directed at changing our child-rearing practices in the direction of greater similarity to the practices characteristic of mankind at large.

AGE OF WEANING

There are 52 societies for which we have our judges' estimates of the age at which serious efforts at weaning are typically begun. For the median case, weaning is reported to begin at the age of about two and a half years. Approximately this age is indeed typical of primitive societies in general, for the estimate for 33 out of the 52 societies falls between the ages of two years and three years.

At the upper extreme there are only two societies for which

the usual age at weaning appears to be greater than three and a half years. The most extreme are the Chenchu tribe of India, who are reported not to wean their children until they are five or six. A case of special interest is provided by the Lepcha, also of India, who generally wean their children by the age of three but in some families do not deliberately wean the youngest child; it is reported that among the Lepcha the youngest child may occasionally be seen nursing up until the time of puberty.

At the lower extreme there are only two primitive societies in our sample who attempt to wean their children before they are a year old. One of these is the Marquesans, whose general attitude toward nursing has already been indicated. The other example is the Chamorro of Guam.

The age of weaning is an aspect of socialization in which our American middle-class group is quite extreme. Our judges' estimate of the typical age of weaning among them was a little over a half year. This is earlier than for any of the 52 primitive societies except the Marquesans alone.

SEVERITY OF WEANING

For most of the societies in our sample there are certain broad uniformities in the way weaning is achieved. It is generally prepared for by the early introduction of supplementary food into the diet, usually during the child's first year. This is usually some form of starchy gruel; if more solid food is used, it is normally premasticated by the mother. The proportion of supplementary food is gradually increased until, by the time of weaning, it may form a large part of the child's diet. When weaning is finally undertaken, some means of discouraging nursing altogether is often employed. The technique of daubing a bitter or peppery substance on the breast is widely reported for this purpose. Separating the child from its mother temporarily and sending it to a relative is not infrequent. More severe measures are rare.

Despite this considerable degree of agreement in general technique among most of the societies, it is possible to discriminate real and sizable differences in the over-all severity or traumatic character of the weaning process. The ratings of severity of weaning were fairly evenly distributed over a wide range, from 6 up to 17.

The upper range of severity of weaning may be illustrated by the customs of the Baiga (with a rating of 15), for whom the ethnographer mentions only techniques of punishment as the way of accomplishing weaning.

The lower extreme, of mild weaning, may be illustrated by the customs of the Kurtatchi (with a rating of 6), among whom weaning is apparently accomplished entirely by building up the satisfaction of eating like an adult, without specific punishment or discouragement of nursing. Blackwood reports of the Kurtatchi (1935, pp. 163–164):

> Weaning is, in the normal course of affairs, a gradual process, other food, beginning with taro, which is given from birth, being gradually increased in quantity and variety. The child, according to the statement of the women, makes, of its own account, fewer and fewer demands upon its mother, who accedes to them till they cease. There would seem, accordingly, to be no shock to the child at weaning.

The median rating among the 39 societies for which confident ratings are available here is 11. This average degree of severity of weaning may be illustrated by the practices of the Kwakiutl, of whom C. S. Ford writes (1941, pp. 32–33),

> Weaning was generally initiated at between two and three years of age, although it might be delayed even longer if the child were sickly. It was accomplished by increasing the amount of supplementary feeding and by punishing the child for suckling. The mother would put some bitter substance on her nipples which, it is said, was very effective in discouraging the child's attempts to nurse. After weaning, thumb sucking was common but was discouraged by taking the finger out of the mouth and giving the child some substitute such as the muscular part of a dried horse clam.

Our judges' evaluation of the practices of our American middle-class group places them about halfway between this median degree of severity and the upper extreme of severity. American weaning practices, then, are above average in severity but are not nearly as extreme as in the initial deprivation of the child's oral interests between birth and the time of weaning.

ANAL TRAINING

INITIAL INDULGENCE

In initial indulgence of the child's free excretory behavior, as in initial oral indulgence, the societies in our sample tend to be gathered toward the upper end of the scale. Ratings given to 22 societies range from 3 to 16, and the median is at 13, only three points below the maximum. The extreme of indulgence may be illustrated by the Siriono of South America. Here the only concern of the parents about defecation in their children appears to be that the child should not play with feces (apparently, according to the ethnographer, because of awareness of a role of feces in contagion); otherwise, there is great freedom. Holmberg reports (1946, pp. 220–222),

> The infant receives no punishment if he urinates or defecates on his parents. Of course, if a mother hears her infant fart or feels that he is about to defecate on her, she holds him away from her body so as not to be soiled, but about the only punishment that an infant is subjected to by defecating on her is that of being set aside for a while until she cleans up the mess.

As there is rather little difference between this extreme case and those which fall at the median of the distribution, there is no need to cite examples to represent the median, which would simply mean slightly less freedom, or shorter duration of freedom, than among the Siriono.

The other extreme, of low initial indulgence of free defecation, is reached among the Tanala of Madagascar where, according to Linton (1939, p. 262),

> Diapers are not used, with the result that the child is constantly soiling its mother; and since the clothes that the mother wears are difficult to replace, we have here an incentive for premature sphincter discipline. In fact, anal training is begun at the age of two or three months, and the child is expected to be continent at the age of six months. If after this time the child soils its mother, it is severely punished.

The practices of our American middle-class group are nearer to the lower extreme than to the upper extreme. Their rating was 8, which was much less extreme than the Tanala, but more extreme than any of the other primitive societies for which this rating is available except the Chagga, who received a rating of 6.

AGE AT BEGINNING OF TOILET TRAINING

The median estimate for the beginning age of serious toilet training falls at the age of two. Slightly over half of the primitive societies (14 out of 25) begin toilet training somewhere between the ages of one and a half and two and a half. At the upper extreme there is one society (the Bena of Africa) where toilet training is not begun until the child is almost five years old. At the lower extreme there are two societies which begin toilet training during the child's first year. Our American middle-class group falls near this extreme, as they are judged typically to start toilet training when the child is only a little over six months old; this is earlier than is reported for any of the primitive societies reviewed with the single exception of the Tanala.

SEVERITY OF TOILET TRAINING

As may be judged from the account already given of early interference with free defecation among the Tanala, this society provides a good example of extreme severity in toilet training. For a more detailed account of the severe punishments sometimes employed in toilet training we cite Herskovits' description of toilet training among the Dahomeans (1938, *1*, 272–273), although the information here is fuller about urination than defecation.

> A child is trained by the mother who, as she carries it about, senses when it is restless, so that every time it must perform its excretory functions, the mother puts it on the ground. Thus in time, usually two years, the training process is completed. If a child does not respond to this training, and manifests enuresis at the age of four or five, soiling the mat on which it sleeps, then, at first, it is beaten. If this does not correct the habit, ashes are put in water and the mixture is poured over the head of the offending boy or girl, who is driven into the street, where all the other children clap their hands and run after the child singing,
>
> > *Adida go ya ya ya*
> > "Urine everywhere."
>
> In Whydah, the child is taken to the lagoon and washed, this being repeated a second time if necessary. If the habit is then not stopped, a live frog is attached to the child's waist, which so frightens the offender that a cure is usually effected. In Abomey, however, beating is the customary punishment.

At the extreme opposite to these practices are those of the Siriono, for whom Holmberg reports (1950, p. 75),

> Almost no effort is made by the mother to train an infant in the habits of cleanliness until he can walk, and then they are instilled very gradually. Children who are able to walk, however, soon learn by imitation, and with the assistance of their parents, not to defecate near the hammock. When they are old enough to indicate their needs, the mother gradually leads them further and further away from the hammock to urinate and defecate, so that by the time they have reached the age of 3 they have learned not to pollute

the house. Until the age of 4 or 5, however, children are still wiped by the mother, who also cleans up the excreta and throws them away. Not until a child has reached the age of 6 does he take care of his defecation needs alone.

Mild toilet training such as has just been described for the Siriono is dependent upon delaying the training until the child has reached an age when he can talk and understand well, and has developed motives which lead him to do things in the way that his parents and other members of the community approve. When these conditions are met, it is possible to achieve toilet training merely by building up new habits of defecating at the appropriate time and place which will supplant the earlier responses of free elimination without the need of punishment. When this method is used, toilet training may indeed be so easy that it does not appear as a conscious problem. When one of us, doing field work among the Kwoma of New Guinea, asked about toilet training, his informants were puzzled as to why this was anything to ask questions about. All they could say at first was, "Why, you just tell the child what to do and he does it."

For 20 societies for which the ratings were made with confidence the severity of toilet training varied from the rating of 18 given to the Tanala and 17 to the Dahomeans down to the rating of 6 given to the Siriono. The societies were rather evenly spread out over this range with some tendency for more of them to approach the lower extreme than the upper extreme. The median rating was 11; the practices characteristic of this degree of severity may be illustrated by those of the Navaho, which have been described as follows by Leighton and Kluckhohn (1947, p. 35):

> . . . bowel control is not expected of the Navaho child until he is old enough to direct his own movements and merely accompany an elder at night and in the morning. The mother or an older sister takes the child out when she herself goes to defecate and tells the little one to imitate

her position and her actions. After a time, the youngster who continues to wet or soil himself is unmercifully teased by all present. However, in the normal case, these functions soon come to be taken for granted. . . . Moreover, little feeling of disgust for urine or feces is inculcated. There is no exaggerated emphasis upon the unpleasantness of odors or consistency of excreta. The child is not thoroughly washed each time it soils itself.

Here the method is basically that of the Siriono, but apparently because of an earlier expectation of completion of the training there is more difficulty felt in achieving it, and some degree of punishment plays a part in the process.

Our American middle-class group was judged to be quite extreme in the severity of toilet training. They were given a rating of 18 on the basis of Davis and Havighurst's account. This is the same rating that was given to the Tanala, the most severe of the primitive societies reviewed.

Sex Training

In comparison with the two systems of behavior we have considered thus far, the sexual system as we have defined it includes a much greater variety of behavior. As has been indicated in the preceding chapter, this fact was recognized in the way our judges were instructed to go about their analysis of the ethnographic data on child rearing. They were asked to look for evidence on four separate aspects of sexual behavior: masturbation, heterosexual play, homosexual play, and immodesty. On each of these they were to make the judgments about initial satisfaction, age at beginning of socialization, and degree of socialization anxiety, if the evidence permitted. Then they were to put the evidence on all four of these aspects of sexual behavior together, along with any evidence in the ethnographic reports referring to sexual behavior as a whole, and make parallel judgments with respect to the socialization of sexual behavior in general.

The outcome of these instructions was that in certain respects the analysis of the separate aspects of sexual behavior is more useful than the analysis of sexual behavior as a whole, and in certain respects the opposite is true. The judges found that evidence about the age at socialization was rare in the case of sexual behavior, and that when available it usually referred specifically to some particular aspect of sexual behavior. Consequently judgments about age of socialization are useful only for the separate aspects (and indeed, even here, there are a sufficient number of such judgments to be useful only in the case of two aspects, heterosexual play and immodesty). Judgments about the satisfaction and the anxiety resulting from the socialization process, on the other hand, were made with confidence for sexual behavior in general in more cases than for any one aspect of sexual behavior. For purposes of relating sexual satisfaction and anxiety to other aspects of behavior, in later chapters, sexual behavior in general will be more useful; for purposes of relating the age of sexual socialization to other aspects of behavior, the specific behavior of heterosexual play and immodesty will be more useful. This same emphasis will be followed in the descriptive account of socialization of sexual behavior to be given here.

For one of our four aspects of sexual behavior, that of homosexual play, there was evidence about its socialization from so few societies that there is little point in attempting to construct a picture of world-wide practices from so small a sample. For those few societies, of course, this evidence was taken into account in arriving at judgments about the socialization of sexual behavior in general. But no attempt will be made here to give a descriptive account of the range of child training practices with respect to homosexual play. We will discuss each of the other three aspects in turn and will then consider the socialization of sexual behavior in general.

MASTURBATION

Initial indulgence of the young child's genital self-stimulation is in general rather high in the 17 societies for which confident ratings are available. The ratings vary from a high of 19 down only to 11, with the median at 15. The more indulgent practices may be illustrated by those of the Alorese of Indonesia, who are given a rating of 19. In Alorese infancy, "one of the favorite substitutes for offering the breast in an effort to pacify a child is to massage its genitals gently," and at a slightly later age, "sex experiences during this early period of childhood seem confined to masturbation, which goes on freely in public. Little boys are commonly seen standing on the fringe of an adult group manipulating their penes with complete self-engrossment" (DuBois, 1944, pp. 37 and 45).

The least indulgent of the primitive societies reviewed may be illustrated by the Manus of New Guinea, who received a rating of 11, and even here indulgence certainly does not approach the low extreme that would be possible. Margaret Mead reports of the Manus (1930, pp. 165–166),

> Variations of the sexual picture are slight. The spirits are not concerned at all with any aspect of sex which does not involve heterosexual activity on the part of Manus women. All other types of sex behaviour are enveloped in the prevailing atmosphere of shame, but escape the stigma of sin. Masturbation is practised by the children but always in solitude, and solitude is hard to find. It seems to have no important psychological concomitants; engendering as it does no very special shame in a society where every act of excretion is lamentable and to be most carefully hidden.

Our American middle-class group were given a rating of 10, just barely below the least indulgent of these primitive societies but still not extremely low on the basis of the absolute estimate of the judges.

Socialization anxiety developed in connection with masturbation was unfortunately judged with confidence for an even smaller sample of societies—only 10. The ratings vary from 16 down to 5, with a median rating of 10. The upper extreme of severity of socialization of masturbation is approached by the Manus. As their treatment of masturbation appears to be constant at various periods of childhood, the passage just quoted to illustrate their low initial indulgence of masturbation will apply equally well to the severity of socialization.

The lower extreme in severity of socialization is found in the Pukapukans, of whom the Beagleholes write (1941, p. 293),

> Masturbation is extremely common among children of both sexes to the age of about 12 years. . . . The general attitude of adults to masturbation in children and sex organ manipulation is one of good-humored toleration; that is, it is considered amusing if called to their attention. But for the most part adults never feel called upon to notice. . . . All adults know that masturbation goes on among children. It is regarded as their game, natural to children of certain ages, and that is all there is to it.

Since masturbation is evidently not a common practice among adults in this society, the implication is simply that masturbation (and its accompanying homosexual and heterosexual play) gives way to adult sexual intercourse around the time of puberty through the positive reward value of the latter activity at that time, and that there is never occasion for punishing masturbation.

Our American middle-class group is rather extreme in the severity with which children are punished for masturbation, as they are given the same rating by our judges as the most extreme of the primitive societies.

HETEROSEXUAL PLAY

The treatment of heterosexual play in young children is one of the aspects of child training practices that appear to show the widest variation on an absolute basis. Both in initial indulgence and in severity of socialization the ratings by our judges reached very close to both the upper and lower limits of the scale.

The initial indulgence of heterosexual play in various societies varied from practices which received a low rating of 4 to practices which received a high rating of 20. The 26 societies for which confident ratings were made were spread out fairly evenly through this wide range, with the median falling at 13.

The most indulgent initial treatment of heterosexual play may be illustrated by the customs of the Baiga (Elwin, 1939, p. 230).

> Baiga children grow up free and unrestrained. . . . Their sexual consciousness is developed very early. Parents may insist on their children going to work and to work hard, but they rarely interfere with their pleasures. . . . Even when they see their children indulging in erotic play, they simply laugh tolerantly. "Sometimes we say, 'Why do it now? Wait a little.' But the children grow excited, so what should they do?" Lahakat might be expected to adopt this tolerant attitude; but Dhan Singh, a much stricter and chaster man, echoed it. "If a child of seven goes to a girl, what does it matter? It does no harm. But of course when they are grown up and go to the bazaars, then there is something in it." Sujji of Kawardha told me that "if I catch my young daughter with a boy I let her alone. I don't beat her or abuse her; otherwise the neighbours may say, 'Is she your wife or your daughter that you are so jealous? Why are you making trouble, you impotent old man? Let her do what she likes.' "

An opposite extreme in heterosexual indulgence appears to be found in the Wapisiana, if we may judge from the fact that the sexes are reported to be kept apart from childhood, with boys and girls never being allowed to play together (Farabee, 1918, p. 94).

The customs of the Tikopia are representative of the societies which are close to the median in initial indulgence of heterosexual play. Here sexual play between young boys and girls appears to be rare, even though it is not severely punished nor is it prevented by separation of the sexes (Firth, 1936, p. 474). One may infer that there is some moderate degree of subtle interference with the free development of heterosexual interests.

Judgments of the age at which serious training in inhibition of heterosexual play is begun vary from about the age of six (for the Arapesh and the Teton) to about the age of twelve (for the Chagga), with a median at 8. These judgments are available for only 17 societies, however, and this is an instance where this restricted group may not be very representative, as it seems likely that for many other societies the information was lacking simply because the interference with heterosexual play is more or less continuous from the time that children first give any sign of interest in it.

In the later socialization of heterosexual play the range of severity was judged to be almost as wide as in the degree of initial indulgence, as the ratings varied from a low of 4 to a high of 17, with a median of 12.

The extreme of high severity in heterosexual training in childhood is found among the Chiricahua, as is illustrated in the following extracts from Opler's report (1941, pp. 77, 79):

> While the child is very young and is still unable to comprehend the social forms which differentiate one class of relationship from another, he is little inhibited. But with his introduction to the ideas clustering around the sibling and cousin relationships comes the first pressure toward reserve between the sexes. Soon this trend is fortified by the increasing separation of boys and girls for play and amusement. Since the youngster is with members of his own sex so much of the time, the feeling of shyness when he is in the company of the other sex becomes pronounced. . . . Sexual precocity is rare and sternly discouraged. The one account of such misbehavior which was obtained was that of a seven-year-old boy charged with trying to throw down little girls and molest them. The mothers refused to allow their children to associate with him. An informant, when he was questioned about sexual play among children, claimed that he had never heard of children engaging in sex games but added that, if two children had been caught at

"such a thing," the parents "would certainly have whipped both of them."

The other extreme of low severity amounts to no attempt to train children out of heterosexual play, and instead simply letting it be replaced by fully adult heterosexual behavior as soon as the adolescent is physiologically equipped for it. As has already been implied in the discussion of masturbation, the Pukapukans illustrate this practice. Another instance of it is found in the Marquesans among whom, after freedom in heterosexual play in childhood, "regular intercourse began before puberty with patterns of group sexual play, two or three girls in the gang serving a number of boys in rapid succession with the other boys looking on. Occasionally there were individual affairs. . . . [And between puberty and marriage] except for taboos in the case of siblings and parents, there was complete sexual license among these young people" (Linton, 1939, pp. 168–169).

Typical of the middle range of this variation in severity of treatment of heterosexual play are the Hopi, who received a median rating of 12. Heterosexual play among the Hopi is disapproved of, but the principal technique used in preventing it is simply that of keeping boys and girls separated for the most part. Each sex is expected to play and otherwise associate primarily with its own members. The significance of this requirement in relation to sexuality is pointed up by warnings about the supposed bad consequences of sexual play. According to Dennis (1940, p. 78),

> Young children are warned against erotic experimentations with members of the opposite sex by the pretense that even children may bear babies. A girl is told that if a girl of eight or nine years were to have a baby, all the people would die and the world would come to an end. In addition the girl is appealed to not to disgrace her family. A boy is told that sexual experience will cause him to stop growing so that he will be a dwarf. He is also warned that if he has sex relations at an early age he will grow old prematurely. Both

boys and girls are told that if they start acting as grown-ups in sexual matters their parents will cease to support them; i.e., sexual maturity and economic responsibility go together.

With respect to the degree of anxiety that is attached to one's own sexual impulses, it is interesting to compare the practices of the Hopi as described by Dennis with those of our own society. The warnings used by the Hopi specifically refer to the harmful effects of the sexual behavior of children, not of adults. This encourages the child to make a differentiation, so that he is not necessarily learning to react permanently with anxiety to his own sexual impulses.

We are not able to make quantitative comparisons between our American middle-class group and primitive societies with respect to treatment of heterosexual play, because our judges were not able to make ratings on the basis of Davis and Havighurst's publications. It is probably symptomatic of the generally successful early prevention of sexual play in this group, and of the attitudes responsible for the effort at prevention, that these authors evidently did not expect inquiry about heterosexual play to be fruitful or acceptable in interviewing mothers in our society. It is our impression that the American middle class is less indulgent initially and more severe in socializing with respect to heterosexual play than the average of these primitive societies, but we have no accurate basis for reporting just how near to the extreme of these societies they stand.

IMMODESTY

Initial indulgence of the child's spontaneous immodesty varies a good deal. At the upper extremes are societies in which young children are naked, are allowed to adopt any postures and display their body freely without interference or even with encouragement, and are not at first trained to avoid taking an interest in the concealed or private parts of other people. Typical of this extreme are the Trobrianders, who receive the highest rating of 17 in initial indulgence of immodesty tendencies. Malinowski (1927, p. 55) says of them: ". . . there is no putting of any veil on natural functions, certainly not in the case of a child . . . these children run about naked, . . . their excretory functions are treated openly and naturally, . . . there is no general taboo on bodily parts or on nakedness in general . . ."

At the opposite extreme are societies in which clothing is used practically from the start, and in which inhibitory training occurs as soon as the child is capable of responding to it. Low initial indulgence of immodesty is usually evidenced indirectly, by implication, as in the following passage about the Western Apache, who received a rating of 9 on initial indulgence of immodesty. "Exposing private parts is strictly avoided, and even small girls and babies of no more than a year and a half are taught not to do it. One day a small girl of five was playing with other children of her own age. Her maternal grandfather happened to see that she was lying on her back with her feet in the air so that her underdrawers showed. He called her name in a stern voice, and the little girl, knowing instantly what he meant, changed her position" (Goodwin, 1942, p. 456). This passage of course also illustrates both early and severe subsequent training into modesty.

Our American middle-class group were judged to be relatively nonindulgent of the child's natural immodesty, as they received a rating of 9, just one point above the lowest of the primitive societies.

The age at which serious training in modesty is initiated was found to be extremely variable. The median judgment was about five and a half years. But there was no clustering of most of the societies near to this median age. Most of the 18 societies for which these estimates are available are spread out rather evenly from the age of three to the age of eight and a half. At each extreme there is one rather deviant case—the Western Apache were judged to begin modesty training between one and one half years after birth, while the Marquesans were judged to delay it until about the age of ten. The judges were not able to make an estimate for the American middle class on the basis of the documents they were using, but it is clear from common knowledge that the age of beginning modesty training is very early here.

Severity of modesty training was rated confidently for only 11 societies. The ratings varied from 7 to 18, with the median at 15. Fairly severe training may be illustrated by the Navaho, who received a rating of 17. Among the Navaho, say Leighton and Kluckhohn (1947, p. 54), cautions addressed to children about sexual matters are in general practical and unemotional. "The only places where admonitions have a strongly effective quality is with reference to incest and modesty. . . . Youngsters are . . . conditioned into a strong sensitivity against exposure of their sexual organs, even before close relatives of the same sex. After puberty especially they are told, 'when you have to urinate, you want to do it by yourself. You don't want your grandfather or your brother to see you. If you do this before people, you'll burn yourself, they say.' "

The other extreme may best be represented by the Yakut who, with a rating of 7, are judged to be less severe by several points on our scale than any of the other societies for which a confident rating was made here. There is no one account to cite in demonstration of the meaning of this low rating. The fact is simply that several ethnographers, in describing the nakedness of children and the near-nakedness of adults inside Yakut houses, imply a nearly complete absence of modesty training.

Severity of training for modesty is one aspect of child training in which the practices of our American middle-class group are not at all extreme. The middle class was given a rating of 14 here, one point below the median of the primitive societies with which a comparison can be made.

OVER-ALL SEXUAL BEHAVIOR

Over-all ratings were made of initial indulgence and of severity of socialization with respect to sexual behavior in general.

These ratings were based on the evidence about the three aspects of sexual socialization already reviewed plus (for a few societies) the treatment of homosexual behavior. Here the judges were able to make confident ratings on a good many more societies. In a few cases this may have been because the ethnographer reported primarily in general terms about the socialization of the child's sexuality. More often it was because somewhat insufficient evidence about each of several aspects of sexual behavior, if it indicated a consistency, might justify a more confident judgment about sexual behavior as a whole than about any one aspect.

In initial indulgence of infantile sexuality the ratings for 31 societies vary from 20 down to 7, with a median of 13. An example of high indulgence is provided in the following concise statement by Linton (1939, p. 168) about the Marquesans, who were given a rating of 19:

> Sexual play was a regular practice among the children from the earliest period. The adult attitude toward it, if not one of active encouragement, was at least that of mild amusement. Intercourse was frequently witnessed by the children in the dwelling and also at the periods of license which followed the feasts. . . . Sexual techniques were learned through imitation of the adults. Masturbation in childhood was inducted by the parents; whether it was practiced afterward in the face of opportunity for intercourse, it is impossible to say. Homosexuality was present in the form of mutual masturbation, but I have no data as to its frequency. . . . Clothing was assumed shortly before puberty.

For examples of extremely low indulgence of infantile sexuality, we are not able to cite passages which concisely refer to all the aspects of sexual behavior which were included in our analysis of this system. The following statement by Linton (1939, p. 295) about the Tanala, who received the lowest rating of 7 on over-all sexual indulgence, does make reference both to masturbation and to social sexual play in general: "Sexual play between children is forbidden and masturbation was not observed. This can only mean that such sexual practices, if they exist at all, must be carried on in secret and receive no social approval. What laxity there is in dealing with these sexual situations is instituted after puberty."

A case of average over-all treatment of the child's initial sexual propensities may be illustrated by the Alorese, whose rating falls exactly at the median. During the earliest years of childhood there appears to be no imposition of modesty training and no interference with masturbation. Heterosexual and homosexual play, on the other hand, is evidently subject to mild interference by adults from the time it first appears (DuBois, 1944, pp. 45, 69–70).

Our American middle-class group was judged to be fairly near the lower extreme with a rating of 9 for initial sexual indulgence. According to this judgment there are only two of the 31 primitive societies who are more extreme in interfering with the child's initial sexual propensities (the Tanala and Ontong-Javanese), though there are three additional societies which share the rating of 9 (Chiricahua, Maori, and Western Apache).

Over-all severity of socialization in training children out of their initial sexual habits shows a wide range, the ratings varying from 18 down to 5, with a median rating of 12.

The society which was considered by our judges to be most severe is the Kurtatchi. It will be noted in the passages which follow that the Kurtatchi are by no means as severe as could be imagined. There is a certain allowance for heterosexual play at first, and later for homosexual play, but evidently of an inhibited sort. The severity of the threats and warnings used in imposing inhibitions, and the extremity of the separation of the sexes, were judged to outweigh this slight freedom in play. Blackwood (1935, pp. 100, 174, 182) says of the Kurtatchi,

> Small children who finger their own genitals or those of their companions are always promptly reproved by an older child or an adult. Sometimes a boy will pretend to cut off

a smaller boy's penis with a knife or a sharp shell. . . . While they are little, children of both sexes play together, but as soon as the boy reaches the ages when he puts on the *upi*, which may sometimes be as young as seven or eight (approximately), but usually, apparently, about nine or ten, he is forbidden to play or have any close converse with the girls and women. . . . Even before the age of segregation, the little boys seemed more often to be playing by themselves than with the little girls. . . . On the whole, it seemed to me that there was comparatively little sexual interest in their games and behaviour to each other. The segregation of the boys wearing the *upi* may perhaps have some bearing on this. I have seen imitations of the act of coitus performed by children; they were done quite openly, but amounted to no more than taking up the appropriate position. . . . These regulations [about boys wearing the *upi*] are—or were at the time of my visit—still strictly binding, or, if broken, so much care is taken that the delinquents are seldom found out. Their effect is to keep the boys completely away from the women and girls, from which it follows that sexual advances are forbidden. One or two cases were reported to me of boys indulging in sexual intercourse while still wearing the *upi*, but they were spoken of with bated breath, and clearly considered very great enormities and quite exceptional. This, I believe, indicates the actual position and was not merely the statement of the conventional standpoint. In the olden days, discovery would have been punished with death for both parties.

At the other extreme are societies such as the Pukapukans, the Siriono, and the Marquesans. Here the extracts descriptive of initial sexual indulgence indicate the character of the socialization, for in these societies there is no sharp discontinuity of cultural expectations up to the time of marriage. The child's initial sexual behavior differs, of course, from his post-pubertal sexual behavior. But the transition from the one to the other is accomplished simply by the child's being permitted and encouraged to engage at each age in the sexual behavior which seems best fitted to his capacities and interests at that age, with little or no evidence of positive training out of the earlier behavior.

Sexual socialization that is representative of the average of the 29 primitive societies may be exemplified by that of the Alorese. Their over-all rating for severity of sexual socialization was 13, one point above the median; they provide a more useful example than the societies right at the median, because there is fuller information. In each of the four aspects of sexual behavior which were taken into account, the Alorese are about average in the severity of their socialization practices. In her account of sexuality during later childhood among the Alorese (1944, pp. 69–70), DuBois says,

> The masturbation that little boys pursue so casually and freely during early childhood seems to disappear after the acquisition of a loincloth. At least it is no longer to be observed, and adults say that "children forget about it." . . . There is marked modesty on the part of adults about the careful adjustment of loincloths, and as soon as a child wears his first one he begins adopting the same attitude. When a child is careless, he is laughed at and shamed by older children and adults. Within a year or two most children have learned to manage this garment. . . . Sex play during this period is frowned upon by adults, but it undoubtedly occurs, both in homosexual and heterosexual forms. . . . It is said that if such [homosexual] behavior comes to the attention of any adult the children are scolded, but that it is not considered an offense of sufficient magnitude to warrant corporal punishment. . . . Play groups of boys often join groups of girls in field houses for several days at a time. Adults are usually suspicious of such alliances and are inclined to warn the girls against the boys. These play groups usually imitate adult relationships. This

may at times take the form of attempted intercourse, performed either secretly in pairs or within a group of age-mates. . . . Such behavior is not approved by adults, but when reported or discovered it is likely to be shrugged off as mere play.

Our American middle-class group was given a rating of 15 on over-all severity of sexual socialization, and thus falls half way between the median and the upper extreme of the primitive societies on which we have comparable ratings.

DEPENDENCE TRAINING

INITIAL NURTURANCE

Indulgence of the young child's initial tendencies to be dependent was found in general to be rather high. The median rating was 15, and all but four of the 38 societies for which confident ratings were made were within 3 points of this median, between 12 and 18. There was only one society with a rating above these limits, the Kwoma with a rating of 19, and three societies with ratings below these limits, the Dobuans and Yakut with a rating of 11 and the Ainu with a rating of 9.

The upper extreme of indulgence of the child's initial dependence is shown in the following passages from Whiting's account of Kwoma infancy (1941, pp. 24–30):

Kwoma infants up to the time they are weaned are never far from their mothers. It is, in fact, very seldom that they are not actually in physical contact with her. Having turned over most of her household duties to her co-wife or some female relative, the mother may hold the child all day and give it her undivided attention. She sits either on the earth floor or on a bark slab under the porch of the family dwelling with the baby nestling on her outstretched legs. At night the infant sleeps cuddled by her side. Whenever she has to move, she carries the child with her cradled in her arm, sitting on her neck, or, less frequently, straddling her hip.

. . . Crying . . . constitutes an injunction to the mother to discover the source of the trouble. Her first response is to present the breast. If this fails to quiet him, she tries something else. If she believes that the child is crying because he is too hot, she moves him away from the heat of her body. If she thinks he is cold, she cuddles him. If his crying calls her attention to a mosquito on him, she brushes it off and scratches the bite. If she suspects that sores from yaws are hurting him, she tries to move him into a more comfortable position. If he seems to be crying because he is sick, she tries to distract his attention by crooning to him, rocking him gently, and patting him. . . . When the infant begins to talk, he learns an even more efficient technique for securing help. A mother does not always know the trouble when her infant cries, but his words elicit immediate and appropriate help. . . . Thus during infancy the response to discomfort which is most strongly established is that of seeking help by crying or asking for it. . . . A motive which becomes strongly established during infancy is the wish to be near to and touch the mother. Almost all the pains and discomforts which an infant experiences are reduced while he is either sitting in his mother's lap or lying by her side. He is fed there, he sleeps there, and he is warmed and cooled, scratched and petted there—always while in bodily contact with his mother. . . . As regards prestige, the Kwoma infant enjoys in a sense the most dominant social position that he will ever attain. His every command is obeyed, and all his wants are attended to.

Much of this pattern of extreme indulgence which is described for the Kwoma is encountered in the rest of the societies which are rated near or above the median, but usually the indulgence is not quite so thorough. Among the Pukapukans, who are rated exactly at the median, the mother is similarly solicitous of the child's needs and eager to gratify them. But the mother does not carry the child about with her. The child is not left alone, but is not in such continuous physical contact with the mother. The mother, moreover, does not continue for long to be exempt from her normal economic responsibilities. When she returns to her work in the fields, the infant is left in care of an older child or female relative, and one may surmise that the nurturance of the infant under these conditions is not likely to be quite so efficient and meticulous as when the mother herself is responsible (Beaglehole and Beaglehole, 1938, p. 276).

The lower extreme of lack of indulgence of the infant's dependence is found among the Ainu. A general impression of their lack of indulgence is given concisely in the following passage from Howard (1893, p. 67):

> What about the babies during the day? you may ask. Answer: They were being trained to the same abstinence as their mothers. Put into the hanging cradle I have previously described, it was known quite well the poor little helpless creatures could not get out, and for the rest they were free to do whatever they were able. This usually meant a good deal of kicking and screaming until tired of it, followed by exhaustion, repose, and resignation. The arrival of the mother and the very late but natural supper she brings with her, quickly satisfies her protesting infant.

The practices of our American middle-class group were given a rating of 13 by our judges, thus falling two points below the median of the primitive societies surveyed. Only six out of 38 societies have a lower rating, and two more have exactly the same rating as the American middle-class group.

AGE AT BEGINNING OF INDEPENDENCE TRAINING

The median age at which serious efforts at independence training are begun is a little above three and a half years. The estimates of this age are spread out rather evenly, for most of the primitive societies, between two and four and a half. There are no societies for which independence training appears to be seriously begun before the age of two. There are six societies, however, in which the beginning of this training seems to be delayed until some age between five and six.

Our American middle-class group was judged to start independence training typically around the age of two and a half, earlier than most of the primitive societies but not aberrantly early. Comparison between the United States and various primitive societies as to age of this training is not adequately given, however, by the beginning age alone. American customs are rather unusual in that independence training is completed at a very late age. Where many primitive societies expect their children to become very thoroughly independent in a short time, American parents require a high degree of continued dependence into adolescence and even early maturity. This very slow attainment of the degree of independence expected of full adults is of course not unknown among primitive societies, but American customs certainly appear to be more deviant in this respect than in the age at beginning of independence training.

SEVERITY OF INDEPENDENCE TRAINING

Ratings of the severity with which children are trained out of their initial dependence into the degree of independence expected of them as older children vary from a high of 17 to a low of 7, with the median falling exactly half way between the extremes, at 12.

The Kwoma will serve as a useful illustration of severe imposition of independence training. They are not quite at the extreme, having a rating of only 16. But they are especially useful as illustrating that severe socialization of dependence may follow extreme indulgence of dependence during an earlier period. As we have already seen, the Kwoma are exceedingly indulgent of the infant's needs and develop through learning strong drives for dependence upon the mother. This continues until the time of weaning, typically during the child's third year. At the same time that the child must give up nursing and learn to depend entirely on the diet of his parents, he is required to give up much of his general dependence upon his mother and other adults. Whiting reports, for example (1941, pp. 33–37),

> When a child is weaned he may no longer sit in his mother's lap by day nor lie by her side at night. This is apparently felt as the most severe frustration experienced at this period of life. No longer is it possible to attain the vantage point from which all drives have hitherto been satisfied. . . . With weaning, then, many of the demands which the Kwoma child has learned to make during infancy become no longer successful. His mother no longer responds in the same helpful way to many of his requests. His demands to be taken into her lap, scratched, patted, or warmed, are now ignored. When she no longer heeds his demands, he becomes more vociferous. Unless he is in serious danger, however, she still does not cater to him. He then reverts to the earlier response of crying. When this fails, he tries other responses in his repertory. . . . If a child is too vociferous and persistent in his demands, he is actually punished. . . . In the realm of prestige, the Kwoma child during the period of weaning plunges from the very top to the very bottom of the social hierarchy. Most of the commands which he issues are now ignored, and the help which he expects is denied him. Furthermore, he has to learn to obey the commands of others during this period. His control over his social environment is at a minimum.

The other extreme of mild socialization with respect to the transition from dependence to independence is reached by the Arapesh of New Guinea, close neighbors of the Kwoma. The mildness of the transition in this case is facilitated by the fact that the change is not very great; dependent attitudes are conspicuous in the adult behavior of the Arapesh. Margaret Mead reports (1935, pp. 42, 47–48),

> When the child begins to walk the quiet continuous rhythm of its life changes somewhat. It is now becoming a little

heavy for the mother to carry about with her on long trips to the garden, and furthermore it can be expected to live without suckling for an hour or so. The mother leaves the child in the village with the father, or with some other relative, while she goes to the garden or for firewood. . . . As the child grows older, it is no longer confined so closely to the care of its own parents. Children are lent about. An aunt comes to visit and takes home the four-year-old for a week's stay, handing him on to some other relative for eventual return to his parents. This means that a child learns to think of the world as filled with parents, not merely a place in which all of his safety and happiness depend upon the continuance of his relationship to his own particular parents. . . . There is no insistence at all upon children's growing up rapidly, or acquiring special skills or proficiencies, and there is a corresponding lack of techniques for training them physically. . . . The result is that the child grows up with a sense of emotional security in the care of others, not in its own control over the environment.

An average degree of severity in independence training may be illustrated by the practices of the Lepcha. The Lepcha are reported by Gorer to delay this training until the child is physically equipped for the degree of independent mastery called for. At about the age of four the parents formally recognize the child's increasing abilities by granting him certain privileges and at the same time definitely requiring greater independence and acceptance of training for adulthood. At this time.

When a child stops being a baby and becomes a young Lepcha the world becomes a more difficult place for him. Instead of being treated with a rather impersonal kindness, he is now treated with a rather impersonal neglect. He has the compensation of adult equipment—the knife and haversack which are the outward sign of physical independence —but he is also judged by adult standards; he is capable

of committing adult crimes, and has to show that he pos-
sesses the adult virtues. . . . Full adult status is a goal
they have to work towards; they see this goal and the
greater number of children are very anxious to grow up.
. . . It is only temperamentally or socially maladjusted
children who appear to be oppressed by the neglect and
occasional harsh treatment which is part of their education,
and who do not see the desirable goal of full status approaching constantly nearer (Gorer, 1938, pp. 307–308).

Severity of independence training in our American middle-
class group is not at all atypical. In fact, it received a rating of 12,
which places it exactly at the median of our sample of primitive
societies. This median position was gained, however, by the
averaging of somewhat discrepant ratings by the several judges,
for one judge rated the middle class as rather severe in independence training and another judge rated it as rather mild. We
questioned the judges later about their ratings here in order
to discover the reason for this discrepancy. The judge who considered independence training to be mild gave special emphasis
to the fact that middle-class children are not forced or even permitted to fend for themselves outside the house until a relatively
late age when skills are well developed; the judge who considered independence training to be severe had given special
emphasis to the fact that middle-class parents put considerable
pressure on their children to dress themselves, learn manners,
and help around the house at a relatively early age when these
responses are difficult for them to learn. There is a real discrepancy here, then, between two aspects of independence
training—the freedom of the child in acting on his own initiative
independently of adult surveillance, and the responsibility of
the child for taking an adult role in the household economy. Had
these two aspects been very differently treated in many societies,
as they are in the American middle class, we might have found
our judges' ratings of independence training to be generally
unreliable because of the differing emphasis the judges placed

on these two aspects. In fact, there was no such general unreliability. The outcome of the ratings of the American middle class does suggest, however, that independence training in future research may need to be broken down for analysis in much the same way that we have already broken down sexual training and aggression training.

AGGRESSION

For aggressive behavior, as for sexual behavior, we instructed our judges to try to analyze separately several aspects of behavior which might fall under this category. Five aspects of aggression were singled out for separate attention: temper tantrums, physical aggression, verbal aggression, property damage, and disobedience. For very few societies, however, was the evidence adequate to permit our judges to make separate judgments about the socialization of each of these aspects. For none of the five aspects, in fact, are there confident judgments on a sufficient number of societies to justify us in trying to present a picture of the range of child training practices. We will only attempt to do so for aggressive behavior as a whole.

In the case of aggressive behavior we found the distinction between initial indulgence during a period of relative freedom, and severity of socialization at a time when a determined effort was made to socialize the child, less relevant than for the other four systems of behavior we have reviewed. For the most part the attitude of a society toward aggression in children seemed to be continuous, that is, not varying much with the age of the infant or child. The judges did make separate judgments for initial indulgence and socialization anxiety, and in a few cases there is a quite appreciable difference between these two ratings for a single society. But for the most part there is a high correlation between the two, a society rating high in initial indulgence and low in severity of socialization. For this reason we will not attempt to give examples of child training practices separately for these two, though we will of course report the range of ratings made in each case, as these ratings will both be referred to later in our study.

Thus it follows that age at beginning of socialization is not a very meaningful concept for aggressive behavior. It was not generally possible, either for aggression as a whole or for separate aspects of aggression, to recognize any approximate age as the time when demands were imposed upon children to start changing from an initial freedom to a greater degree of control. Usually the demands were essentially of a single character right from the start. Consequently our judges made very few judgments of age of socialization in the case of aggression, too few to be of any value to report. Hence we will deal here only with indulgence and severity of socialization, and not with age.

These introductory remarks should not be taken to mean that the judgments made about child training practices with respect to aggression are based on poor evidence or are otherwise less dependable than the judgments for the other systems of behavior. It is simply that the same scheme of analysis was not applicable in full detail; where it was applicable, the results seem to be quite as meaningful as for the other systems of behavior.

The ratings for initial indulgence of aggressive tendencies varied from a high of 17 to a low of 5. The median was at 11, and the American middle class received a rating of 10.

The ratings for severity of socialization varied from a high of 21 to a low of 5. The median was at 14. Our American middle-class group, with a rating of 16, was in this instance judged to be rather above the median in severity; seven out of 31 primitive societies received a higher rating, and three more received exactly the same rating as the American middle class.

The extreme of low initial indulgence of aggressive tendencies and very severe socialization is illustrated by the Harney Valley Paiute, who received a rating of 6 for initial indulgence and 21 for severity of socialization. The ethnographer reports,

If siblings fight among themselves, the older ones are whipped. If a child strikes his parents, they hit him back. Children are told that a big owl or a wildcat will take them off if they do not mind. They are told that if they get angry when they eat they will swell up. Over and over again they are told that they should love their parents and their siblings and should not be angry with them nor fight with them. They are severely punished for destroying bird's eggs or hurting any bird or animal.

Probably more important than this direct punishment is the fear of aggression which they acquire by observing their parents and hearing them discuss sorcery and fighting. If there is a fight in the community, mothers gather up their children and take them away. They are frightened that sorcery will be "thrown around" and will accidentally or purposefully hit the children. Children see their parents reacting with anxiety to the danger of sorcery. They observe that their parents are afraid to express aggression overtly for fear of being accused of sorcery. They are admonished never to laugh or make fun of other people lest they be attacked. They are warned always to be polite, to speak to people and to speak pleasantly. They hear much gossip about sorcerers and how dangerous such individuals are.

The result is that a child is afraid to express aggression for fear of punishment from his family directly, or because of fear of punishment by others. He shares his family's anxiety about expressing aggression. Furthermore, because of certain beliefs connected with sorcery and the acquisition of bad power, he develops a fear that he will express his aggression unconsciously (Beatrice Whiting, 1950, pp. 68–69).

An approach to the opposite extreme of permissiveness and encouragement with respect to aggression may be illustrated by the Siriono. With respect to disobedience (which we have considered as one aspect of aggression), Holmberg reports that an unruly child among the Siriono is never beaten. "At worst, his mother gives him a rough pull or throws some small object at him." Male children are strongly encouraged to learn the use of weapons and to employ them to kill birds and animals as early as they are possibly able. The treatment of inter-child aggression is described as follows:

> Within play groups aggression is freely expressed. When boys are playing with their bows and arrows (boys' arrows always have blunt ends, and their bows shoot with little force), accidents sometimes occur, and occasionally one child shoots another intentionally, even though boys are admonished not to point their weapons at any human target. When such accidents or shootings occur (children are seldom wounded as a result of them), a fight usually breaks out, and the child who has been hit often strikes back at the boy who shot him. Adults generally take no part in these fights (they usually laugh at them), but the loser almost always runs crying to his parents for protection. . . . Considerable teasing and torturing—such things as pinching the genitals, poking fingers in the eyes and scratching —of young children by older children takes place. A young child most often protects himself from such attacks with a brand of fire or a digging stick, and if he catches off guard the older child who molested him, he may burn him rather severely or give him a sharp rap on the head. Older girls, too, sometimes tease young children by pretending to suck from their mothers' breasts, and this invariably arouses aggression in the latter, who sometimes strike their tormenters with considerable force. Under such circumstances, older children are not allowed to express counter aggression (Holmberg, 1946, pp. 227, 230–234).

An average sort of treatment of aggression may be exemplified by the practices of the Kwoma, who received a rating of 13 for initial satisfaction and a rating of 11 for socialization anxiety in aggression. Whiting (1941, pp. 30, 36–37, 57–63) reports on the treatment of aggression in the Kwoma at various periods of childhood. In infancy, loud crying is the principal aggressive response made.

> A parent will say, "The infant is cross." Nevertheless, a mother helps her infant even if he is crying angrily. In fact, the louder he cries, the more effort she expends trying to aid him, so that aggression is rewarded rather than punished. . . . Aggression still plays a minor role in the life of a Kwoma during the weaning period. In some ways aggressive behavior is less successful at this time than it was during infancy. Although the child becomes more adept at killing mosquitoes and eliminating similar minor dangers, he is now punished for becoming angry with his parents. . . .

As the child grows older, he continues to be punished for aggression toward his parents and other people who are older than he. But he is permitted to be aggressive toward his younger brothers and sisters, so long as serious injury is not threatened.

Over-all Indulgence and Severity

The most meaningful facts about initial indulgence and severity of socialization in the child training practices of a society are those we have already reviewed, those about the treatment of particular kinds of behavior on the part of children. There may be some interest, however, in the average degree of indulgence or severity in the treatment of all kinds of behavior on the part of children. Davis and Havighurst (1947, p. 10) express such an interest when they say, "Indeed, the culture of *middle-class* Europeans and Americans probably exerts more severe pressure upon the young child—upon both his bodily processes and his emotional development—than does the culture of any other people in the world!" These authors are here making a judgment about the average indulgence and severity of socialization in the American middle class in comparison with all other societies the world over. A similar judgment not made so explicit seems to underlie much of the criticism that has been directed in recent years at this aspect of our culture. Is the judgment correct?

So far as we know, such judgments have previously been based entirely on an informal method of judgment with no systematic comparison between our society and an adequate sample of other societies. Our systematic analysis of child training practices in a sample of primitive societies the world over can provide the basis for a somewhat more adequate evaluation of such judgments.

The comparison that we can make must be based upon the average degree of indulgence and of later severity of socialization in the five systems of behavior that we have been considering. It will be valid only to the extent that these five systems provide a sufficient sample of the systems of behavior in connection with which socialization must be imposed.

In order to make this comparison we believe it is best to include all of the 47 primitive societies for which judgments of at least an intermediate degree of confidence are available for all five systems of behavior. (If we confined the sample to societies for which confident judgments are available for all five systems of behavior, the sample would be limited to 15 cases for initial indulgence and 10 cases for severity of socialization.)

The average degree of initial indulgence is found to vary from an average rating of 10 for the Tanala and Dobuans to an average rating of 17 for the Siriono. The median is at 13. Our American middle-class group has an average rating of 10, and they are thus extremely low in average indulgence of these five initial tendencies in their children. They are not, however, outside the range of primitive societies, as might possibly be supposed from the statement by Davis and Havighurst. They are tied with the two most extremely non-indulgent out of the 47 primitive societies in the sample.

The average degree of severity of socialization has a slightly wider range, from an average rating of 8 for the Tikopia up to an average rating of 16 for the Dobuans. The median is at 12. The American middle class has an average rating of 15, tied with the Ashanti who stand in second place among the 47 primitive societies in the sample. Again, then, the American middle class is rather extreme in the severity of its socialization practices but it does not fall outside the range of the primitive societies.

We must conclude, therefore, that if our measures can be trusted for this present purpose Davis and Havighurst have exaggerated, but only a little, in their judgment of the severity of the pressure put upon children in the American middle class.

Leighton and Kluckhohn have made a comparative judgment about the Navaho which is similar in nature to Davis and Havighurst's judgment about the American middle class. It also may serve to illustrate the difficulty of making clear and dependable comparative judgments without a systematic method of comparing cultures. Leighton and Kluckhohn (1947, p. 111) say, "In spite of the fact that Navaho infants receive a maximum of protection and gratification, when they grow to be adults they are very moody and worry a great deal."

If this comment is taken to refer to initial dependence indulgence it would appear to be, like the comment on our culture by Davis and Havighurst, somewhat exaggerated. The Navaho are indeed above the median in initial dependence indulgence according to our judges (with a rating of 16), but are not quite at a maximum. Out of 38 societies there were 9 which were judged to be equally indulgent and 8 which were judged to be more indulgent with respect to dependence; the maximum rating was 19. If the comment is instead taken to refer to over-all indulgence and the average of our five initial indulgence scores provides an appropriate basis for making a similar comparison, the comment is even less accurate. On average initial indulgence in the five systems of behavior in the Navaho stand exactly at the median of our sample of 47 primitive societies. Finally, however, if Leighton and Kluckhohn are understood simply as comparing

Navaho culture with American culture as a reference point, their comparison is quite correct, since the Navaho are considerably more indulgent than Americans both in dependence and in the average of all five systems of behavior.

IN CHAPTER 4 we have reviewed separately the variations among human societies in a number of specific aspects of child training practices. The fact that we have analyzed a number of aspects of these practices also permits us to explore the interrelations among them. This exploration, which we will report in this chapter, rounds out our factual report on child training. Then we will turn to the testing of hypotheses about the effects of these practices on other customs by way of their influence on personality.

INITIAL INDULGENCE AND SEVERITY OF SOCIALIZATION

A first problem in the interrelation of various child training practices is one to which we have already alluded in the preceding chapter. This is the problem of the relation between initial indulgence and subsequent severity of socialization with respect to any single system of behavior. If a society is highly indulgent of its infants with respect to some system of behavior, does this enable us to predict that this society when a time comes for firmer socialization pressures will then be among the least severe in the way the socialization is imposed? Or if a society is initially rather non-indulgent, does this mean that at the time of major socialization of this system of behavior the socialization will be unusually severe?

We alluded to this problem in the preceding chapter in connection with aggressive behavior. There we reported that our judges had difficulty making a clear distinction between initial indulgence and subsequent severity of socialization. That is, practices in the treatment of aggression in children tend to be rather uniform for various ages, and it is usually not possible to recognize, in accounts of child training practices, an age at which there is a shift from greater leniency to stronger demands for conformity to adult norms. Judgments were none the less made separately for initial indulgence and for subsequent severity of socialization, but in the case of aggression the judges often felt that in doing so they were rating essentially the same facts about the practices of a society. (They were rating these facts, however, on two opposed scales, degree of indulgence being the reverse of degree of severity.) The other system of behavior for which there most often arose the same difficulty that we have mentioned for aggression was sexual behavior; here, too, there appeared in some cases to be little distinction between an earlier and a later period. For the other three systems of behavior it was generally possible to make a distinction between an initial period of lesser interference with the child's spontaneous tendencies and a later period of greater interference.

For oral, anal, and dependent behavior, and to a lesser extent for sexual behavior, the relation between initial indulgence and severity of socialization thus promises to be a factual matter about the actual relationship found between the two sets of ratings. If the relationship between indulgence and severity of socialization for a given system of behavior turns out to be close, this should indicate that these two distinguishable practices tend to be determined by some common factor. If the relationship is slight, this should indicate that the two practices are independently determined.

The relationship between initial indulgence and later severity of socialization for each system of behavior may be summarized by a coefficient of correlation, a statistical measure which expresses the closeness of relationship between two variables.[1]

1. All correlation coefficients reported in this book are Pearson product-moment coefficients; a fuller account of their meaning may be found in any standard text on general statistics.

The correlation coefficient may have any value from zero (indicating a complete absence of relationship) to 1 (indicating perfect one-to-one relationship). If the coefficient is positive, it indicates that high values of one variable tend to be associated with high values of the other variable. If the coefficient is negative, it indicates that high values of one variable tend to be associated with low values of the other variable. Such coefficients have been calculated for each of the five systems of behavior, to measure the relationship between initial indulgence and later severity of socialization. All five of the coefficients are negative, indicating uniformly that a society highly indulgent with respect to any system of behavior will tend to be less severe than average in the socialization of that same system of behavior.

The highest correlation coefficient, -0.81, was found for aggressive behavior; this confirms the judges' impression that the two variables were hard to distinguish for this system of behavior, and came close to being inverse measures of the same thing. For anal and sexual behavior, however, the negative correlations are found to be very nearly as high as for aggression (-0.76 and -0.74, respectively). It would appear that in these two cases also there is a marked tendency for initial indulgence and lack of subsequent severity of socialization to be consistent with each other or expressive of a single general attitude toward the particular system of behavior. For oral behavior there is a considerably less close inverse association between indulgence and later severity of socialization, represented by a correlation coefficient of -0.60. Finally, for dependent behavior the relationship is very low indeed, as the correlation coefficient is only -0.18.[2]

Dependence thus stands out as the one system of behavior

2. In each instance the correlation is based only on those societies for which confident judgments are available for both variables. The number of societies which meet this criterion varies; the numbers of cases on which the five coefficients are based are, in the order given in the text, 25, 17, 25, 37, and 27. All of the correlations are highly significant statistically except the one for dependence which is so low as to give no dependable evidence of any true relationship.

for which there is almost no connection between the degree of indulgence of the very young child and the severity with which socialization is later imposed. In general, then, human societies make in effect a sharp distinction with respect to dependence between an early period and a later period, a distinction so sharp that the determinants of treatment of dependence in the child in the two periods are almost completely independent of each other. It was partly to bring out this point that we chose the Kwoma to illustrate child training practices with respect to dependence in the preceding chapter. The Kwoma illustrate that a high degree of indulgence of dependence during the earliest years may perfectly well be combined with a very severe method of training the child out of dependence at a later age. The combination of practices represented by the Kwoma is not of course typical; but enough societies show a marked difference in treatment of dependence initially and during socialization so that there is no consistent relationship between initial indulgence and severity of socialization for dependence.

It is interesting that oral behavior is the system which most closely approaches dependence in this respect. Both are systems in which the requirements of infancy differ very radically from the requirements of adulthood. An infant must be allowed to be dependent or it cannot survive; likewise, under conditions of primitive life, an infant must be allowed to suckle or it has a greatly reduced chance of surviving. Adult norms of independence and of eating cannot be imposed upon the infant. In the other systems of behavior, on the other hand, adult norms can at least symbolically be imposed upon the infant without seriously threatening its survival. The infant can be punished for sexual or aggressive behavior without any damage other than psychological, and he can learn some degree of inhibition. In the case of toilet training the early acquisition of inhibition may be more doubtful, but the life of the infant is not threatened by severe treatment. We would infer that because of these facts the general attitude of a society toward any one of these three systems of behavior is likely to be expressed in early as well as later treatment of this behavior in a child. In the case of dependence, on the other hand, and to a lesser extent oral behavior the manifestly different requirements of infancy tend to prevent this generalization and permit other determinants to affect the customary practices with respect to infant care.

AGE AND SEVERITY OF SOCIALIZATION

A second problem in the interrelation of child training practices has to do with the relation between the age at which socialization is begun and the severity with which it is imposed. When socialization of a particular system of behavior is begun unusually early, is it likely to be more severe or less severe than in the society which begins socialization at an average age?

This question can be answered for those systems of behavior for which judgments were obtained of the age at which socialization begins. Since these judgments were possible for relatively few societies, we decided not to reduce the numbers still further by using only those for which the judgments about severity of socialization were made with maximum confidence. Consequently we have included here societies for which these judgments were made with only an intermediate degree of confidence.

The relationship between age and severity of socialization is in every case negative. That is, early socialization is found to be relatively severe, and late socialization is found to be relatively mild. The degree of relationship varies considerably. It is highest for modesty training, where the correlation coefficient is —0.77. For three of the other aspects of socialization the correlation coefficient is also moderately high: for heterosexual play it is —0.53; for toilet training it is —0.52; and for oral behavior, —0.41.[3] For dependence training, however, the correlation co-

3. Sears and Wise (1950) report that children in our society are more disturbed the later they are weaned. Since one of the components of our severity of weaning judgment was signs of emotional disturbance, these findings appear to be somewhat contradictory to ours. The age ranges of the two findings, however, are quite different. Sears and Wise's group

efficient between age at beginning of training in independence and severity of this training is only —0.11.[4] Each of these correlations, except the one for dependence, is statistically significant; that is, we may be sure that the appearance of a negative relationship did not arise through sampling error and random errors in the process of judgment. We cannot be sure, however, whether the judgment of severity of socialization was unconsciously biased by the age factor. Although our judges were instructed to try to keep the factors of age and severity distinct, it is still possible that punishment of a year-old infant would be rated as being more severe than punishment of the same severity in the case of a four- or five-year-old. Such a possibility cannot be ruled out as perhaps contributing to the correlations reported above.

If the relationship is not entirely due to the bias of the judges, there are two distinct processes which may account for it. One has to do primarily with the child, and the other with the adults who are socializing the child. As the child matures he becomes better able to learn easily, so that socialization can to that extent be achieved more easily, and milder techniques can be successful. On the other hand, moral attitudes in the parents may influence both the severity and the age of socialization. Severe disapproval of sexual behavior, for example, may lead parents both to begin very early to stamp it out and to take strenuous steps in doing so; a mild moral attitude, on the contrary, may lead parents both to disregard sexual behavior in their children until a late age, and to use mild and casual disciplinary techniques when the time comes when it cannot be altogether neglected. We have no way of judging from our data which of these two general processes is the more important in producing the relationships that we have found.

---

varied in age of weaning from birth to approximately seven months (only 5 of 70 cases were weaned later than this), whereas the age range represented in our study was from six months to five and a half years.

4. The numbers of cases on which these correlations are based are, in the order in which the correlations are given, 15, 17, 25, 46, and 41.

A factor which might tend to produce a positive relation between age and severity, instead of the negative relation we have found, has been pointed out by Sears and Wise (1950). The longer a child practices an initial habit, and is rewarded, the stronger this habit should become and the stronger should be the parental interference required for socialization.

The fact that the relationship between age and severity is so much lower for dependence than for the other systems may be tentatively interpreted as related to this factor of progressive strengthening of the initial habit. Dependence is the one system of behavior which to the greatest extent depends for its motivation upon the learned incentive-value of its goal, an incentive value which should be increased in strength with continued indulgence. Hence as the child grows older and is continuously indulged in his dependence upon parents, it may become increasingly difficult to train him out of this dependence. This would make for a positive correlation between age and severity of socialization in the case of dependence. But at the same time the factors which make for a negative correlation are presumably working here as well as in other systems of behavior. The effect may be that the two relationships approximately cancel each other out, and the observed fact is an almost complete lack of relationship for dependent behavior between age and severity of socialization. If this suggestion is correct, a similar outcome is to be expected when it becomes possible to apply a similar analysis to other systems of behavior—such as aggression—in which acquired drives also play a paramount role.

RELATIVE DEGREE OF INDULGENCE AND SEVERITY IN
THE FIVE SYSTEMS OF BEHAVIOR

A third problem is that of the relative treatment of the five systems of behavior. Which system of behavior is most greatly indulged, and which is the least indulged, among primitive societies the world over? For which system of behavior is socialization most severe, and for which least severe? Are there appreciable differences in these respects among the five systems, or are there only such minor variations as might arise by chance as a result of our having data on only a small sample of societies?

In the attempt to answer these questions, the most relevant judgments are the rankings made by our judges of the relative indulgence and of the relative severity of socialization in the five systems of behavior for each society separately. All three of our judges made these rankings with confidence for 31 societies in the case of indulgence, and for 32 societies in the case of severity of socialization. We will confine our report to these societies, which best permit a direct comparison among the five systems of behavior.

This use of judgments must, however, be regarded as somewhat doubtful because of the likelihood of a cultural bias in the judges. Elsewhere in this book we have made use of rankings only for the purpose of ordering societies along a single dimension of variation. The rankings of severity of weaning, for example, have been used to place various societies in order from least severe to most severe with respect to weaning. That this use of the rankings has some objective meaning is indicated by the fact that it led to certain consistent relationships with an independent analysis of quite different customs. In the present case, however, we have to go further and make a comparison between the absolute values of judgments about two different dimensions. We have to assume now that when oral anxiety is ranked first among the five anxieties, for example, it really is first. For other purposes we have only had to assume that when oral anxiety is ranked first it is relatively greater than when it is ranked lower than that. While this assumption of absolute meaning for the rankings which has to be made here may be correct, it is much more doubtful than the assumption of relative meaning, and we have no results which give any evidence as to whether it is correct.

For whatever they are worth, we present our findings on this point in Table 2. There are very sizable differences among the five systems in general degree of indulgence, and of severity of socialization. Dependence is the system of behavior which our

TABLE 2. Relative Indulgence in the Five Systems of Behavior

This table represents the rank order of indulgence and severity of socialization based on the combined rank score of our three judges (represented by the numbers in parenthesis).* Confident judgments only are included. For initial indulgence the system listed first is most indulgent, that listed last, the least indulgent. For severity of socialization the system listed first is most severe, that listed last, least severe.

INITIAL INDULGENCE

Sample of Primitive Societies		American Middle-Class Group	
1. Dependence	(6.4)	1. Dependence	(3)
2. Oral	(7.3)	2. Aggression	(6)
3. Sexual	(9.7)	3. Oral	(10)
4. Anal	(10.2)	4. Sexual	(12)
5. Aggression	(11.5)	5. Anal	(14)

SEVERITY OF SOCIALIZATION

Sample of Primitive Societies		American Middle-Class Group	
1. Aggression	(7.8)	1. Anal	(4)
2. Dependence	(8.1)	2. Aggression	(7)
3. Sexual	(9.1)	3. Sexual	(9)
4. Oral	(9.8)	4. Oral	(11)
5. Anal	(10.2)	5. Dependence	(14)

* For a given society a rank score could have any value from 3 (meaning that all three judges agreed that this system ranked first among the five systems in that society, in indulgence or in severity) to 15 (meaning that all three judges agreed that this system ranked fifth among the five systems).

judges report to have the highest degree of initial indulgence, on the average, and oral behavior is second. Aggression is the system of behavior with the lowest average degree of indulgence. It may be of interest to note that our American middle-class group is judged to be similar to the typical primitive tribe in indulging dependence more strongly than other systems of behavior. In one respect, however, its pattern of initial indulgence is not typical of primitive societies; aggression is judged to be the second most indulged system in our American middle-class group, whereas it is on the average the least indulged in primitive societies. There was close agreement among the three judges on this point; every one of the judges considered dependence to be most indulged and aggression next most indulged in young children of our American middle-class group.

In subsequent socialization there are two systems of behavior that essentially share the top position as characteristically most severely treated. These are aggression and dependence, whose mean rank scores of 8.1 and 7.8 are very close together. Oral behavior is third, sexual behavior fourth, and anal behavior is in general the system with mildest socialization. Again, our American middle-class group presents a somewhat unusual pattern with anal training judged to be the locus of the most severe socialization rather than the least, and dependence least severe as compared to second most severe in the world-wide sample.

INTERRELATIONS AMONG THE FIVE SYSTEMS

The final problem with which we will concern ourselves in this chapter has to do with the interrelations among socialization practices in the five systems of behavior. Does a society which is highly indulgent in its treatment of one system of behavior tend to be highly indulgent of other systems of behavior also? Is severe socialization in one system of behavior likely to be accompanied by severe socialization in other systems as well? Does a society tend to impose socialization in all systems at about the same time? These are the specific questions we have in mind in speaking of the interrelations among the five systems of behavior.

In Table 3 we present the correlation coefficients which permit an answer to these questions. In general, the answer is simply that there is no consistent relation between the way one system of behavior is socialized and the way any other system of behavior is socialized. Out of 30 correlation coefficients included in this table, only 3 are significant at the 5% level of confidence. Since these three are in fact highly significant, they probably represent genuine exceptions to the simple generalization we have stated. Two of the exceptions have to do with the relation between dependence and oral behavior; for both initial

TABLE 3. Interrelations Among Systems of Behavior in Child Training Practices

> The table is divided into three parts, dealing with separate measures of child training practices. Each entry is a correlation coefficient, expressing the relationship between the two systems (or aspects) of behavior represented by the row and column in which the entry appears, with respect to the measure dealt with in that part of the table. After each coefficient appears, in parentheses, the number of cases on which it is based.

INITIAL INDULGENCE

	Anal	Sexual	Dependence	Aggression
Oral	−0.18(21)	−0.18(27)	+0.39(35)	+0.07(27)
Anal		+0.17(18)	−0.02(21)	+0.14(25)
Sexual			−0.17(25)	+0.07(23)
Dependence				+0.14(25)

SEVERITY OF SOCIALIZATION

	Anal	Sexual	Dependence	Aggression
Oral	+0.07(19)	−0.14(25)	+0.57(26)	−0.13(23)
Anal		+0.22(13)	−0.17(16)	−0.24(16)
Sexual			−0.16(20)	+0.34(21)
Dependence				−0.07(20)

AGE OF SOCIALIZATION

	Anal	Modesty	Heterosexual	Dependence
Oral	+0.17(25)	+0.09(15)	−0.02(17)	+0.12(36)
Anal		−0.40(11)	+0.04(11)	+0.04(24)
Modesty			+0.85(7)	+0.23(17)
Heterosexual				+0.26(16)

indulgence and severity of socialization there is a significant positive relation here. This seems meaningful in view of the fact that the feeding of the child is one of the principal ways in which the young child is dependent upon its parents, and that information about the treatment of the child's oral needs was necessarily one of the bases for making a judgment about the treatment of his dependence upon his parents. Indeed, it is perhaps surprising that there is not also a significant correlation between these two systems in the age of socialization. The other exception has to do with two aspects of sexual behavior for which age of socialization was separately judged; there is a very high positive relation between the age of socialization for modesty and heterosexual training, so high that it is statistically significant even though only 7 cases are available for its calculation. Apart from these three instances, there is little suggestion even of any tendency for the correlations to be consistently in one direction. For indulgence and severity of socialization taken together, there are exactly as many negative correlations as there are positive ones. Only in the case of age of socialization is there any marked imbalance, with a tendency for most of the correlations to be positive, although very low in magnitude.

We may conclude for indulgence and severity, and with less certainty for age, that the practices of a society for one system of behavior are almost entirely independent of its practices with respect to other systems of behavior.

This finding is a factual matter of some interest. It suggests that the aspects of child training practices we are dealing with here do not grow out of cultural attitudes toward children such as might produce general laxity or general strictness, but grow rather out of antecedents specific to each system of behavior. What some of these antecedents are has been suggested in an informal report by Murdock and Whiting (1951), to which we will refer more fully in our final chapter.

This finding also has some incidental meaning for the major object of our present report. The absence of correlations among the several systems of behavior suggests that the ratings of child training practices were not a function of some spurious general factor such as adequacy of information. We had some fear, at the outset of our study, that perhaps a full report of child training in any society would lead to a judgment, for example, of severe socialization in every system of behavior, just because it would mention punishments used in each system, and that a relatively sparse report would lead to judgments of mild socialization just because of the absence of detailed accounts of punishment techniques. Had this happened to any appreciable extent, there should be consistently positive correlations among the various systems of behavior.

CHAPTER 6. *The Analysis of Customs Relating to Illness*

In the previous chapters we have described our antecedent variables, that is, the various aspects of child training which we consider relevant to the hypotheses we are going to test. In this chapter we will present a general description of the way in which we analyzed the consequent variables, explanations for illness and techniques of therapy. The relation between the antecedent and consequent variables will then be considered in the following chapters.

As we have indicated in Chapter 1, customs relating to illness and the threat of death are the cultural data which we propose to use as indices of personality characteristics of the typical members of a given society. There are several reasons for this choice, which we would like to present before proceeding to a description of the way in which we analyzed these data.

Our first reason for the choice of customary reactions to illness lies in the fact of their universality. Sickness and death occur in all societies, and customs relating to them have grown up everywhere. These include beliefs about the causes of illness as well as preventive and therapeutic practices. We were thus assured that there would be a comparable set of customs in all the societies of our sample.

As in the case of the five socialization problems, illness and death not only are a universal problem but have given rise to a diversity of customs. We were thus assured of the variations which are required for testing hypotheses about the personality integration of culture.

Another essential point is that customs relating to illness are a part of what Kardiner (1945) has called the projective systems of a culture. These customs are for the most part magical and unrealistic. By and large, the beliefs with which we will be concerned do not accord with theories scientifically established by modern medicine, and the therapeutic practices, although they may be effective as psychotherapy, generally do not have the physiological effects which are produced today by surgery or the use of antiseptics and antibiotics. The magical medical theories and practices of primitive societies seem much more likely to be retained because of their compatibility with personality variables than because of their practical physiological utility.[1]

We are thus proposing to use these customs relating to illness as a sort of projective test for a society as a whole. Our rationale is essentially the same as that which commonly underlies the interpretation of fantasy produced by individual subjects on such clinical tests as the Rorschach or the Thematic Appreception Test. The securities and anxieties found in fantasy are likewise assumed to be little structured by reality and to be expressive of the securities and anxieties which are of basic importance in the personality of the individual.

There is of course the important difference between our indices of personality and those provided by a projective test that our indices are provided by genuine customs which are to some extent conformed to by each individual as a result of specifica-

---

1. We are not contending that the medical beliefs and practices of primitive societies altogether lack a realistic basis. Indeed, the Western European's scorn for the adaptation of the "primitive man" to his environment has often been followed by an adoption of the "primitive" man's wisdom. We are only arguing that the opportunity for realistic influence on these customs under prescientific conditions is less than for many other customs, and that the likelihood of an important influence of personality is greater. It must also be recognized that customs relating to illness are influenced by additional factors besides personality variables and realistic physiological effect. Their adjustive functions in integrating the life of a society and in social control have often been noted by anthropologists.

tions provided to him rather than solely because of his relevant past experience. We do not assume that an individual explains illness in a particular way, or uses a particular therapeutic technique, solely as an outgrowth of certain characteristics of his own personality. He most often will have learned the explanation or the therapy as a result of its being initially specified to him by older members of his society. But not every explanation or therapeutic technique that is invented in a society, or is taught to one of its members, is well learned or later repeated. In this as in other phenomena of culture there is change. Our supposition is that those customs which survive continual change, or emerge from it, will tend to be those that are best learned or most often created because they resemble the fantasies to which the members of a society would individually be led by the personality characteristics they have in common. It is to the extent that these customary responses to illness do represent uniformities resulting from common experience, that we may hope to make use of them as indices of personality characteristics of members of a society. But we recognize, as we would not have to in the case of a projective test, that their value as indices of personality characteristics will be reduced to the extent that they are reactions which are now being learned by members of a society solely as a result of their being specified as customary behavior.

Customary reactions to illness, fortunately, have long attracted the attention of fieldworkers in anthropology. As a result the ethnographic accounts of these customs are extremely rich and diverse. At first glance the beliefs and practices about illness, found in various societies, might appear so diverse and complex as to baffle any attempt at systematic comparison of one culture with another. Closer scrutiny, however, reveals several variables which provide a basis for the comparative study of these aspects of culture. We will give a brief general account of these variables, first for explanations of illness and then for therapeutic practices.

Our analysis of explanations of illness is based on five variables which promised to be significant.

1. AGENCY. Perhaps the most striking of these variables has to do with the character of the *agent* who is believed to play some role in the etiological sequence leading to illness. In every culture of our sample personal agents were to at least some extent specified as playing such a role. But the cultures differed in the character of the agent and in the importance of the role played by various kinds of agent. The agent may be a living person with supernatural powers (e.g., as sorcerer or black magician). He may be the ghost of an ancestor or other dead member of the society. He may be some other sort of human spirit, a god, or the spirit of some animal. A society may believe in all of these as agents causing illness, but believe some to play an important role and others an unimportant one. Another society may believe in only one or two of these agencies of illness.

2. PATIENT RESPONSIBILITY. A second major variable on which theories of disease may be compared is the degree to which the patient himself is believed to be responsible for his own sickness. In some cultures the patient is believed to be primarily responsible, and the role of any agent is only incidental. In others, the agent is conceived as an arbitrary and malignant being who causes sickness with little regard to anything the patient may have done or failed to do. All degrees of blame of the patient between these two extremes are also found.

3. ACT. A third major variable has to do with what particular act or failure to act, on the part of the patient, is believed to be a contributory cause of sickness. It may be believed, for example, that a person gets sick because of breaking a food taboo or a sex taboo, because of sacrilege, or because of failure to perform some ritual.

4. MATERIALS. The fourth variable has to do with the *materials* involved in the production of illness. The term "materials" is

used very broadly here; it includes not only such obvious items as poisons, exuviae, and menstrual blood, but also spirits, magical weapons or reified aggressive wishes insofar as these appear to be thought of as being (like real materials) put into the patient's body, taken out of it, used in ritual, etc. The materials to which the origin of illness is attributed are extremely diverse.

5. MEANS. The last of the variables used in the analysis of theories of disease consists of the *means* by which these materials have an effect. The means were classified into five categories: ingested, introjected (i.e., more or less magically taken or thrust into the body), brought into contact with the body, removed or lost, and used in ritual.

It should be noted that all of these variables may be involved in the analysis of a single explanation of illness. The Kwoma, for example, believe in sorcery. The *agent* is a living person, either a specialist in sorcery or anyone who has sufficient skill in sorcery. In order to bring about illness, the sorcerer may obtain crumbs of food which remain from a meal eaten by his intended victim (the *materials*), and with these he performs a ritual (the *means*). As far as this particular belief is concerned, the degree of *patient responsibility* may be judged to be reasonably low, inasmuch as blame is clearly put on the sorcerer rather than the victim, yet not as low as it might be. One *act* of the patient mentioned as contributing to his illness is carelessness with his exuviae, an act which makes possible the sorcerer's ritual (Whiting, 1941, pp. 136–143).

A given society, moreover, typically holds to more than one explanation of illness. Among the Kwoma there is one which is very similar to the one just described; it is that a sorcerer may bring about illness by placing a certain white powder in his victim's food. And certain minor ailments may be caused by a spirit instead of a sorcerer (Whiting, 1941, pp. 141 and 134).

In view of this diversity of explanation of illness in a single society, it appeared desirable to obtain some quantitative measure of the custom potential of each aspect of belief which was analyzed. This required a specification of how custom potential was to be judged. The following criteria were decided upon as being both theoretically relevant and capable of application to the available data.

1. The number of diseases, according to the theory held in the particular society, to which this aspect of explanation was applied. Thus, if all diseases were believed to result from some action of the patient, the rating of patient responsibility would be higher than if only a part of them were. This criterion follows from the use of probability of evocation as a measure of the habit potential of a response.

2. The frequency of occurrence in the particular society of the disease to which this aspect of explanation was applied. Thus, if tuberculosis were endemic in a society, whereas cholera were rare, the theory about tuberculosis would be given more weight if it differed from the theory about cholera. This criterion also follows from the use of probability of evocation as a measure of the habit potential of a response.

3. The seriousness of the disease. Theories about diseases which are often fatal would be given a higher rating than those about minor ailments. This criterion follows from the fact that we were considering beliefs as responses to anxiety, and that it seemed appropriate to stress those beliefs where evidence was clearest that strong anxiety was an important part of the stimulus situation.

4. The strength with which the belief was stated and held to. Here evidence of the strength of conviction and the emotional support of the belief was taken into account. This criterion is suggested by the use of amplitude or intensity of response as a measure of habit potential.

On the basis of these criteria our judges were instructed to rate custom potential on a 5-point scale, or to report that a given aspect of explanation was stated by the ethnographer to be absent, or that no relevant data were available. This scale was then applied to over 200 aspects of explanation subsumed under the five major variables of disease causation discussed above (i.e., agency, patient responsibility, act, materials and means). These aspects of explanation are so numerous that they will not be presented in detail here; those which were made use of in obtaining the results reported in this book will be described as the occasion arises.

For most aspects of explanation the most frequent judgment was, "No relevant data." In general, we have treated this judgment the same as, "Stated absent" (which was rarely made). In doing so, we are certainly falling into error in some specific cases. We have used in this study, however, only societies for which there was some considerable information about explanations of illness.[2] For these societies it is reasonable to suppose that, usually, when an explanation is not mentioned it is genuinely either not present or of very slight importance.

Since most aspects of explanation appeared to be absent in most societies, our treatment of the data was reduced to a categorical rather than a quantitative one. That is, we simply divided societies into those in which the explanation was present and those in which it was absent, disregarding the quantitative variation in judgments of custom potential for the former group. For certain aspects of explanation of illness, however, which will be dealt with in Chapters 11 and 12, absence was rare and we have hence retained the quantitative approach in analyzing the results.

The analysis of customs relating to illness was made independently by two research assistants, one a graduate student in anthropology and the other a recent college graduate who had majored in psychology. To minimize the possibility of bias, these two judges were kept ignorant of the ratings made on the child training variables and of that portion of the ethnographic reports dealing with child training. Like the judges of child training practices, these judges were instructed to indicate (on

2. Several societies on which the child training material met our criterion of adequacy were omitted from our sample because of inadequate coverage of customs relating to illness.

a two-point scale) the degree of confidence they felt in each judgment. With their task so much oriented toward determining whether there was or was not evidence for the presence of a given explanation, however, these judges found that if they were able to make a judgment they were generally confident of it. Hence few judgments were made with a lower degree of confidence; for the sake of simplicity we have treated these few judgments just as though they had been confident judgments.

For specific items of an explanation, which were not universally found, the judge tended generally to report the custom potential to be high in any society where the explanation was present. Few points on the rating scale were actually used. The judges reported difficulty in making discriminations among these points, and in fact the two judges did not agree very well with each other in their exact ratings on such items. This provided a second reason for reducing the data here to the form of categorical judgments of presence or absence. On the present-absent dichotomy, when we measured agreement between judges on sample items in a way [3] that would be roughly comparable to the reliability coefficients for the quantitative judgments of child training practices, we found that the degree of agreement appeared to be at least of the same general order that had been found there for the confident judgments. In other words, the analysis of explanations of illness reaches an acceptable degree of reliability.

In the pooling of judgments by the several judges, disagreements between judges become more difficult to deal with for categorical variables than for quantitative variables. In the case of quantitative variables (those of child training practice, and reactions to illness dealt with in Chapters 11 and 12), we have resolved the disagreement by simply adding together the ratings of the several judges. In the case of categorical variables, however, the disagreement is between a judgment of absence and a judgment of presence. A procedure akin to averaging

3. We used for this purpose the tetrachoric correlation coefficient (cf. Edwards, 1946, pp. 116–117).

would create a third, intermediate category of uncertain presence. To be sure, the introduction of such a category seems quite meaningful, for on the whole such disagreement probably means that the custom is present but not very conspicuous or important. But in the absence of any strong reason to preserve this third category, its introduction would unnecessarily complicate the presentation and statistical analysis of the results. We therefore placed the cases of disagreement in the "present" or in the "absent" category according to which would come nearest to dividing the total number of societies into two groups of equal size. The exact meaning of "present" and "absent" thus varies slightly from one context to another, and we will indicate what it means in each instance; it always has the uniform meaning, however, of a division of the societies into two groups according to the evidence for the presence or absence of the custom being discussed.

ANALYSIS OF THERAPEUTIC PRACTICES

Therapeutic practices were analyzed by a schema very similar to that used for explanations of illness. We were again able to use as variables *agency* (the persons taking part in therapy), the *acts* responsible for cure (acts of either the patient or his therapist), the *materials* employed in the cure, and the *means* by which these materials are brought into play. Degree of patient responsibility did not seem to be generally capable of being judged, and was not employed in the analysis of therapy; a somewhat similar variable was provided, however, by the *degree of isolation* of the patient during illness. Finally, an additional variable in the analysis of therapy was the *effect* of the therapeutic practice as conceptualized in the particular culture (e.g., as placating the agent responsible for the illness, or as removing foreign material from the patient's body, or as restoring the patient's soul to his body).

We have thought it essential to give a fairly full introductory account of our analysis of child training practices and our analysis of explanations of illness, because the results of those analyses are drawn upon in various places throughout the rest of this book. In the case of therapeutic practices, there is no such reason to give a full introductory account of our methods. Results deriving from this analysis are dealt with only in Chapter 10. It seems simpler, therefore, to present further details about the method of analysis used for therapy only as they are necessary in Chapter 10. The account which has been given in the previous section of this chapter, of the handling of methodological problems in the analysis of explanations of illness, applies equally to the analysis of therapeutic practices. The same two judges analyzed both of these sets of customs relating to illness.

IF A YOUNG child has certain experiences in connection with nursing and weaning, psychoanalytic theory holds, he may come to have an oral fixation. By "oral fixation" is meant that oral matters continue to have for him an actual or potential importance greater than they would have for someone who had not had these experiences. An oral fixation might be manifested in a variety of specific ways—for example, in a great interest in smoking and eating candy, in an exaggerated concern about the quality of what one eats, or in an approach to other people which has a metaphorical resemblance to a desire to incorporate them into oneself by swallowing them.

Oral fixation is but one example of the general concept of fixation in psychoanalytic theory. Fixation, it is held, may occur with respect to any of the strongly motivated basic interests which at various times are conspicuous in children and which are curbed or restricted in some way during the process of socialization. It is with this general phenomenon of fixation that we propose to deal in this and the three succeeding chapters.

We have been able to bring cross-cultural evidence to bear on the problem of fixation. This does not mean, however, that the evidence we present will serve to validate or invalidate all the psychoanalytic hypotheses that are associated with the term "fixation." In particular, such a caution needs to be given about the idea that our evidence might relate to the psychoanalytic conception of a regular sequence of "psychosexual development" in infancy and childhood.

The concept of fixation as it is used in psychoanalytic writings is closely associated with the idea of a regular and more or less universal sequence of psychosexual development. In broad outline this sequence begins with an oral stage, in which the infant's pleasure-striving is centered on the activities of the mouth. It proceeds to an anal stage, in which the young child's pleasure-striving is centered on excretory processes. Finally, this stage gives way to a genital stage in which the genital organs gain primacy as the locus of the major strivings for bodily pleasure. Fixation is conceived of as involving a partial failure of progression from one of these stages to the next.

Psychoanalytic theory thus imbeds the concept of fixation in a context of hypotheses about a developmental sequence of pleasure-strivings. The association thus established may be so strong that some readers may suppose the idea of regular stages of development to be an essential part of the concept of fixation. On the contrary, it seems clear to us that the concept of fixation refers to a possible process which may adequately be examined in isolation from this particular developmental sequence within which psychoanalytic theory supposes it to occur. It is our intention here to investigate the general process of fixation, and to do so without making any assumptions about a uniform sequence of psychosexual development. The aspect of psychoanalytic theory with which we are here concerned, then, has to do with a general process and the factors which determine it, rather than with specific sequences which in our opinion are much more likely to vary radically among individuals and among societies.

The essence of the notion of fixation, as we understand it then, is the idea that events occurring in childhood with respect to a particular system of behavior, e.g., oral or sexual behavior, may bring about a continued importance or prepotence of that system of behavior, in comparison with the importance it would have had in the absence of those events. But now what are these events that might bring about fixation? On this question we will review briefly what psychoanalytic theory has suggested, and what revisions in that theory are suggested by more general theory of behavior.

An excellent and concise statement of psychoanalytic theory about the origins of fixation is offered by Fenichel in the following passage (1945, pp. 65–66):

> What are the factors responsible for evoking fixations? Unquestionably there are hereditary tendencies that account for the various erogenous zones being charged with different amounts of cathexis or different degrees of ability for discharge. Little is known about such constitutional factors. Psychoanalysis did succeed, however, in studying the kinds of experience that favor the development of fixations.
>
> 1. The consequence of experiencing excessive satisfactions at a given level is that this level is renounced only with reluctance; if, later, misfortunes occur, there is always a yearning for the satisfactions formerly enjoyed.
>
> 2. A similar effect is wrought by excessive frustrations at a given level. One gets the impression that at developmental levels that do not afford enough satisfaction, the organism refuses to go further, demanding the withheld satisfactions. . . .
>
> 3. One frequently finds that excessive satisfactions as well as excessive frustrations underlie a given fixation; previous overindulgence had made the person unable to bear later frustrations; little frustrations, which a less spoiled individual could tolerate, then have the same effect that a severe frustration ordinarily has.
>
> 4. It is understandable, therefore, that abrupt changes from excessive satisfactions to excessive frustrations have an especially fixating effect.
>
> 5. Most frequently, however, fixations are rooted in experiences of instinctual satisfaction which simultaneously gave reassurance in the face of some anxiety or aided in re-

pressing some other feared impulse. Such simultaneous satisfaction of drive and of anxiety is the most common cause of fixations.

Fenichel has here stated five sequences of events which may, according to psychoanalytic theory, produce fixation.[1] All five seem likely to be of importance. But only two of the sequences, the first two in Fenichel's list, appear to refer to basic processes. The other three sequences refer instead to special conditions influencing the first two sequences, or to the effect of the combined presence of both of the basic sequences in a single life history. For this reason it is Fenichel's first two points that require our attention as possibly pointing to important basic processes.[2]

The first of the origins of fixation listed by Fenichel is excessive satisfaction. The second is excessive frustration. It will be noted that these two antecedents to fixation bear a close resemblance to the two basic socialization variables chosen for this study. Our initial satisfaction variable corresponds to Fenichel's "satisfactions at a given level" and our socialization anxiety to his "frustrations at a given level." This correspondence is no

1. With Fenichel we would agree that constitutional factors probably play a part too; but since our study throws no light on them, and is concerned only with experiential factors, we will neglect constitutional factors in our discussion of fixation.

2. Two of Fenichel's additional points may be recognized as relevant to our method of measuring the effects of child training practices, as presented in Chapter 3. The notion that abrupt changes have an especially marked effect (Fenichel's fourth point) was taken account of in measuring socialization anxiety, though we made the assumption uniformly for all instances of frustration through socialization (see above, p. 53). The contribution of extraneous anxiety (Fenichel's fifth point) was taken account of in measuring initial satisfaction (see above, p. 51). The remaining point made by Fenichel (his third point) is neither postulated nor directly tested in our study. It would, however, as Fenichel states it, lead to an expectation that given indices of fixation would be correlated in the same direction with initial satisfaction and with socialization anxiety, an expectation which, as will be shown in succeeding chapters, is not confirmed by our data.

accident. In formulating our variables of satisfaction and anxiety our intention was to use them in testing hypotheses suggested by the psychoanalytic view which Fenichel is summarizing. Before turning to the fundamental question of the relation between these two contrasting variables of gratification and frustration we wish to call attention to several points on which our assumptions as to the probable determinants of fixation differ from those stated or implied by Fenichel.

A first point of difference has to do with Fenichel's phrase "at a given level." This phrase refers to the Freudian hypothesis of stages or levels of psychosexual development. Associated as it is with this developmental hypothesis, the psychoanalytic account of fixation lays special stress on the three systems of behavior for which the three major levels of development are named in psychoanalytic terminology—oral, anal, and sexual behavior. We, on the contrary, intend no special stress on these three systems of behavior. The process of fixation as we deal with it should be equally pertinent to the dependent and aggressive systems with which we also deal. It should also be pertinent to other systems of behavior which share with these five the general feature of involving initial habits which must be interfered with in the course of socialization. It might of course be argued that dependent and aggressive behavior are already embraced in the Freudian account of fixation, the former under the rubric of oral dependence and the latter under the rubrics of oral and anal sadism. We prefer, however, to assume that dependence and aggression may more usefully be treated as separate systems of behavior.

A second point of difference also has to do with the notion of levels of development. It might be inferred from Fenichel's account that the effect of gratification or of frustration will vary radically according to the time when it occurs, because of the position at which that time falls in a regular sequence of psychosexual development. Thus it might be inferred that oral frustration would lead to fixation if it occurred in the first year of life, during the supposed oral period of development, but that it would not lead to fixation if it occurred at the age of three, when the child has presumably passed from a period of oral dominance to a period of anal dominance. From our description of how initial indulgence and socialization anxiety were analyzed in our study (see above, pp. 50–55), it will be seen that no such assumptions were introduced.[3]

A third point of difference has to do with the word "excessive." Fenichel is quite typical of psychoanalytic writers in specifying that fixation results from *excessive* gratification or from *excessive* frustration. This terminology raises the question, At what point does gratification or frustration become excessive? There is no *a priori* answer to this question, so that even if one were proceeding from this psychoanalytic assumption it would be safer to measure these variables along a continuous scale rather than to judge whether they were present in excess. The same terminology suggests that any degree of gratification or frustration less than excessive would have no fixating effect, whereas any excessive degree would have a uniform fixating effect. The presence of a threshold effect here, and even the absence of quantitative variation above it, is indeed conceivable. We considered, however, continuity much more likely, and this provided a further reason for our use of quantitative judgments. It seemed likely to us that initial satisfaction and socialization anxiety would function as variables which, as they increased in degree, would have an increasing effect.

Now a fourth point of difference brings us back to more fundamental considerations. Fenichel cites two quite different kinds of antecedent conditions, gratification and frustration—which are in a sense direct opposites—and suggests that they lead to a single consequence, that of fixation. Even the specific terms used

3. Had we felt it necessary to postulate critical, genetically determined stages at which a particular socialization pressure would have effects quite different from its effects at other ages, we would have found it impossible to conduct this study. The available ethnographic data are not sufficiently precise with respect to age. Insofar as we have obtained positive findings without any such assumption, our study may be seen as adding to the doubtfulness, or at least restricting the generality, of that assumption.

in this context by Fenichel suggest essentially the same effect in the two cases; "a yearning for the satisfaction formerly enjoyed" and "demanding the withheld satisfaction" seem to refer to a distinction only of source and not of effect. Possibly, the same eventual effect could be produced by opposite causes—just as a sensation of cold may under certain conditions be produced by either a very warm or a very cold stimulus. But we feel that a more careful analysis of these two sequences, an analysis made in the light of present principles of learning, suggests that there is an important difference between them, not only in the event that initiates them but also in the nature of the "fixation" which results.

FIXATION AND GENERAL BEHAVIOR THEORY [4]

What, first of all, would we expect to be the consequence of a high degree of gratification in a particular system of behavior? On the basis of principles of learning we would expect the development of a strong habit potential of acquired reward as a response to the stimuli associated with the gratification. Dollard and Miller (1950, pp. 78–79), using the term "reinforcement" where we have been using the term "reward," put the matter as follows:

> When, as the result of learning, previously neutral cues gain the capacity to play the same functional role in the learning and performance of new responses as other reinforcements, such as food for the hungry animal or water

4. It will be noted that we do not consider here the experimental literature which has grown up around the concept of fixation; this literature has been critically reviewed by Sears (1943), and some more recent work is also summarized by Maier (1949). The reason is that these experimental studies have been primarily concerned with the problem of the conditions giving rise to habits of very high potential, where the responses generally are instrumental acts. Our specific interest in personality development has led our attention more particularly to the nature of the habits involved, in psychoanalytic fixation, as habits which give rise to acquired drive and reward.

for the thirsty one, they are described as *learned reinforcements*. . . . Experiments by Wolfe (1936) and Cowles (1937) show how poker chips can acquire learned reinforcement value for chimpanzees. In order to give reinforcement value to the poker chips, Wolfe first trained hungry chimpanzees to insert them into a vending machine which delivered a grape for each token inserted. After sufficient training of this kind, he found that the chimpanzees could be taught to work for the chips by pulling a handle against a weight. Cowles found that after the poker chips had been associated with primary reinforcement, they could be used to reinforce the learning of a variety of new habits. . . . Other experiments on subjects ranging from chickens to children have shown that a variety of sounds and visual stimuli (and hence presumably any cue) can be made to function as a learned reinforcement by repeated, immediate association with primary reinforcement. In the experiments that have been done to date, the acquisition of learned reinforcement seems to follow exactly the same laws as the learning of any other habit.

This account stresses the experimental evidence, mostly from studies of lower animals, for the general nature of the process by which acquired reward is learned. What would be the parallel circumstances and effects in the child undergoing socialization?

We will offer here only a very general answer to this question, reserving for a bit later particular examples for each system of behavior with which we deal. If there is especially high and consistent gratification of one system of behavior, we would expect that the various responses that make up this system, and the stimuli consistently associated with them, would develop a strong potential for evoking acquired reward. These responses and stimuli would become major sources of security or satisfaction, because they would become capable of evoking relaxation in the presence of diffuse drives—such as vague, generalized anxiety—which are capable of being reduced by a general response of relaxation. In terms of cultural concepts, then, a high degree of indulgence of a particular system of behavior in the child training practices of a society should lead to the development in children of a high satisfaction potential in that system.

The psychoanalytic conception of fixation would, however, have a further implication here: that once established, such a satisfaction potential would continue to be high throughout the lifetime of the individuals concerned. Learning theory, on the contrary, leaves this an open question. What is learned can be unlearned. Whether the initial childhood learning is sufficiently retained to have a lifelong influence is, in the absence of detailed analysis of subsequent learning conditions, purely an empirical matter. The psychoanalytic assumption of a generally consistent lifelong influence is, in part, what is being tested in our study.

Now what of the effects of a high degree of frustration? Principles of learning do not at all suggest that the effects will be the same as result from a high degree of reward or gratification. The effects should be quite different—the acquisition not of acquired reward but of acquired drive. A recent statement by Hull (1951, p. 21) may be cited for a general statement of some of the reasoning here:

It is a matter of common observation that situations which are associated with drives themselves become C_D's [i.e., conditions which give rise to a drive]. Consider, for example, the case involving tissue injury. The response leading to escape from the injury gets connected to the stimuli and to the traces of those stimuli which are associated with the onset of injury through the resulting cessation in the drive stimulus discharge (S_D). . . . These antedating stimuli when later encountered will therefore give rise to more or less realistic reproductions of these movements. Now, these antedating stimuli are the new C_D's, and the proprioceptive stimuli activated by the associated internal or "fear" reactions become the S_D's of the *secondary drive* or motivation.

As applied to the child undergoing socialization, learning principles would lead to the following prediction: A high degree of frustration or punishment with respect to a given system of behavior leads to emotional responses, which are drive-producing, and which might be described by such terms as "anxious anticipation of continued deprivation" and "anxious anticipation of punishment." The various responses which make up this system of behavior, and the stimuli associated with them, then come through learning to evoke these emotional responses and thus produce a drive which we might describe as anxiety about continued deprivation and about punishment. In cultural terms, then, child training practices which involve severe frustration of a given system of behavior should lead to the development of a high anxiety potential. Again, while psychoanalytic theory suggests that such an effect, if of high degree, will necessarily be long-lasting, principles of learning suggest rather the possibility of subsequent unlearning, and recommend direct empirical investigation to determine whether the effects are generally long-lasting.

Now if the fixation resulting from severe frustration or punishment consists of a tendency for certain stimuli to evoke acquired drive, it might be expected that the final outcome would be that the person would simply learn to avoid all of these stimuli. It would then be difficult to detect the fixation. Since the person avoids all the stimuli which might arouse anxiety in him, there is in the course of his life as he actually lives it no anxiety to detect. Yet there is reason to believe that the anxiety will in fact be repeatedly evoked. The reason for this lies in the character of the systems of behavior which are crucial for socialization. The need for socializing these systems of behavior arises in part out of the fact that these systems of behavior are critically relevant for adult living and that the person must learn to behave in an acceptably adult manner in each system. He cannot avoid all the responses and stimuli of any of these systems. In the case of the oral and anal systems, the biological requirements of life ensure the continuation not merely of thoughts but of overt behavior. In the case of the sexual system, a biologically determined drive produces at least tendencies toward overt behavior, and similar interests in other people conspire to keep these tendencies active. Aggressive and dependent behavior are repeatedly occasioned by the circumstances of adult social interaction. Thus the person with a high degree of anxiety potential in any of these systems of behavior is unable to escape all stimuli which will evoke his anxiety. The positive pressures toward overt and implicit responses in that system will ensure his being kept in a conflict situation, in which the anxiety will repeatedly be a conspicuous part of his total reaction. Thus the effect of severe socialization in a system of behavior, insofar as it is a permanent effect, should be not only a predictable anxiety if the individual is forced into certain situations, but an actual anxiety because the individual is indeed certain to be forced into those situations to some considerable extent.

Principles of learning suggest, then, that from extreme frustration and from extreme gratification should follow quite different consequences. Yet both sets of consequences may usefully be labeled as fixation, following well-established psychoanalytic terminology. In this event, distinctive labels are also needed. We suggest that fixation which results from a high degree of gratification be called *positive fixation,* and that fixation which results from severe socialization be called *negative fixation.*[5]

5. Alternative terms might be *reward fixation* and *drive fixation,* which would correctly point to the special major feature of each. These terms might, however, mistakenly suggest that the consequences consisted in the former case entirely of changes in reward, and in the latter case entirely of drive. This is, of course, not true. Where new drives are built up, situations become rewarding which would not otherwise have been so.

Examples of what each of these two types of fixation might mean in each system of behavior should now be useful in clarifying the distinction. We will again consider oral fixation as a first example.

EXAMPLES OF POSITIVE AND NEGATIVE FIXATION

Of the various forms of behavior that are regarded in psycho-analytic writings as symptomatic of oral fixation, some could be aptly described as involving primarily the attachment of high drive value to stimuli associated with oral functions, and these we would call instances of negative fixation. One clear example of this is the behavior which consists of exaggerated worry about the possibility of not being adequately fed. When a person who demonstrates this behavior begins to get hungry or to think about his next meal, he reacts to this stimulation with increased drive. The drive may come from his having learned to make, under some of these conditions, the internal responses that actually produce more intense hunger. Or it may come only from more diffuse emotional responses which create a general drive of anxiety. In either case the behavior is such as to permit the inference that a rather high drive state is evoked by thoughts of future eating or the need for food. We speak of this as a case of *acquired* drive because we assume, as does psychoanalytic theory, that a person *acquires* this habit of internal responding as a result of what has happened to him when hungry (typically, in infancy and early childhood). A person who is frustrated through being fed too little or too seldom will generally be very hungry and emotionally aroused at the time when he is fed. Through this frequently occurring association he learns to respond to any of the cues of hunger and food

---

The development of acquired rewards, on the other hand, means that the sight or thought of the goal object or situation may now act as an incentive, producing drive which motivates behavior toward seeking the goal. This latter point will be referred to again in our chapter on the origins of guilt, though it does not seem pertinent to our tests of hypotheses about fixation.

thoughts with the extremer hunger and emotional excitement which have been associated with drive reduction.[6]

A second manifestation of negative oral fixation is fear of punishment or of guilt as a reaction to oral activity or to the temptation to engage in oral activity. Here some class of oral activity (e.g., especially pleasurable eating, kissing, sucking a drink through a straw) evokes in the person anticipations of being criticized or even self-criticism, and these anticipations or criticisms function as drive. Here again it is assumed that the person who reacts in this way does so as a result of previous learning; he has been punished and has learned to punish himself, for certain forms of oral activity. As a result of the anxiety acquired in this training he never engages in the exact oral activity for which he was punished (e.g., obtaining milk by nursing from breast or bottle). But the high anxiety acquired through excessive punishment and frustration is manifested in the generalization of the anxiety to other oral activities which in another person would not evoke anxiety.

Now if these forms of oral fixation involve primarily acquired drive, there are others which involve primarily acquired reward and these we would call positive fixation. A good example is provided by thumbsucking. A significant fact about thumbsucking is that it appears to have a generalized drive-reducing or rewarding value (Davis and Havighurst, 1946). That is, almost any sort of tension in the child, whether it originates in hunger, fear, embarrassment, or guilt, is likely to evoke thumbsucking, and the thumbsucking seems to have some effect in reducing the intensity of the discomfort. What is most conspicuous appears to be not the presence of drive associated with oral activity, but the very diffuse reward-value of this particular oral activity. This would appear, then, to be a case of acquired reward. The origins might lie in an especially strong and frequent

6. We have stated this process of acquisition of drive in terms of a reinforcement theory of learning, as does Hull in the passage we have quoted from him above (p. 137). It could equally well be stated in terms of a contiguity theory of learning.

association of oral activity with drive reduction, especially with the reduction of varied emotional drives.

Another example of positive oral fixation may be provided by a case described briefly by Abraham (1927, pp. 261–262). This is the case of a woman who had practiced masturbation for many years, although she had a horror of heterosexual activity. Then she was frightened by reading a warning against the evils of masturbation, and succeeded in giving up this practice altogether. At this time, Abraham says, she developed ". . . a violent longing for sweets. She bought and consumed sweets in the greatest secrecy and with feelings of pleasure and gratification the intensity of which surprised her." It is evidently supposed here that the acquired reward value of oral activity was such that a particular oral activity was capable of producing some reduction of the drive for genital pleasure, as well as of generalized anxiety.

Not all the specific items of behavior which are said to represent oral fixation can be clearly recognized as having their probable origin in a particular one of these two processes, positive and negative fixation. Some items of behavior may depend on the presence of both types of fixation; others may grow out of negative fixation in some individuals, but out of positive fixation in other individuals. Consider, for example, the hypothesis that a strong habit of smoking is a consequence of oral fixation. Are we to say that a strong anxiety about basic oral pleasure, leading to smoking as a substitute, or a strong reward potential of all oral activity, is more conspicuous here? There might be ways of making a judgment here in the individual case, but there seems to be no basis for making a broad generalization about which component is on the whole predominant. Despite this limitation, we believe that separate analysis of the two general processes underlying fixation is important. If theory suggests that there are two separate processes, those of positive and negative fixation, scientific progress requires their separate analysis, even if the two processes are often found operating together.

This distinction between positive and negative fixation is

not relevant only for oral behavior. We have chosen this system of behavior as an example to present at some length. It may be well now to indicate more briefly examples of the distinction for the other four systems of behavior we are dealing with.

In the case of the anal system as in the case of the oral system, psychoanalysts have already suggested a variety of forms of behavior as symptomatic of fixation. Some of these seem to fit clearly the picture of positive fixation that we have drawn on the basis of learning theory, and others fit clearly the picture of negative fixation. Positive fixation may be illustrated here by the person who derives in adulthood a much greater than normal pleasure from excretory processes, and who tends to find some relief from vague anxieties through urinating or defecating. Such a person may feel a prolonged morning visit to the bathroom as one of the most pleasurable periods of the day. Negative fixation may be illustrated by an exaggerated inhibition of excretory processes (as in chronic constipation or extreme modesty about excretion) or by the excessive general ritualism which according to psychoanalytic theory may result from very strong anxieties established in toilet training.

In the sexual system, examples of both extremes are easy to find. On the one hand, there are cases of positive fixation where sexual behavior appears to be a person's major way of giving himself reassurance in the face of anxieties of any sort—where sexual behavior, in other words, produces not only its own intrinsic rewards but also the reward of reduction of anxiety. On the other hand, there are cases of negative fixation where the person responds to external stimuli of sexual import, and to his own sexual impulses, with an anxiety which is entirely disproportionate to any realistic consequences of his present sexual behavior and which therefore seems likely to have arisen from the punishing consequences of the arousal of sexual interest at some time in the distant past. Specific forms of behavior which are common in our society, and which may illustrate negative sexual fixation, are worry about sexual potency and exaggerated fear of diseases of the genito-urinary tract.

In the case of dependence, there are again some people for

whom this form of behavior appears to be a major source of reassurance. Such people, when confronted by difficulties in life, habitually turn to others in a dependent manner; and they do so, perhaps, not so much in the expectation of real help in solving their difficulties as simply because they find that the very act of dependence reduces their anxiety about the difficulties which confront them. This strong and broadly generalized reward value of dependent behavior is what would be expected as a consequence of positive dependence fixation. In contrast, some people become highly anxious when they are threatened with being dependent, or even with seeming to be dependent, on others. This arousal of high anxiety by potential dependence is often a source of unhappiness in marriage and at work, but also one important source of the rugged individualism which is so much admired in American culture. It is the consequence that would be expected from negative dependence fixation.

For aggression, finally, a similar distinction may be made. For some people, anxiety aroused by an awkward social situation, by hunger, or by any sort of frustration, is immediately reduced by some aggressive act in word or deed; and they may persistently act in this way, indicating the strong reward value of aggression for them, even though the aggression so often leads to new sources of difficulty. On the other hand, of course, it is equally clear that many people are made highly anxious by any token of aggression or temptation toward aggression, in themselves or others, and are led thereby not simply to a socially desirable restraint but to a crippling inhibition of mastery over their environment. Here again, then, one sort of behavior suggests the label *positive fixation* and another sort of behavior suggests the label *negative fixation*.

CULTURAL INDICES OF FIXATION

Thus far, in using the term fixation, and the more specific terms of positive fixation and negative fixation, we have been speaking in theoretical terms. The psychoanalytic concept, and our modification of it in light of general behavior theory, call attention to certain forms of adult behavior whose origins might plausibly be supposed to lie in the frustrations and gratifications of childhood. But that there is adult behavior which might plausibly be explained in this way does not prove that the explanation is correct. We have so far offered no evidence that the hypotheses which underlie the concept of fixation have any validity. It is these hypotheses which we propose to subject to the test of cross-cultural evidence in the following chapters.

In order to make such a test, two kinds of measures of customs are necessary. On the one hand, we must have measures of variations in child training practices which, according to the hypotheses we are considering, should produce differences in degree of fixation. These measures we have already described in detail; they are our measures of initial satisfaction and of socialization anxiety in each of the five systems of behavior. On the other hand, we must have measures of variations in other customs which can function as indices of the extent to which fixation in each system of behavior actually characterizes the typical behavior of adults in a given society. We have already indicated, of course, that customary reactions to illness provide the measures we intend to use for this purpose, and in Chapter 6 we have described our general method of analyzing these customs. We have delayed until now, however, after a theoretical discussion of fixation, an account of what kind of indices of fixation we propose to find in customary reactions to illness. We propose, of course, separate indices of positive and of negative fixation.

Positive fixation, we have suggested, should consist primarily of acquired reward. As a result of strong and consistent gratification of a particular system of behavior, the individual should come to respond with relaxation or pleasure to any of the component responses and the stimuli associated with that system of behavior. Evidence of positive fixation in a particular system of behavior, then, would be provided by evidence that those responses and stimuli do have acquired reward value, that they are sources of security for one individual to a greater extent than for other individuals.

Applying this reasoning on the cultural level, we arrived at a general intention to use customary therapeutic practices as indices of positive fixation. Therapeutic practices are responses to anxiety about illness and possible death; they are responses that appear to have a direct function of reducing the anxiety somewhat. To the extent that this drive-reducing power of therapeutic practices does not derive from a real physiological effect of the practices in reducing the severity or the painfulness of the illness, then from what does it derive? Our general assumption was that it might be derived by generalization from the satisfaction potential established for certain forms of behavior in other anxiety-arousing situations. Specifically, we assumed that responses which had acquired a high satisfaction potential as a result of child training practices, had acquired in this way a strong tendency to reduce generalized anxieties of all sorts, might be evoked by anxiety about illness. On this basis it would be predicted, for example, that if the child training practices of a society were such as to make oral behavior especially rewarding to its members, then in the face of anxiety about illness they might resort to some sort of oral behavior as a therapeutic practice.

Negative fixation, we have suggested, should consist primarily of a tendency for the responses and stimuli associated with a given system of behavior to evoke acquired drive. As a result of deprivation and punishment with respect to this system of behavior, that is, the individual should come to respond to this system of behavior with internal states of anxiety and insecurity which would function as a drive. Since the systems we are dealing with are all ones which continue to be repeatedly activated, these emotional states should be repeatedly elicited. The person's responses in this system, then, should continue to be accompanied by emotional concern. An implication of this is that this system of behavior should be a conspicuous source of worry or tension in the individual's life. It is also a locus of conflict, and the existence of conflict may further increase the associated drive state.[7] An index of negative fixation in a particular system of behavior, then, would be provided by evidence that this system of behavior is a locus of conflict, of anxiety, of worried preoccupation.

Applying this reasoning, too, on the cultural level, we arrived at a general intention to use customary explanations of illness as our major indices of negative fixation.[8] Explanations of illness are responses to the anxiety aroused by illness; they are responses which consist of identifying what is to be feared. Illness first of all, of course, is the state that is to be feared; but what objects, persons, or events are to be feared as likely to bring on this state? Our assumption was that in the absence of a realistic basis for identifying the sources of illness, their identification should arise by generalization from the sources of other major anxieties or conflicts. Specifically, we assumed that it might arise by generalization from the circumstances of the major anxieties established in the members of a society as a result of the customary child training practices of the society. If lasting anxiety about the oral system was characteristic of members of a particular society, for example, then anxiety about illness might evoke by generalization responses of worrying about oral matters as a possible source of illness.

The specific indices we used for each system of behavior will be described in the chapters in which we make use of them. In the next chapter (Chapter 8) we will turn to our test of the hypothesis of negative fixation. Since the outcome there must be taken into account in interpreting our results on positive fixation, we will deal with positive fixation afterwards, in Chapter 10. Meanwhile, in Chapter 9 we will round out our evaluation

7. Cf. the recent theoretical article by Brown and Farber (1951) on the motivational effects of a state of conflict.

8. Subsequently, as will be shown in Chapter 10, we found reason also to regard certain therapeutic practices as another possible index of negative fixation.

of the hypothesis of negative fixation by considering various alternative explanations that might be offered for our findings. In Chapter 10, then, after discussing our findings on positive fixation we will be ready for a general discussion and evaluation of all our findings on fixation.

CHAPTER 8. *A Test of Negative Fixation*

IN THIS chapter we present our major test of the hypothesis of negative fixation. The general hypothesis, expressed in terms of individual behavior, is as follows: In any system of behavior, variations in the severity of socialization will give rise to variations in the degree of anxiety associated with that system, and through continuation of this anxiety into adult life will give rise to variations in the extent to which that system of behavior is a focus of worry or concern in the adult. Using the idea of personality integration of culture which we have outlined in Chapter 2, we predict from this psychological hypothesis certain associations between distinct customs. Customary severity of socialization in each system of behavior has been analyzed, for each society in our sample, with respect to the degree of anxiety to which it should give rise. Explanations of illness which ascribe it to events associated with a given system of behavior have been taken as an index of the extent to which that system of behavior is a focus of worry or concern in the typical adult member of the society. The hypothesis of negative fixation, in the specific form in which we propose to test it cross-culturally, may then be expressed as follows:

In any society, the greater the custom potential of socialization anxiety for a system of behavior, the greater will be the custom potential of explanations of illness which attribute illness to events associated with that system.

THE CHOICE OF INDICES OF NEGATIVE FIXATION

The primary indices of negative fixation, as was stated in the last chapter, were drawn from our judgments on explanations for illness. The portions of our analysis of explanations that were useful for this purpose were those dealing with the acts of the patient which might cause illness, the materials (in a broad sense) which might cause illness, and the means by which these materials brought illness about. For each system of behavior, then, we sought for explanations which specified acts, materials, or means which had a similarity to that system of behavior and its circumstances. In judging this similarity, we relied for the most part upon simple common sense judgment that identical or similar elements were involved. In a few cases, where the similarity is less apparent to common judgment, we have instead been guided by specific psychoanalytic hypotheses about the generalization of childhood fixations. The basis for the judgment of similarity will be indicated for each explanation of illness as it is introduced below.

ORAL EXPLANATIONS

1. Ingestion, i.e., eating or drinking, is the act of the patient which is believed responsible for illness; or food or poison is believed to be the material responsible for illness (but only classified here if the means involved entering by the mouth). Ingestion, and the material swallowed, are of course placed here because of their obvious relevance to any generalized concern about oral activity.

2. Verbal spells and incantations performed by other people are the material responsible for illness. This was selected as the one item which indicated concern about specifically oral activity in other people. We were led to include it by the psychoanalytic hypothesis that basic attitudes toward oral activity, acquired in connection with feeding and sucking in infancy, are generalized to the activity of the mouth in speaking.

ANAL EXPLANATIONS

1. Defecation is responsible for illness; or feces, urine, or their odor is the material responsible for illness. This item was in-

cluded because it provides direct evidence of anxiety about excretory functions and their products.

2. Carelessness with one's exuviae is responsible for illness; or the use in ritual of any of the following exuviae is responsible —food leavings, nail parings, hair cuttings, sex excretions, saliva, other excretions, menstrual blood, other blood, or unspecified exuviae. We assumed that generalization would often be made from excretory products to other exuviae. We excluded these other specific exuviae, however, if the belief referred to some use of them other than in ritual—to their being eaten, for example—for we felt they were then likely to reflect some other kind of anxiety; this distinction is not of great importance, for where illness is ascribed to exuviae it is generally in connection with their use in ritual.

3. The use of charms, curses, spells, or incantations in ritual is responsible for illness. This item was included because we assumed for this purpose the validity of the psychoanalytic hypothesis that compulsiveness, and hence a reliance upon ritual, is a common outgrowth of severe toilet training (since acceptance of toilet training involves acceptance of ritual of time, place, and manner, rather than generalized inhibition). A more complex or indirect causal sequence is assumed here than for the rest of our items. It is assumed that in a society with severe anal training the general personality of adults will involve a high degree of ritualism, and hence a person who blames his illness upon actions of another will suppose those actions to be of a kind characteristic for his society—that is, ritualistic.

4. Failure on the part of the patient to perform some ritual is responsible for illness. The reason for the inclusion of ritual is the same as in the preceding item. But here the connection is more direct; it is assumed that a person of compulsive character, when he blames himself for something that has gone wrong, will blame it on some lapse from his usual compulsive ritualism.

Certain other explanations which obviously belong in this list, such as attributing illness to getting dirty or soiling things, had to be omitted because there were no instances in which our two judges agreed in reporting their presence in a culture.

SEXUAL EXPLANATIONS

1. Sexual behavior is the act responsible for illness. This item provides direct evidence of anxiety about sexual behavior.

2. Sexual excretions or menstrual blood are the material responsible for illness. This item provides direct evidence of anxiety about materials associated with sexual behavior or with the sexual organs. In the case of menstrual blood, however, it must be recognized that the assumption that this anxiety arises by generalization from anxiety about sexual behavior is a tentative assumption which may well be in error.

DEPENDENCE EXPLANATIONS

1. Soul loss is responsible for illness; that is, a person gets sick because his soul has left his body. The fact that makes this explanation similar to the circumstances of dependence training is that when the soul leaves the body it is generally believed to go to commune with spirits, commonly ancestral spirits. The explanation may thus indicate concern about a metaphorical, supernatural dependence upon parent-figures.

2. Spirit possession is responsible for illness; that is, a person gets sick because an alien spirit has entered his body. This explanation, like the preceding one, seems to show concern about a metaphorical, supernatural dependence, though the parent-like character of the supernatural creature is not so clear. (One of the two judges almost never used this category, and instead merely noted that a spirit was the agent of disease, not specifying whether it entered into the patient's body. We here counted it as agreement if the other judge rated spirit *possession* as present, and this judge noted the presence of a spirit as the agent.)

We had expected to have as a third item here the attribution of illness to actual dependent behavior. Our judges failed to find this explanation, however, in the societies included in our sample.

AGGRESSION EXPLANATIONS

1. Aggression or disobedience to spirits is the act of the patient responsible for illness; or aggressive wishes, whether of the patient or someone else, are the material responsible for illness. These beliefs seem to be obvious indices of anxiety about aggression.

2. Poison is the material responsible for illness only if it produces illness by being introjected (i.e., brought into the body magically) or brought into contact with the body. It seemed to us that attributing illness to poison (real or imaginary) would clearly indicate concern about aggression rather than about oral activity only if it was thought of as being gotten magically into, or being brought into contact with, the body rather than as being ingested.

3. Magical weapons are the material responsible for illness only if they produce illness by introjection or contact; or other solid objects are the material responsible for illness only if by introjection. Here, in contrast with the previous item, we are dealing with materials which are uniformly imaginary. Their similarity to actual instruments of aggression seemed to warrant their being taken as evidence of anxiety about aggression. In the case of solid objects other than standard weapons this assumption seemed justified only if the object was thought of as, like a weapon, penetrating the body; mere contact with solid objects would include a variety of explanations which could well have no relevance to aggression.

We have then a measure of the presence or absence, in the adult members of each society, of a certain index of negative fixation in the oral, anal, sexual, dependence, and aggression systems of behavior. It is the index provided by the custom potential, as measured by presence or absence, of explanations of illness which specify events associated with the particular system of behavior.

Before proceeding to a test of our hypothesis a few comments should be made concerning the method which we used to obtain our final judgment of presence or absence of explanations corresponding to each system. It will be noted that the list of explanations for each system of behavior contains from two to four numbered items. About half of these items correspond exactly to single entries in the rating sheet used by our two judges who rated the material on explanations of illness. In the other instances the numbered item includes several separate entries from the rating sheet. The reason they are grouped together as a single item is that they represent closely similar entries on the rating sheet which may possibly have served as alternatives. That is, they are sufficiently similar in meaning so that a fact classified under one entry by one judge might well have been classified under another entry by the other judge. The grouping we have made here is an attempt to correct for over-refinement in our rating sheet.

The unit of agreement that we have attended to is the numbered item in the lists presented above. If our two judges agreed in finding evidence for the explanation, or any of the explanations, described in an item, for a given society, that item was considered to be present in the culture of that society. The several items listed, for example, under oral explanations were then considered to be equally acceptable as evidence of adult concern about oral matters. If for any one of those items the two judges agreed in finding it present, the society was considered to have an oral explanation of illness; if such an agreement was lacking, the society was considered not to have an oral explanation of illness. We have been able to use this method of dividing cases uniformly throughout this chapter, for it happens that for each of the five systems of behavior it yields a division which is reasonably close to dividing the societies into two groups of equal size.

A second question of a technical nature is, for which societies should the test of the hypothesis of negative fixation be made? We have decided to make the principal test by including only those societies for which the judgments of socialization anxiety are of the highest degree of confidence—that is, those societies for which in the particular case all three judges of the child training material made a confident judgment. This is a suitable restriction here because, since the societies are fairly evenly divided between those in which a given kind of explanation is present and those in which it is absent, it still leaves a sizable group of societies in each of the two categories, present and absent. That the results would not differ very greatly in general import if they were based on a less restricted sample of societies will be shown in the next chapter.

RESULTS OF THE TEST

The main results obtained in testing the hypothesis of negative fixation will first be presented in detail with the names of all the societies involved in making the test. The test is, of course, made separately for each of the five systems of behavior.

In Table 4 we present the results which permit a test of the hypothesis of negative fixation for the oral system of behavior. The societies for which confident ratings are available for oral socialization anxiety are listed in two columns. In the left-hand column are listed the societies in which oral explanations (as defined in the previous section) are absent, and in the right-hand column are listed the societies in which oral explanations are present, according to the criteria of presence and absence which were described in the previous section. For convenience in understanding the results, the societies are divided within each column into those that are above and below the median ratings in oral socialization anxiety. The hypothesis will be confirmed to the extent that more societies appear in the upper

TABLE 4. Relation Between Oral Socialization Anxiety and Oral Explanations of Illness

(The name of each society is preceded by its rating on oral socialization anxiety.)

	Societies with oral explanations absent	Societies with oral explanations present
		17 Marquesans
		16 Dobuans
		15 Baiga
		15 Kwoma
		15 Thonga
		14 Alorese
Societies above the median on oral socialization anxiety		14 Chagga
		14 Navaho
		13 Dahomeans
		13 Lesu
		13 Masai
		12 Lepcha
		12 Maori
		12 Pukapukans
	13 Lapp	12 Trobrianders
	12 Chamorro	11 Kwakiutl
	12 Samoans	11 Manus
	10 Arapesh	10 Chiricahua
	10 Balinese	10 Comanche
	10 Hopi	10 Siriono
Societies below the median on oral socialization anxiety	10 Tanala	8 Bena
	9 Paiute	8 Slave
	8 Chenchu	6 Kurtatchi
	8 Teton	
	7 Flathead	
	7 Papago	
	7 Venda	
	7 Warrau	
	7 Wogeo	
	6 Ontong-Javanese	

right-hand quadrant and the lower left-hand quadrant of the table, rather than in the other two quadrants, for to that extent it will be true that societies low in oral socialization anxiety tend not to have oral explanations of illness and that societies high in oral socialization anxiety do tend to have oral explanations of illness. It will be seen at a glance that for the oral system of behavior the results appear to give strong confirmation of the hypothesis. A very large majority of the societies do appear in the quadrants predicted by the hypothesis, and it would appear that custom potential of oral socialization anxiety is indeed associated with the custom potential of responding to illness with oral explanations.[1]

1. This association between oral socialization anxiety and oral explanations of illness represents the most striking single confirmation of any of our hypotheses. It may, therefore, be appropriate at this point to call attention to something we have already mentioned in Chapter 2—that establishing the influence upon a particular custom of one set of antecedents does not exclude the possibility that other antecedents also influence this same custom. Even with the very close association found here, it will be seen that several societies with moderately high oral socialization anxiety fail to have oral explanations of illness, and that several societies have oral explanations even though their child training practices are such as to yield low oral socialization anxiety. Some of these societies may be only apparent exceptions, failing to conform to the generalization because of inaccuracies of ethnographic reporting and of our analysis. Some, on the other hand, may represent instances where the presence or absence of oral explanations is more strongly influenced by other factors. We would suspect, for example, that the Siriono (with a rating just below the median for oral socialization anxiety) may have an oral explanation for illness as a result of the oral insecurity which results from the chronic uncertainties of their food supply (cf. Holmberg, 1950). A similar point should be made about the societies which do conform to the generalization we are making here. In some instances, the confirmation may have arisen by error, through inaccuracies in the ethnographic reports or in our analysis. In some other instances the presence of an oral explanation in a society which does have high oral socialization anxiety, for example, may actually have been more importantly influenced by some factor which we are not studying. We are seeking to test the general

We have also included for each society in the table the exact value of the rating of oral socialization anxiety. We have done so because some readers may wish to have this more detailed information, rather than mere indication of a society's being above or below the median, and also because these exact values will be made use of in making statistical tests of the significance of the results.

Table 5 provides the data for a comparable test with respect to the effects of anal training. Here there are many fewer societies appearing in the table; this simply means that confident ratings from many fewer societies were available for anal sociali-

TABLE 5. Relation Between Anal Socialization Anxiety and Anal Explanations of Illness

(The name of each society is preceded by its rating on anal socialization anxiety.)

	Societies with anal explanations absent	Societies with anal explanations present
Societies above the median on anal socialization anxiety	17 Dahomeans 16 Ontong-Javanese 13 Pukapukans 12 Slave 11 Balinese	18 Tanala 15 Chagga 15 Lesu 15 Manus 11 Hopi 11 Navaho
Societies below the median on anal socialization anxiety	10 Wogeo 9 Papago 8 Teton 8 Western Apache 6 Siriono	10 Paiute 9 Alorese 9 Lepcha 8 Kwoma

validity of certain hypotheses about cultural integration. Where we establish the validity of those hypotheses, we do not thereby disprove other hypotheses (except contrary ones); nor do we supplant the interpretative study of single cultures (where the purpose is that of understanding the single culture rather than testing generalizations).

zation anxiety than for oral socialization anxiety. In this system of behavior there is only the slightest suggestion of confirmation of the hypothesis of negative fixation.

The results for sexual behavior are presented in Table 6. Here the distribution of societies among the four quadrants of the table gives no suggestion at all of confirmation of the hypothesis of drive fixation, as each quadrant has exactly the same number of societies. When the exact values of sexual socialization anxiety are looked at, however, it may be seen that there is a slight tendency in the direction predicted by the hypothesis.

TABLE 6. Relation Between Sexual Socialization Anxiety and Sexual Explanations of Illness

(The name of each society is preceded by its rating on sexual socialization anxiety.)

	Societies with sexual explanations absent	Societies with sexual explanations present
Societies above the median on sexual socialization anxiety	16 Wogeo 15 Chamorro 15 Dobuans 14 Chagga 14 Navaho 13 Samoans 13 Tanala	18 Kurtatchi 17 Chiricahua 16 Arapesh 16 Manus 16 Western Apache 15 Kwoma 13 Alorese
Societies below the median on sexual socialization anxiety	12 Hopi 10 Chenchu 9 Trobrianders 8 Masai 7 Murngin 6 Comanche 5 Siriono	12 Kwakiutl 12 Teton 9 Chewa 8 Baiga 8 Maori 6 Lepcha 5 Pukapukans

For dependence, the system of behavior reported on in Table 7, there is more striking confirmation of the hypothesis of drive fixation, though not as striking as in the case of the oral system.

TABLE 7. Relation Between Dependence Socialization Anxiety and Dependence Explanations of Illness

(The name of each society is preceded by its rating on dependence socialization anxiety.)

	Societies with dependence explanations absent	Societies with dependence explanations present
		17 Kwakiutl
Societies	17 Dobuans	16 Azande
above the	16 Kwoma	15 Alorese
median on	15 Lesu	15 Balinese
dependence	15 Navaho	15 Maori
socialization	13 Samoans	14 Chiricahua
anxiety	13 Trobrianders	14 Pukapukans
	13 Western Apache	14 Siriono
	11 Comanche	12 Marquesans
	11 Ontong-Javanese	11 Lepcha
Societies	10 Bena	11 Manus
below the	10 Chagga	11 Palaung
median on	10 Hopi	9 Tikopia
dependence	10 Kurtatchi	
socialization	10 Paiute	
anxiety	9 Papago	
	9 Wogeo	
	7 Arapesh	

Finally, in Table 8, results are presented for aggressive behavior. Here the evidence in support of the hypothesis is quite
strong, very nearly as strong as in the case of oral behavior.

TABLE 8. Relation Between Aggression Socialization Anxiety and Aggressive Explanations of Illness

(The name of each society is preceded by its rating on aggression socialization anxiety.)

	Societies with aggressive explanations absent	Societies with aggressive explanations present
		21 Paiute
		18 Chamorro
		18 Chiricahua
Societies		17 Lepcha
above the		17 Palaung
median on		16 Alorese
aggression		16 Kwakiutl
socialization	17 Kiwai	15 Papago
anxiety	15 Arapesh	15 Zuni
	14 Rwala	14 Maori
	14 Teton	14 Sanpoil
	13 Western Apache	12 Lamba
	12 Chagga	12 Pukapukans
Societies	12 Thonga	11 Kwoma
below the	11 Wogeo	11 Navaho
median on	10 Lesu	7 Murngin
aggression	9 Chenchu	
socialization	8 Masai	
anxiety	8 Siriono	
	7 Comanche	
	7 Manus	
	5 Dusun	

To facilitate an over-all view of these results, we have drawn
up a summary of them which we present in the upper part of
Table 9. Here the names of the societies are omitted, and we
present instead just the number of societies which fall into each
quadrant of each of the five detailed tables.

TABLE 9. Relation Between Socialization Anxieties and Explanations of Illness: Frequency Tables

(Each entry states the number of societies which have the indicated combination of characteristics.)

PRESENCE (+) OR ABSENCE (−) OF EXPLANATIONS OF ILLNESS CORRESPONDING TO A GIVEN SYSTEM OF BEHAVIOR

		Oral		Anal		Sexual		Dependence		Aggression	
		−	+	−	+	−	+	−	+	−	+
Rating of socialization anxiety for the given system of behavior	High	3	17	5	6	7	7	7	8	4	12
	Low	13	6	5	4	7	7	10	5	11	5
Ranking of socialization anxiety for the given system of behavior	High	4	17	10	10	7	10	7	11	7	11
	Low	13	4	9	8	12	6	13	6	14	3

These results which we have presented in detail are all based on the *ratings* of socialization anxiety by our judges. It will be recalled (pp. 56–58) that we also have available another measure of socialization anxiety, *rankings* by the judges of the relative custom potential of socialization anxiety in the five systems of behavior within a single society. It is possible to test the same hypotheses by use of either the ratings or the rankings. As we indicated earlier, we felt it preferable in general to use the ratings. For purposes of comparison, however, we present here in the lower part of Table 9 the parallel results which are obtained through the use of rankings. Although the ranking scale runs in an opposite direction from the rating scale, we have arranged this table so that *High* and *Low* have the same meaning for both ratings and rankings.

The results obtained with rankings are closely similar to those obtained with ratings. For three systems of behavior (oral, sexual, and dependence) somewhat stronger confirmation of the hypothesis is obtained through rankings than through ratings; in the case of sexual behavior, this difference is quite substantial. Considering together the results obtained with ratings and with rankings, we may conclude that there appears to be striking evidence in confirmation of the hypothesis of negative fixation for oral behavior, dependence, and aggression, but only very slight evidence in favor of the hypothesis for the anal and sexual systems. In no case is there any suggestion of a relationship opposite to that predicted.

But just how good is the evidence in support of the hypothesis for any of the five systems of behavior? The question might be raised whether these results may not have arisen by chance, through the accidents of sampling societies and the unreliability of judgment. The fact that for all five systems of behavior there is some evidence of an association in the predicted direction, and in no case in the opposite direction, argues against this possibility. It is better, however, to have a quantitative test of the possibility, and without one there can be little basis for judging how much confidence should be placed in a positive conclusion. The standard procedures of statistical reasoning permit such a test. A test could be made directly on the frequency tables given in Table 9. A more adequate test, however, which takes account of quantitative variation in the measures of socialization anxiety, is possible in connection with a second way of summarizing the main results.

This second way of summarizing the results is to compare the average socialization anxiety, in each system of behavior, of societies which do and do not have the corresponding explanations of illness. The facts which must be drawn on, for the results based on ratings, have already been presented in Tables 4–8; they consist simply of the division of societies into those with

and those without a given explanation of illness, together with
the exact rating of the corresponding socialization anxiety. We
have calculated the mean value of these ratings, then, for societies with and without each type of explanation of illness, and
the means are presented in the first two lines of Table 10.

Parallel calculations may be made for the *rankings* of sociali-

TABLE 10. Relation Between Socialization Anxieties and Explanations
of Illness: Mean Differences

		SOCIALIZATION ANXIETY IN EACH SYSTEM OF BEHAVIOR, MEASURED BY RATINGS				
		Oral	Anal	Sexual	De-pendence	Ag-gression
Mean *rating* for societies where corre-	Present	12.22	12.10	12.21	13.38	14.82
sponding ex-planation of illness is	Absent	8.94	11.00	11.21	11.71	10.80
Difference between means *		3.28	1.10	1.00	1.67	4.02
t		4.05	0.71	0.66	1.72	3.30
p		<0.0005	<0.3	<0.3	<0.05	<0.005

		SOCIALIZATION ANXIETY IN EACH SYSTEM OF BEHAVIOR, MEASURED BY RANKINGS				
		Oral	Anal	Sexual	De-pendence	Ag-gression
Mean *ranking* for societies where corre-	Present	8.52	9.78	7.81	7.06	5.79
sponding ex-planation of illness is	Absent	11.88	10.16	9.58	9.10	9.00
Difference between means *		3.36	0.38	1.77	2.04	3.21
t		4.05	0.32	1.43	2.12	3.18
p		<0.0005	<0.4	<0.1	<0.05	<0.005

* The differences between means have been so calculated that the direction of difference has the same meaning for ratings and for rankings.

zation anxiety. These have been made, and the resulting means are entered in the first two lines of the lower half of Table 10.

For every system of behavior, and for both ratings and rankings, the results as measured by means are perfectly consistent in supporting the hypothesis of negative fixation. In every instance, the group of societies which have a given explanation of illness give evidence of higher average socialization anxiety in the corresponding system of behavior than do the societies which lack that explanation of illness. The exact value of this difference between the mean anxiety of the two groups is in each instance presented in the third line of each half of the table.

It is from these mean differences that it is possible to proceed to a statistical test of the dependability of our findings. For this purpose the difference may be expressed as a ratio of the variability found in the data by a standard statistical technique which is referred to as t.[2] The value of t for each comparison is presented in the fourth line of each half of Table 7. The final step is to consult the appropriate statistical table to determine the level of statistical significance of each result. The level of statistical significance is expressed in terms of a probability, which is entered in the final line of each half of the table with the label of p, for probability. This entry expresses the probability that a mean difference as large as was found and in the predicted direction could have occurred by chance, through random variation in the sampling and analysis of data. It is customary to consider a p as low as .05 as significant, and a p as low as .01 as highly significant. Applying these criteria to our results, we find that there is significant confirmation of the hypothesis of negative fixation for three systems of behavior—oral, dependence, and aggression—regardless of whether ratings or rankings are used. In the case of aggression the result is highly significant regardless of which measure is used. In the case of oral fixation the result is far beyond the level considered highly significant both for ratings and rankings. For the other

2. For a fuller account of t, see for example McNemar (1949) or Edwards (1946).

two systems of behavior, anal and sexual, the results are not statistically significant regardless of which measure is used.

From these main results, then, we may conclude that consistently for every system of behavior there is some evidence in support of the hypothesis of negative fixation. For three systems of behavior this evidence is statistically significant, and for two of these it is highly significant. The result is that for oral, dependent, and aggressive behavior we may conclude with considerable confidence that the process of negative fixation is operative. For anal and sexual behavior we cannot place much confidence in the hypothesis that negative fixation is operative. We have then very strong evidence for the general hypothesis of negative fixation. But we also have tentative evidence that it is a more important process for some systems of behavior than for others.

RELATIONSHIP OF INDICES OF NEGATIVE FIXATION TO INITIAL SATISFACTION

We have shown that explanations of illness are related in the predicted way to pertinent aspects of child training practices. The aspects of child training to which we have related explanations of illness are such that the term "negative fixation" seems clearly appropriate. But it may now be asked whether our evidence really points distinctively to a process of negative fixation as differing from positive fixation. May it be that the evidence presented thus far carries a distinctive suggestion of negative fixation simply because we have not yet presented parallel evidence which would indicate that the same explanations of illness are related in the same way to aspects of child training which have to do with the development of acquired reward rather than acquired drive? If our sharp distinction between positive and negative fixation is justified, the explanations we have taken as indices of negative fixation should not turn out to be in fact equally suitable as indices of positive fixation.

To deal with this question we must consider the relationship between explanations of illness and the initial satisfaction potential developed in each system of behavior as the result of the child training practices of a society. We have described on pp. 50–52 how we measured this satisfaction potential for each system of behavior. As in the case of socialization anxiety, the satisfaction potential for each system of behavior was measured in two ways—by an absolute rating, and by a ranking relative to the other four systems of behavior.

For the sake of simplicity we will use here only one of the two methods of analysis which were applied to our main results earlier in this chapter—the one which deals with mean differences and permits an adequate statistical test of the possibility that the findings might have arisen solely by chance variation. We accordingly present in Table 11 a set of figures which are exactly parallel to those of Table 10, except that the measures of child training which are used are those of initial satisfaction in each system of behavior instead of socialization anxiety.

If a high initial satisfaction for a given system of behavior were associated with presence of the corresponding explanation of illness, this would be represented by a positive difference in the third line of each part of Table 11. It will be seen that the outcome is consistently contrary to this. Though most of the differences are not statistically significant, every one of the differences is negative. In every instance, that is, presence of an explanation of illness tends to be associated with low initial satisfaction of the corresponding system of behavior, not with high initial satisfaction.

These results then, far from disturbing our tentative conclusion that explanations of illness are specifically related to negative fixation, actually appear to suggest new support for that conclusion. For these results may be expressed in another way; they show that explanations of illness tend to be related to *low* initial satisfaction of the corresponding system of behavior. This suggests the possibility that low initial satisfaction is not mere absence of something positive. A society was placed low on a scale of satisfaction for a given system of behavior if

TABLE 11. Relation Between Initial Satisfactions and Explanations of Illness: Mean Differences

INITIAL SATISFACTION IN EACH SYSTEM OF BEHAVIOR, MEASURED BY RATINGS

		Oral	Anal	Sexual	De-pendence	Ag-gression
Mean *rating* for societies where corresponding explanation of illness is	*Present*	13.96	10.91	13.14	14.00	9.69
	Absent	14.45	13.09	14.00	15.85	12.44
Difference between means *		−0.49	−2.18	−0.86	−1.85	−2.75
t		0.68	1.68	0.64	2.84	2.49
Number of societies		51	22	31	38	31
p †		<0.5	<0.2	<0.6	<0.01	<0.02

INITIAL SATISFACTION IN EACH SYSTEM OF BEHAVIOR, MEASURED BY RANKINGS

		Oral	Anal	Sexual	De-pendence	Ag-gression
Mean *ranking* for societies where corresponding explanation of illness is	*Present*	7.52	10.65	10.40	7.41	12.13
	Absent	6.20	10.05	8.90	5.26	11.05
Difference between means *		−1.32	−0.60	−1.50	−2.15	−1.08
t		1.39	0.56	1.15	2.59	1.05
Number of societies		36	36	36	36	34
p †		<0.2	<0.6	<0.3	<0.02	<0.4

* The differences between means have been so calculated that the direction of difference has the same meaning for ratings and for rankings.

† Because the differences are not being used here to test a single hypothesis, but rather to decide between alternative hypotheses which would lead to opposite predictions, the values of p indicate the probability that so large a difference *in either direction* would arise through random error.

child training practices included such practices as depriving the child of regular satisfaction right from the start, or interfering with normal degree of satisfaction. A low rating, in short, may indicate not mere absence of satisfaction, but also definite anxiety or insecurity. In other words, it may be said that low values for initial security give another measure of anxiety which may be called *initial anxiety*. If this position is taken, we would predict essentially the same consequences for initial anxiety as for the later socialization anxiety.

Now one difficulty stands in the way of drawing such a positive conclusion from these findings. That is that the two measures of child training customs—initial satisfaction and later socialization anxiety in a given system of behavior—are not entirely independent of each other. We have already shown in Chapter 5 that for four of the systems of behavior these two measures have a rather sizable negative correlation with each other, so that a society which is rated high on initial satisfaction is very likely to be rated low on socialization anxiety, and vice versa. The implication of this for the present results is that they cannot be interpreted with any high degree of precision. It may be that the negative relationship between explanations of disease and initial satisfaction is essentially due to the fact that socialization anxiety is related positively to the former and negatively to the latter. This means that initial satisfaction or rather initial anxiety, so far as one can tell from the over-all character of these results for the several systems of behavior, may not in and of itself have any effect on explanations of disease. Indeed, it is even possible that the effect of initial satisfaction potential might really be the opposite of what it appears. High satisfaction potential might genuinely have some slight tendency to produce the corresponding explanation of illness, a tendency which is simply completely covered up by the opposite effect of the relation of these two variables to socialization anxiety. All that one can conclude with certainty for these over-all results is that if there is some tendency for high initial satisfaction to produce the same effects as high socialization anxiety, the tendency is very much stronger in the case of socialization anxiety; for the effect of socialization anxiety is so much stronger that it produces large and statistically significant differences even though this supposed effect of high initial satisfaction would be working in a contrary direction in the case of all the results we have presented in this chapter.

Fortunately, there is one out of the five systems of behavior for which we can go beyond this conclusion with some certainty. That is dependence behavior. Here, it will be recalled from Chapter 5, the relation between initial satisfaction and socialization anxiety is very low. It is represented by a correlation coefficient of only −0.18 (where the corresponding coefficients for the other four systems of behavior varied from −0.60 to −0.81). This is low enough to be, for the present purposes, a practically negligible degree of relationship. In the case of dependence, then, we can study separately the effects of initial satisfaction and of socialization anxiety with assurance that the results will have some independent meaning.

It will be observed from Table 11 that for dependence behavior the results here give clear support to our suggestion that high initial satisfaction and high socialization anxiety do not have the same effects on personality. The results obtained here are highly significant statistically; in fact they are more significant than those obtained for socialization anxiety in the dependence system. The explanations of illness which we found earlier to be positively related to high socialization anxiety with respect to dependence—attribution of illness to soul loss or to spirit possession—are positively related not to a high initial satisfaction potential for dependence but to a low satisfaction potential for dependence. Another way of stating this is to say that early-established *insecurity* or *initial anxiety* about dependence has, in this instance, the same effect as *socialization anxiety* about dependence established at a later point during independence training. We would not suggest that initial anxiety and socialization anxiety have in every detail the same effect. But they do share this effect—that of establishing dependence as a system of behavior about which the person is concerned or driven, and from which he tends to generalize his worries to other areas of anxiety or insecurity.

So far as our data have permitted us to make a test, then, we find that the adult behavior we have taken as an index of negative fixation tends to support our hypothesis that it is related to anxiety developed during infancy and childhood. We have found this index—the presence of explanations of illness which indicate worry about a particular system of behavior—to be positively related to the degree of socialization anxiety developed by a society's child training practices with respect to a given system of behavior. We have found no evidence that this same index has any positive relation to high initial satisfaction in the given system of behavior, as would be suggested by an indiscriminate notion that the same sort of fixation is produced by either extreme frustration or extreme gratification. We can say with certainty that if there is any such positive relation to high initial satisfaction potential, it is of much smaller degree than the relation to socialization anxiety. The facts suggest rather that high initial satisfaction potential is negatively related to explanation of illness—in short, that similar negative fixation may be produced by the anxiety developed through initial deprivation in a given system of behavior or by the anxiety developed in the course of later socialization. In the case of one system of behavior—dependence—for which technical difficulties do not prevent a proper test of this notion, it is clearly confirmed.

We may conclude, then, that the custom potential of explanations of illness which reflect worry or concern with a particular system of behavior is a function of the degree to which that system of behavior has motivational or drive value for typical members of a society—motivational value which may originate either in initial deprivation or in severe training out of an initially permitted freedom.

CHAPTER 9. *Negative Fixation: The Question of Alternative Interpretations*

IN CHAPTER 8 we have presented evidence in confirmation of our hypothesis of negative fixation. From the hypothesis of negative fixation we predicted a positive relation between the custom potential of socialization anxiety in a given system of behavior and the presence of explanations of disease which suggested anxiety or worried preoccupation about that system of behavior. Our data agreed with the prediction; a positive relation was indeed found. We interpret this agreement as a confirmation of the prediction which led to our analysis of the data.

Yet it is perfectly possible that the positive relationship we have found in our data might be more plausibly explained in some other way. We have tried to consider with care various alternative explanations that have occurred to us, and to see whether our data could yield any evidence which would indicate the plausibility of each of them. In this chapter we will consider these alternative explanations. For some we are able to report highly pertinent evidence, for others only arguments or indirect inferences which have some bearing on their plausibility. Consideration of all of these alternatives is pertinent to an interpretation of our findings. Consideration of some of them is, however, of a more general interest as well, because of a relevance to broad problems of method in social science.

THE RESULTS AS AN EFFECT OF
AMOUNT OF INFORMATION

In having to depend sometimes on rather inadequate information we faced a possibility that apparently positive results might emerge simply as a result of that inadequacy. The serious possibility of this sort that occurred to us was the following: The division of societies into those which, by our standards, have a given type of explanation and those which do not is without doubt partly a division according to adequacy of information. That is to say, some of the societies which are judged not to have that explanation are so judged because of lack of information, whereas few or none of the societies which are judged to have it are so judged because of lack of information. Now it is possible that the measures of socialization anxiety might also reflect in part the general adequacy of information, a high rating or ranking of socialization anxiety being more likely for societies with full information about child training. If both of these possibilities should actually be true, then each of the correlations between a measure of socialization anxiety and the presence of a supposedly corresponding type of explanation might be a spurious resultant of over-all adequacy of information about the various societies.

Our data supply evidence which seems to indicate that this particular explanation can be quite decisively rejected. Three lines of evidence are pertinent.

1. This interpretation seems to require that the ratings of socialization anxiety in the several systems of behavior should show consistent positive relationships with each other because of the common influence upon them of adequacy of information. But we have shown in Chapter 5 (p. 116) that this is not the case.

2. If the alternative interpretation just suggested were the true one, each type of explanation of disease should be positively associated with the ratings of socialization anxiety in every system of behavior, and not primarily the one system that our hypothesis would predict. In order to check on this interpretation, we have determined the direction of association of ratings of socialization anxiety for each system of behavior with each of the four types of explanation of sickness for which no association was predicted from our hypothesis. There are 20 associations to be tested. Of these, 12 are positive and 8 are negative.

None of these are significant at the 1% level. Of the 12 positive associations one is significant at the 5% level (that between dependence anxiety and aggressive explanations); of the 8 negative associations two are significant at the 5% level (those between anal anxiety and aggressive explanations, and between sexual anxiety and dependence explanations). The outcome is clearly very different from that obtained for the five associations which are predicted from the hypothesis.

3. An interpretation in terms of general adequacy of information could apply only to the results obtained with *ratings* of socialization anxieties, and not to the results obtained with *rankings* of socialization anxieties. Greater adequacy of information about a society could conceivably lead to a uniformly higher *rating* of socialization anxiety for each system of behavior. It could not, however, lead to a uniformly higher *ranking* of every socialization anxiety; wherever the ranking is made, it necessarily involves giving the rank of 1 to one of the five systems of behavior, 2 to another system and so on through 5. Hence if adequacy of information were entirely responsible for the associations between explanations of illness and ratings of socialization anxieties, it would be expected that the corresponding associations between explanations of illness and rankings of socialization anxieties would be approximately zero. To the extent that the associations with ratings of anxieties might be partly due to adequacy of information, the associations with rankings would be expected at least to be of smaller magnitude and significance. It is apparent from Tables 9 and 10, presented in the previous chapter, that exactly the opposite is true. There is a fairly consistent tendency for the results obtained through the use of rankings to indicate closer relationships (as shown in Table 9) than the results obtained through the use of ratings; with respect to the statistical significance of the results (as shown in Table 10), there is no consistent difference between the outcomes of these two methods of measurement.

It is quite clear, therefore, that our findings on negative fixation cannot be explained as a product of variations in adequacy of information.

THE RESULTS AS AN EFFECT OF SOME GENERAL CULTURAL VARIABLE

Another possibility that perhaps merits consideration is that the results might reflect neither specific relationships pertaining to particular systems of behavior, nor a general relationship dependent solely on adequacy of information, but instead a general relationship genuinely pertaining to the over-all character of the cultures studied. It is conceivable, for example, that a general cultural variable such as the amount of free-floating anxiety might underlie the associations between ratings of socialization anxieties and presence or absence of corresponding types of explanation of sickness. A culture characterized by strong vague anxieties might be greatly concerned about every aspect of child training and hence train the child severely and produce high anxiety; at the same time it might be expected to have an elaborate and strongly felt set of theories about illness, which would be so full and rich that they would be likely to include almost every possible type of explanation.

Such possible interpretations as this may, however, be rejected as decisively as the interpretation in terms of adequacy of information. Exactly the same evidence applies here. A general factor would have to predict consistently positive relations among the various socialization anxieties, and between ratings of each socialization anxiety and every type of explanation, and a lack of relation between rankings of socialization anxieties and explanations of illness. This is equally true whether the general factor resides in the adequacy of information or in the true characteristics of the cultures which are being studied.

THE RESULTS AS AN OUTCOME OF RANDOM VARIATION

Another possibility, so important that we have already given it some attention in presenting the results, is that our correlations might have arisen solely through random variation. There are several important sources of random variation which affect the evidence on which our conclusions are based. One source is the selection of societies for our sample. Another is the variation arising through the inaccuracies and omissions in the ethnographer's reports. Finally, there is the variation introduced by the unreliability of our judges' analyses of the ethnographic evidence. Any or all of these sources of variation might conceivably have led to associations in the data which would appear to confirm our hypothesis.

There are two lines of evidence which are relevant to this alternative interpretation of our results as a product of random variation.

1. One is the fact that certain associations—those of oral and aggressive anxiety with the corresponding explanations of disease—reach very high levels of statistical significance, and the association for dependence reaches the generally accepted level of 5%. The statistical procedure by which this outcome is reached is one which takes into account variability created by the unreliability of the ethnographic reports and of the judging process as well as that inherent in the behavior realities upon which the data are based. Furthermore, the relationship is in the predicted direction for each of the five systems; this alone is an improbable outcome on a basis of random variation, disregarding the statistical significance of some of the separate relationships. All this evidence permits the rejection of the possibility that these results are due to random variation.

2. Although this first line of evidence is itself sufficiently conclusive, there may be some value in citing evidence of a second sort. This evidence pertains to the effect upon our results of including more uncertain judgments. Our results have so far been presented only as based upon those societies in which, for a given system of child behavior, the data were sufficiently good so that all three judges of the childhood material were confident of their judgments. We may compare these results with those which would be obtained by inclusion of all the societies for which there is any judgment at all. Here we would reach an extreme of unreliability, for one of our judges was instructed to at-

tempt a rating (and mark it as very uncertain) even if he could find only the most indirect basis for an inference, and this one judge obviously made a wild guess in many cases where there was no adequate basis for a judgment at all. Consequently, it is useful also to compare results obtained by including along with the most confident judgments only those which meet the intermediate criterion of confidence which we have defined in Chapter 3.

In Table 12 we present a comparison among the results obtained with judgments which reached each of these three criteria of confidence. The upper part of the table is based on the *ratings* of childhood training. Here, for each of the five systems, we present the mean difference in rated anxiety between societies which do and societies which do not have the corresponding explanation. This difference is given (a) in the first line of the table for only those societies, selected because three judges made confident judgments, on which the tables in the preceding chapter were based; (b) in the second line of the table for all societies which meet our criterion for an intermediate degree of confidence; and (c) in the third line of the table for all the societies for which we have any judgment at all. In the lower half of Table 12 an exactly parallel comparison is made for the results based on ranking.[1]

If our results were due to random variation, there would be no reason to expect any consistent variation in the results according to the degree of confidence with which the judgments were made. In fact, there is a consistent variation. In the case of the results based on rankings there is perfect consistency. In nine instances where less confident judgments are added to the body of data, the magnitude of the mean difference is

1. It should be explained that where a rating or ranking was not made by all judges, we of course had to estimate a value and add it to the ones that were made, in order to have a scale for these cases comparable to that for the other cases. If two judgments had been made, they were averaged as an estimate of the third. If only one judgment had been made, it provided the estimate of the other two.

TABLE 12. Relation Between Socialization Anxiety and Explanations of Illness: Effect on Mean Differences of Including Less Confident Judgments

Types of judg-   Mean differences in socialization anxiety *ratings* be-
ment included   tween societies with and without the corresponding
                  explanation of illness, for each system of behavior
                  (the number of societies on which each mean dif-
                  ference is based is indicated in parentheses)

	Oral	Anal	Sexual	De-pendence	Ag-gression
Most confi-dent only	3.28(39)	1.10(20)	1.00(28)	1.67(30)	4.02(32)
Also those of intermediate confidence	1.64(65)	1.71(49)	1.48(61)	1.02(57)	2.81(64)
Also those of least confidence	1.41(75)	1.11(74)	1.30(74)	0.53(75)	1.93(75)

Types of judg-   Mean differences in socialization anxiety *rankings* be-
ment included   tween societies with and without the corresponding
                  explanation of illness, for each system of behavior
                  (the number of societies on which each mean dif-
                  ference is based is indicated in parentheses)

	Oral	Anal	Sexual	De-pendence	Ag-gression
Most confi-dent only	3.36(38)	0.38(37)	1.77(35)	2.04(37)	3.21(35)
Also those of intermediate confidence	3.12(48)	0.01(48)	1.29(48)	1.60(49)	3.08(49)
Also those of least confidence	2.05(75)	0.23(75)*	0.72(75)	1.06(75)	1.94(75)

* This one difference is in a direction contrary to that predicted by the hypothesis of negative fixation.

diminished; and in the tenth instance it is reversed in direction. In the case of the results based on ratings there is an inconsistency for toilet training and sexual training, the two systems for which our results are not statistically significant when based on the confident judgments.[2] For the other three systems of behavior the same consistency appears here.

These comparisons tend to confirm what has already been indicated by the statistical significance of the results as we first presented them: that it is highly unlikely that our results are due to chance and would fail to appear with another selection of cases or with more reliable techniques. This conclusion is particularly warranted in the case of oral, dependence, and aggression training.

THE RESULTS AS AN EFFECT OF BIAS IN THE JUDGES

In dealing with complex and diffuse materials, such as the sum of ethnographic data on childhood training or on explanations of illness for a primitive society, there is a very real danger that a judgment based on these materials will be influenced by the preconception or bias of the judge. We were aware of this danger

2. For the sake of consistency we have based our conclusions about the statistical significance of the findings, presented in the previous chapter, entirely on the societies for which confident judgments were available. For any reader who is tempted to draw a definite conclusion that negative fixation does not occur in the anal and sexual systems, however, we should at this point indicate the level of significance reached by the results for these systems when societies with judgments of intermediate confidence are included. For ratings in the anal system the difference of 1.71, as entered in Table 9, when expressed in ratio to variability yields a t of 2.08 and a p of less than .05. This significant finding greatly weakens the case for an argument that the anal system yields no evidence for negative fixation. On the other hand, a definite argument for negative fixation in this system is in its turn weakened by the fact that for *rankings* the corresponding difference, as may be seen in Table 9, is almost zero. For the sexual system the value of t for the ratings is higher when judgments of intermediate confidence are included (1.57 against the 0.66 reported in the previous chapter); for the *rankings*, t is lower when judgments of intermediate confidence are included (1.13 against the 1.43 reported in the previous chapter). In no case do the results for the sexual system reach ordinarily accepted standards of statistical significance.

and took it into account in planning this research. The precautions to which we were led have been described in Chapter 3. Those precautions are sufficient to guarantee that the results could not be attributed to any ordinary bias in the judges. The possibility of some extraordinary bias should now be faced as well.

By an extraordinary bias we refer to the possibility that some one of our judges might quite deliberately have falsified his or her judgments in order to yield the findings we have reported. Such an occurrence seems so unlikely (both on general grounds and from our knowledge of the persons who were our judges) that it may not merit serious consideration. It must be admitted, however, that if such deception had taken place, it might account for a very considerable part of our results, which are based on the pooled analyses of several judges.

Fortunately, we can provide a check on this possibility. There were three judges for the material on childhood training. There were two judges for the material on explanations of illness. The associations between variables of childhood training and explanations of illness may therefore be tested separately for six different pairings of judges. If our over-all results are due to bias in one of our judges, they should be confirmed consistently only for the results obtained through that one judge's analyses and not for the results obtained through analyses by the other judge or judges who analyzed the same material. This check has been made. For the results obtained with the use of ratings there are 30 associations to be tested (each of the five predicted associations between socialization anxieties and explanations of illness being tested separately for each of the six pairings of judges). For the results through the use of rankings there are another 30 associations to be tested.

The outcome of this test is very clear. For the *ratings*, every one of the 30 associations is positive—that is, in the direction predicted from the hypothesis of negative fixation. For the *rankings*, 29 of the associations are positive and only one negative. Our results apparently do not depend upon peculiarities of judgment in one judge then, but are confirmed separately by the results obtained with various judges.

There is another problem of bias which must be considered—cultural bias which may have been shared by all our judges as participants in present-day American culture. Orlansky (1949, p. 25) has made a comment on our method which may usefully raise the question, though he does not indicate just what relevance he considers the comment to have to the interpretation of our results. He says that we ". . . have experimented . . . with the use of independent ratings by observers of the 'custom strength' of various childhood disciplines, and of the 'habit strength' to which they give rise. The effort to objectify their procedures is commendable, but it runs the risk of substituting a cultural bias for a personal one—i.e., all American raters or all American psychologists may agree in weighting a particular discipline as 'severe' or 'lenient' in terms of our values; Chinese or Hopi observers, however, might weight the same disciplines differently."

If such a suggestion were intended to mean that our results are an artifact—a product of preconceptions shared by all our judges rather than of real consistencies in the data—it would have the same status as the possible explanation in terms of personal bias. In the case of personal bias we were concerned lest a judge's preconceptions about the relation between child training and adult personality, together with his knowledge about both aspects of a single culture, might influence his judgments. Unless steps had been taken to prevent this, it would have been possible that a uniform cultural bias in every judge might have the same effect. But it could not have in this study, because the step we took against personal bias—of allowing each judge to work with only one of the two aspects of culture we were dealing with—would equally prevent any influence of a cultural bias about how child training and adult personality should go together. The finding of a correlation between child training and adult personality in our study thus could not possibly be an artifact of such a bias.

The possibility of cultural bias remains pertinent, however, to the question of how our results are to be interpreted. That is, while they cannot be an artifact of cultural bias in our judges, such a bias might affect in some other way the meaning that should be given to the results. As a specific example we will consider the association we found between oral socialization anxiety and oral explanations of illness. The judgments of anxiety were more complex than those of explanations, and cultural bias seems more likely there; so to simplify discussion we will refer only to the possible effects of cultural bias on the judgments of anxiety. There seem to be two possible effects which are distinguishable.

1. It is possible that the judges are making consistent and stable judgments as they move from one society to another, but that cultural bias leads them to believe they are judging "oral socialization anxiety," whereas what they are judging should from a culture-free point of view have some quite different label. Suppose, for example, that our culture is so peculiar that the conditions we and our judges take as producing oral anxiety actually produce in other cultures oral security. In that event the label we have used would be grossly misleading, and our results would really indicate that oral explanations of illness tend to go along with high oral security rather than high oral anxiety. Now this is rather a far-fetched example, which we offer merely to make clear what kind of effect this first one is. The fact is that we have not been able to think of any really plausible alternative explanations of our results in terms of this sort of effect of cultural bias. It is quite possible, however, that other people with a more critical set toward our interpretation may be able to. If they do, the question that would be raised would not have to do with whether the consistent relations we find are produced by cultural bias; it would have to do with whether cultural bias leads us to give our variables inappropriate labels, and hence to interpret inadequately the behavior significance of the consistent relations among those variables.

2. The other effect of cultural bias which we believe to be

more importantly involved in our study is an effect on reliability rather than on the validity or meaning of the findings. In making judgments of oral socialization anxiety our judges were evaluating (among other things) the effect of physical punishments used in weaning. Now we were aware that they might have a tendency to evaluate this effect by reference to the effect that physical punishment would be expected to have in our society. Our instructions were intended to reduce this cultural bias by asking them to take into account the context of the specific culture as it could be judged from the entire account of child training practices. But this is of course not a very full context, and there is no doubt that less freedom from cultural bias was achieved here than could be achieved by thorough study of the entire culture being judged. That, however, we could not permit because of the possibility that a bias about the relationship between child training practices and adult personality could then produce a correlation as an artifact. So to some extent the effect of physical punishment upon oral anxiety, for example, was probably judged for each culture by criteria deriving from our culture rather than from the context of the culture being judged. The result of this would be to introduce a variable inaccuracy in the judgments, some societies being judged higher in anxiety and some being judged lower in anxiety than they would have been if the entire cultural context had been accurately taken into account. The result of such variable inaccuracy would be to reduce the chances of our obtaining any significant findings, but not to alter the interpretation of those findings which are significant. Hence, while this effect of cultural bias was undoubtedly present in our study, it is relevant to the interpretation of results primarily where our results are negative. That is, where we fail to obtain significant findings on a particular point, it is quite possible that the reason is because of especially great unreliability [3] of the judgments used there, arising in part out of these variable effects.

3. The unreliability referred to here is one we have no way of assessing in this study; it is lack of agreement between analysts who come from widely different cultural backgrounds.

THE RESULTS AS AN OUTCOME OF JOINT DIFFUSION

Another possibility to be considered is that our results may reflect only a historical accident magnified by the effects of diffusion. Could it be that severe weaning and an oral explanation of illness are found together in many cultures because they once happened to be together in a culture which has greatly influenced subsequent cultures, these two characteristics having been taken over bodily along with others, without any relation to their functional connection? On this hypothesis the cultures that lack both these characteristics will be ones that have been little influenced by the primary culture that is postulated, and the remaining cultures that have only one of the characteristics will predominantly be ones to which the diffusion of that primary culture has been less thorough.

Such an explanation of our results would seem to require that the societies with the two characteristics upon which any of our associations are based should be societies whose histories and geographic location are such that they are likely to have a common origin or to have borrowed from one another. This is not required, however, of those societies which lack both characteristics. If severe weaning and oral explanations of disease were both found almost exclusively in North American Indian tribes, for example—generally being found together in these tribes and generally being both absent in tribes elsewhere in the world—it might be suspected that this explanation is a likely one. The fact is that when we look at the data from this point of view, we do not note any startling tendencies of this sort. A subjective impression of this sort, however, may well differ from one person to another, and some more systematic and objective evaluation would be desirable.

The simplest way we have thought of to organize evidence on this point is to test our findings separately for each of five regions into which the world may for convenience be divided. These regions are defined by physical geography but have a real social meaning in relation to the possibility of diffusion. In general (though certainly with exceptions) migration and intersocietal contact are very much easier within any one of these regions than between regions. The regions are (1) Africa, including Madagascar, 13 societies in our sample; (2) Asia, including the Japanese and Andamanese islands and Lapland of northern Europe, 11 societies in our sample; (3) North America, 18 societies in our sample; (4) South America, 7 societies in our sample; (5) Oceania, including Australia, Indonesia and the Philippines as well as the Pacific islands, 26 societies in our sample.

It should be noted that this attempt to check on the possible effects of diffusion differs from previous attempts to do this in correlation studies. Beatrice Whiting (1950) used the device of retesting her hypotheses by including only one society in each cultural area. Murdock's method (1949, p. 193) was to note the frequency distribution by major culture area of the variables of social structure. Our method, which we believe to be more adequate than either of the above, involves testing the assumed relationship separately within each of five more or less geographically independent regions of the world.

For each of these five regional samples we have tested the hypothesis of negative fixation in the same way that we did for the over-all data in Table 7, that is by determining the mean difference in socialization anxiety between societies having and not having the corresponding explanations of illness. We did not, however, for this purpose restrict the societies to those for which all three judges of the childhood material had made a confident judgment; in too many instances, this would have made a test impossible or have made it depend on a single case. On the other hand, we did not consider it sensible to include all societies, even those for which a single judge made a very uncertain judgment. We decided to use the intermediate criterion for confidence of judgment. Within each region, for societies where the judgments of socialization anxiety met this criterion of confidence, the mean rating or ranking of each anxiety was determined for societies which do, and for societies which do not, have the corresponding explanation of illness. The difference between these two means was then looked at to see whether it was in the direction predicted by the hypothesis of negative fixation, or in the opposite direction. In general, these differences are not statistically significant because they are based on such a small number of cases (the numbers being reduced, by elimination of cases with uncertain information, below the numbers given above for each region). Interest centers instead in how many of the differences are in the predicted direction. The results are presented in Table 13.

TABLE 13. Relation Between Socialization Anxiety and Explanations of Illness: Direction of Mean Differences for Societies Within Each of Five Major Regions of the World

(The entries are based on the mean difference, in rating or ranking of a given socialization anxiety, between societies with and societies without the corresponding explanation of illness. A + indicates that the difference is in the direction predicted by the hypothesis of negative fixation; a — indicates that the difference is in the contrary direction; a 0 indicates that no test of the hypothesis was possible, because the corresponding explanation did not occur in the small sample of societies available.)

SYSTEM OF BEHAVIOR, AND TYPE OF MEASURE

	Oral		Anal		Sexual		De-pendence		Ag-gression	
REGION	Rtg.	Rkg.	Rtg.	Rkg.	Rtg.	Rkg.	Rtg.	Rkg.	Rtg.	Rkg.
Africa	+	+	+	+	+	—	+	+	+	+
Asia	+	+	+	—	+	+	—	—	+	+
North America	+	+	—	—	+	+	+	+	+	+
Oceania	+	+	+	—	+	+	+	+	+	+
South America	+	+	0	0	0	0	+	+	+	+

It is clear that the general hypothesis of negative fixation is confirmed separately within the various regions of the world. For every one of the five regions there is a clear preponderance of positive associations. For one region (South America) every relationship which could be tested is positive. For each of two regions (Africa and Oceania) there are nine positive associations and only one negative. For North America there are eight positive associations and two negative; for Asia, finally, there are seven positive and three negative. With the single exception of the data on dependence from Asiatic societies, moreover, the negative findings are confined to the two systems of behavior—anal and sexual—for which the over-all results are not statistically significant. Otherwise, for the three systems of behavior for which the over-all results are statistically significant (oral, dependence, and aggression training), confirmation of the hypothesis of negative fixation is found uniformly in this region-by-region analysis. For oral and aggressive fixation there are no exceptions at all.

These facts argue strongly against a simple diffusionist explanation of our results. They indicate that the association between child training practices and explanations of illness is not simply spread by joint diffusion but is dependent upon some more or less universal functional relationship between them which creates the association anew within sets of societies living in any single region of the world.

The Results as Reflecting a Reverse Direction of Cause and Effect

For alternative explanations mentioned thus far we have presented either evidence for their rejection or an explanation of why we believe them not to play any very important part in the interpretation of our findings. We come now to an alternative explanation which we believe does properly play an important part; here we see the problem as that of trying as best we can to judge just what that part is. This alternative is the hypothesis that our results are to be explained as being due to an influence of adult personality on child training, rather than an influence of child training on adult personality.

An intrinsic defect of the correlational method of scientific inquiry in comparison with the experimental method, as we have pointed out in Chapter 1, is that it provides no means of adequately testing the direction of the cause-effect relationships that are being studied. Sometimes, when the correlational method is used, it is possible to assemble evidence which properly influences one's judgment of the plausibility of one or another notion of the direction of causal relations, even though it does not provide an absolute test. An excellent example of this is provided by some of Murdock's use of cross-cultural data in his study of social structure (1949). For our study we have no parallel evidence to cite. It may, however, be useful to consider in an *a priori* fashion, for each of our five systems of child behavior, the plausibility of the notion that the results are due to an influence of adult personality on child training. We will do so for each system in turn.

1. ORAL BEHAVIOR. Here our index of adult personality is provided by concern with oral activity and oral materials in the explanation of illness. This specific concern is probably symptomatic of a general tendency to be concerned about oral activity and oral materials in contexts other than that of illness. Now, given that the members of a society typically have this personality characteristic as adults, can a clear prediction be made about the severity of the oral training and, specifically, about the severity of weaning they will therefore impose upon their children? We do not see that any prediction could safely be made *a priori*. We tend to feel that the most plausible prediction would be that this concern with oral matters would make for easy weaning—that concern about oral matters would make parents apprehensive about bad consequences arising from difficulties in this transition, and would lead them to enforce weaning gradually and tenderly. But we mention this argument only to make the point that an opposite argument is by no means a clear one, though certainly tenable.

2. ANAL BEHAVIOR. Here our index of adult personality represents a mixture of concern with excretory matters, carefulness with exuviae, and general compulsiveness as reflected

in emphasis on ritual. Here we think the argument is clear. In a society where adults typically have these personality characteristics, it seems to us that experts would agree rather well in expecting that these characteristics would lead adults to impose rather severe toilet training upon their children.

3. SEXUAL BEHAVIOR. Here again, the prediction that would be made *a priori* seems clear. Adults who feel guilty and anxious about sexual matters should be expected, on the whole, to punish their children for manifestations of sexual interest.

4. DEPENDENT BEHAVIOR. The index of adult personality used here has to do with a fear of intimacy with the supernatural. We have interpreted this as reflecting a general fear of dependence. This personality characteristic in adults might well lead them to train their children rather brutally out of dependence upon parents. We do not feel that this argument is as clear and convincing as the parallel arguments for toilet and sexual training, however, for dependence is a system of behavior in which the roles of different age groups are especially likely to be sharply differentiated (see pp. 108 f. for evidence on this point).

5. AGGRESSIVE BEHAVIOR. Here, as in the case of toilet and sexual behavior, the argument from adult personality to child training practices seems quite clear and convincing. Adults who are guilty and worried about aggression certainly seem likely to be led therefore to treat aggression in their children severely.

Insofar as this sort of *a priori* reasoning has any value, then, it suggests that our results do in part reflect an influence of adult personality upon child training practices. It does not, however, suggest to us that our results are likely to be entirely explained by this sort of causal relation. The system of behavior for which we obtained the most significant results—oral behavior—is the one for which the argument for this sort of causal relation seems to us clearly the least convincing. Two of the systems of behavior for which the expectation of this sort of causal relation is most convincing a priori—anal and sexual behavior—are the systems for which we found almost no statistically significant evidence of any relation at all.

Our own tentative assumption would be that both kinds of relationships are actually occurring—that child training practices influence the adult personality characteristics of members of a society, and that those characteristics in return influence the child training practices for the next generation. In other words the relationship is probably reciprocal. Where these two sequences tend to establish the same association—that is, where adult personality characteristics lead to the same child training practices which led to them—the two sequences should reinforce each other's effects and tend to produce stable cultural characteristics. If instances can be found where the two sequences are irrelevant to each other, then this particular influence for stability would be lacking. If instances can be found where the two sequences tend to produce opposite associations, some sort of alternation among generations might be expected to characterize the cultural history of societies with respect to these particular sequences.

Perhaps the best method of determining the primary direction of influence (if either is primary) is to note cases of historical change. If, for example, a change in child training practices introduced in an American Indian tribe by a visiting nurse or social worker had no effect over generations on the explanations of illness, whereas in other instances a change in adult personality brought about by the changes in the economic system did have an effect on child training practices, we would have some indication of the direction of influence. In our opinion, in any case, the truth is most probably that the causal relations between these two sets of customs are generally reciprocal, that is, each influences the other.

CONCLUSIONS

For the main results on negative fixation, as presented in the preceding chapter, we have in this chapter considered various alternative interpretations which would ascribe the results to some other origin than a process of negative fixation. For several of these interpretations we were able to present evidence or arguments which lead us to feel that they are not strong competitors with the hypothesis of negative fixation as a means of explaining our findings. In the case of the last interpretation, ascribing the results to an effect of adult personality on child training practices rather than the opposite, we cannot entirely reject it and indeed would assume that this interpretation has some validity. We have presented our reasons, however, for not believing it likely that the results could be ascribed entirely to such an effect.

For the other results which will be presented in later chapters we have not made a similar painstaking search for evidence relating to each of these alternative interpretations. We have, indeed, in every case considered the possibility that the results might have arisen through random variation, and have used statistical techniques to evaluate this possibility. And the possibility of a reverse direction of causal relation is of such general importance that we will return to consider it again in the final chapter. In the case of other alternative interpretations we can hardly hope for the less clear-cut results in some of the later chapters to enable us to make an analysis which can lead to such definite rejection of these interpretations as was possible for the results on negative fixation. For this reason we have not even attempted such an analysis. We have simply chosen for this detailed analysis the one, of the two major hypotheses (of positive and negative fixation) with which we started our study, for which the data yielded striking confirmation. The fact that for our results on negative fixation there is satisfactory evidence against an explanation in terms of adequacy of information, personal bias, etc., may create a presumption that such an explanation does not hold true for other aspects of our results either. But such a presumption does not constitute proof, and our findings on negative fixation are certainly more firmly established than other findings to be reported in subsequent chapters.

CHAPTER 10. *A Test of Positive Fixation*

IN THIS chapter we present a test of the hypothesis of positive fixation, together with other findings to which we were led by the outcome of that test.

The general hypothesis of positive fixation, expressed with reference to individual behavior, is as follows: In any system of behavior, variations in its initial indulgence in the young child will give rise to variations in the acquired reward potential of that system and, through continuation of this reward potential into adult life, will give rise to variations in the extent to which performance of responses in that system is a source of security in the adult. As in the case of negative fixation, we use the idea of personality integration of culture to predict from this psychological hypothesis certain associations between distinct customs. Initial indulgence of each system of behavior has been analyzed for each society with respect to the degree of satisfaction to which it should give rise. Therapeutic practices which seem to involve the performance of responses of a given system as a means of reducing anxiety have been taken as an index of the extent to which that system of behavior has satisfaction potential in the typical adult member of a society. The hypothesis of positive fixation in the specific form in which we propose to test it cross-culturally may then be expressed as follows:

In any society, the greater the custom potential of initial satisfaction in any system of behavior, the greater will be the custom potential of therapeutic practices which involve the performance of responses in that system.

But could particular therapeutic practices be found which would permit a test of this general hypothesis? We were not so fortunate here as in the case of explanations of illness. There is not such a wealth of therapeutic practices which obviously have a potential relation to the systems of behavior we are concerned with, and some of the practices which might have this relevance were not actually found in our sample of societies.

One consequence of this relative inadequacy of the material for our purpose is that some of the practices we must attend to are rare, so that it is desirable to include as many societies as possible in the sample to increase the small number of societies having the given practices. For this reason we decided to include here societies for which the judgments on child training reach only an intermediate degree of confidence, as well as those for which the judgments are of maximum confidence. For the sake of consistency we have then adopted this policy for all the tests to be made in this chapter.

In the analysis of therapeutic practices there was even more disagreement between the two judges of this material than was found in the analysis of explanations of illness. As indicated in Chapter 6, we have followed as a uniform rule that of classifying cases of disagreement with either the *present* or *absent* group, according to which classification will more nearly divide the societies into two groups of equal size. Even so, as will be seen, the groups are often of very unequal size.

Certain doubts which we had in advance about our indices of positive fixation should be mentioned here. As we stated in Chapter 2 in our discussion of the custom complex, one of the functions of a belief is to specify the relevant stimuli and responses of the related practice. If this formulation is correct, therapeutic practices should be influenced by beliefs about the cause of illness. Thus if sickness is believed to be caused by the ingestion of poison, the therapeutic practice should involve getting the poison out of the body. Such influences may in many instances override the effects of positive fixation. Some evidence on the relation between explanations of illness and therapeutic practices will be presented later in this chapter, and we will also indicate some of the other difficulties which occurred to us in adopting therapy as an index of positive fixation.

Since what positive findings we have to report in this chapter consist of slight tendencies toward uniformity, rather than single associations of striking significance, we have not felt it useful to print tables of data in full for the single associations. The reader who would like to construct such tables will find in the appendix the data for the findings based on ratings. But we will here present only summary information.

We are now ready to make whatever test we can of the hypothesis of positive fixation, for each of the five systems of child behavior in turn.

INDICES CHOSEN, AND RESULTS OF THE TEST
ORAL PERFORMANCE THERAPY

The therapeutic practice which might be expected to reflect a lasting satisfaction of oral activity is that of swallowing something. What is swallowed may be food, infusions of herbs, other medicines or, in a few instances, any of a variety of other materials. These ingestion therapies are found very frequently. There were 40 societies for which our two judges agreed in reporting the presence of ingestion therapy, and 21 in which one or both of our judges failed to find evidence of ingestion therapy.[1]

The differences between these two groups of societies in initial oral satisfaction are in the right direction to confirm the hypothesis of positive fixation, but the differences are too small to provide any basis for conviction. In the rating of oral satisfaction resulting from child training, the mean value for societies with ingestion therapy is 14.2 and the mean value for societies without ingestion is 13.6. The absolute value of this difference is small, and when it is tested for statistical significance it is found to provide no satisfactory evidence that the difference is based on a real phenomenon rather than on random

1. The numbers mentioned here and in similar later statements refer only to societies for which the pertinent rating of child training is available. For tests made with rankings the numbers of cases are different.

variation. (The value of t is only 0.9.) The ranking of oral security leads to similar results. Societies with ingestion therapy
have a mean value of 6.9, and societies without ingestion therapy
have a mean value of 7.4. This difference too is in the predicted
direction, but it is far from being statistically significant. (The
value of t is 0.5.)

We can draw no definite conclusion about the validity of our
hypothesis for the oral system of behavior, then; these small
differences could have some meaning only if their direction were
confirmed by more significant findings for the other systems of
child behavior.

ANAL PERFORMANCE THERAPY

Therapeutic practices which might clearly grow out of the satisfaction of free excretory behavior developed in early childhood
are not numerous or conspicuous. Defecation and urination as
therapeutic techniques are the only ones actually found which
we judged likely to have this significance. (We included urination on the grounds that generalization from one excretory response to another is highly likely.) There were 14 societies
for which one or both of our judges reported these practices to
be present, and 30 societies for which neither judge reported
them to be present.

When the differences between these two groups of societies
are tested, the result is similar to that obtained for the oral system. The differences are in the predicted direction but are far
from significant. For the results based on ratings the difference
is extremely small, the means for the two groups being 12.1 and
12.0. For the results based on rankings the means are 9.8 and
10.5; this is a larger difference, but it is still far from being statistically significant. (The value of t is 0.1 for the ratings, and
0.7 for the rankings.)

For the anal system as for the oral system, then, we can draw
no definite conclusion.

SEXUAL PERFORMANCE THERAPY

Therapeutic practices which seem likely to grow out of the satisfactions of initial sexual behavior are very infrequent. Our judges
found no instance where masturbation was believed to have
therapeutic value. There were four societies, however, for which
one or both of the judges found some evidence that sexual intercourse was believed to have therapeutic value. Unfortunately,
judgments on the initial satisfaction of sexual behavior in early
childhood are available for only two of these societies (the
Baiga and the Marquesans). A comparison may be made between these two societies and 51 societies for which our judges
found no evidence of sexual intercourse as therapy.

This comparison leads to a strong confirmation of the hypothesis we are testing. The two societies are quite extreme in having child training practices judged likely to produce a very high
satisfaction for sexual behavior. For the ratings of initial satisfaction these two societies have a mean value of 18.5, while
the other 51 societies have a mean value of 12.3. This difference
is highly significant (the value of t being 2.70). For the rankings
of initial satisfaction the means for the two groups are 3.0 and
10.1, and this difference is also significant at the 1% point (t
being 2.51).

DEPENDENCE PERFORMANCE THERAPY

Prayer is the therapeutic technique which seemed to us likely
to grow out of initial dependence satisfaction. Prayer appears
to signify a dependence upon supernatural beings, in the face
of anxiety, analogous to the young child's dependence upon his
parents. There were 30 societies for which one or both of our
judges reported prayer to be used as a therapeutic technique,
and a comparison between these and the 27 other societies permitted a test of our hypothesis.

The results here are in a direction contrary to what would

be predicted from the hypothesis we are testing. The societies which use prayer as a therapeutic technique are societies which, on the average, have child training which is less conducive to the development of initial dependence satisfaction than do the societies which fail to use prayer. For the results based on ratings the means are 14.1 for societies with prayer and 14.9 for societies without prayer. For the results based on rankings the corresponding means are 6.3 and 5.8. While neither of these differences is statistically significant (t being 0.9 for ratings and 0.6 for rankings), they are both in the opposite direction from that predicted by the hypothesis.

AGGRESSION PERFORMANCE THERAPY

The sort of therapy which should reflect a high satisfaction potential for aggression is therapy which is aggressive in character. In our analysis of therapeutic techniques, there were four items which seem clearly to have this character. One has to do with the effect of therapy upon the material responsible for illness; a conception of therapy as involving the destruction of this material appears to signify a reliance upon aggression. The other three items have to do with the effect of therapy upon the agent (person or spirit) responsible for the illness; a conception of therapy as destroying the agent, as tricking the agent, or as forcing the agent to desist from his efforts to produce sickness, again appears clearly to signify a reliance upon aggression. There were 31 societies for which one or both of our judges reported the presence of one or more of these aggressive conceptions of therapy, and these could be compared with 25 societies for which there was no such report.

The results of this comparison are inconsistent. For the ratings of aggression satisfaction in early childhood the differences between the two groups of societies is in the predicted direction, with mean ratings of 11.2 and 10.5; this difference is far from being statistically significant (t being 0.7). For the rankings of aggression satisfaction the difference is reversed in meaning, with means of 11.7 and 11.6; this minute difference is of course also not statistically significant (t being 0.3).

For aggression we can draw no conclusion at all, then, except that our hypothesis concerning positive fixation is in this instance definitely not confirmed.

CONCLUSIONS ABOUT THE RELATION BETWEEN INITIAL
SATISFACTION AND THERAPEUTIC PRACTICE

For the five systems of child behavior considered together, therefore, we must conclude that there is no general support for the hypothesis that initial satisfactions produce positive fixations which will be maintained into adult life and influence the choice of therapeutic technique. For one specific system of behavior— the sexual—confirmation of the hypothesis is so striking that one might be justified in having some confidence of its holding true for this specific instance; we will return to this finding later in the chapter. Any more general support of the hypothesis is clearly lacking in our evidence.

Does this outcome mean that positive fixation is not demonstrable by our methods of cross-cultural comparison, whereas negative fixation is? Before accepting that conclusion we would direct attention at another possibility.

The socialization anxieties with which we have dealt in the preceding chapter are probably, on the whole, anxieties which continue to be reinforced in the later experience of the individual. After the age of principal socialization of a given interest there may still be discontinuities in training, as Benedict (1938) has pointed out. But on the whole, continuity is probably the more common, the person being trained at the time of major socialization into a good approximation of the adult norm for behavior.

The situation is quite different in the case of the initial satisfactions we have dealt with thus far in this chapter. Here we are concerned with an early period of life in which the child may be clearly recognized as being in a distinct cultural category with a role very different from that of the adult. The way he is treated at this age may have little to do with the way he will be treated later. In Chapter 5 we have shown that for the customs of primitive societies this is particularly true for dependence; there is very little relation between how greatly a young child's dependence needs are indulged in a given society, and how severely he will subsequently be trained out of dependence. For the other systems of behavior there is a greater tendency for the initial treatment of the child to be similar to his later treatment. But still the relation is far from perfect.

These considerations lead to a possible reinterpretation of our failure to find consistent evidence of an enduring effect of initial satisfaction. Could it be that positive fixation is intrinsically as real and lasting a process as negative fixation, but that early positive fixations are largely extinguished or unlearned during subsequent socialization and supplanted by later learning of new adult satisfactions, whereas in the case of negative fixation there is not so generally a new learning which will interfere with the old? This should be particularly true where the treatment is discontinuous, that is, where an initial habit is at first highly indulged and later another and incompatible habit is indulged. To test this notion, we must see whether appropriate measures of later satisfaction show any more consistent relationship to the custom potential of therapeutic practices.

PROGRESSIVE SATISFACTIONS
AND THERAPEUTIC PRACTICES

Some test of the notion that later or progressive satisfactions have an influence on therapeutic practices is possible from our analysis of ethnographic data. It is not very satisfactory, but we will none the less present it because of its value as tentative evidence. It is unsatisfactory in part because of inadequacies of the data and in part because of inadequacies of our analysis.

This test depends upon judgments made about another aspect

of child training practices which we have not yet mentioned. This is the aspect which we have termed "progressive satisfaction." In each of the five systems of behavior the child is trained out of certain initial habits and trained into the behavior expected in his culture for that particular system. The habit corresponding to these cultural expectations we have termed the "progressive habit" in each system, in contrast with the "initial habit."

Now in order to arrive at a judgment of its satisfaction potential, it is first necessary to identify the progressive habit. For two systems of behavior, oral and toilet behavior, the character of the progressive habit is quite clear and is relatively constant from one society to another. For oral behavior the progressive habit consists primarily of nourishing oneself in the way customary for adults in the given society—of conformity to adult norms with respect to foods eaten, time and other circumstances of eating, manner of putting food into the mouth, and the like. For toilet behavior the progressive habit similarly consists of conformity to adult norms in excretory behavior.

For the other three systems of behavior—sex, dependence, and aggression—the progressive habit is much more variable from one society to another. For sex it may involve anything from almost complete sexual freedom to almost complete sexual restraint until the time of marriage. For dependence it may involve anything from a stern expectation of thorough autonomy to a continued dependence which varies from the initial behavior primarily in the specific behavior in which it is expressed. For aggression the progressive habit may vary from a rather consistent nonaggression to a positive emphasis on strongly aggressive behavior toward certain social objects. Each of our judges had to formulate, for a given society, his conception of the progressive habit in each system of behavior before he could judge the custom potential of its satisfaction. We have tried to use the judges' notes to sort out these conceptions, but we find that the conceptions vary so widely as to leave unmanageably small numbers of societies in any one category. Consequently, the best we can do is to deal with the progressive habit in each of these three systems of behavior as though it had a constant meaning, recognizing that any result which might emerge would be most tentative until it could be tested by better analysis of a larger number of cultures.

Once a judge had identified the progressive habit for a particular system of behavior in a given culture, his next task was to judge the satisfaction potential likely to be developed for that progressive habit in view of the socialization practices of that society. Here, as in the case of the other measures we have described more fully in Chapter 3, we set down certain theoretical determinants of progressive satisfaction for the guidance of our judges. These were as follows:

1. Duration. It was assumed that the longer the progressive habit was maintained, the greater would be its satisfaction potential. Since in most cases the progressive habit was conceived to be more or less permanent, this determinant did not play a very important part.

2. Idealization. The judge was to look for evidence, in the data on child training, that this progressive habit was idealized in the culture. To the extent that it was idealized, this was taken as evidence that conformity would be rewarded by a variety of positive social responses from others, which would contribute to the development of acquired reward value for the progressive habit.

3. Status gain. The judge was instructed to look for evidence of connection between this particular progressive habit and a gain in status; a close connection was taken as evidence of rewards for conformity which would contribute to the acquired reward value of the habit. For example, if conformity to adult eating patterns is a major criterion for recognizing a person to be now a child and no longer an infant, this would tend to raise the rating of the satisfaction potential of the progressive habit in the oral system of behavior.

4. Praise. Evidence that the child is consistently praised for conformity to a particular progressive habit was taken as evi-

dence of specific rewards which would contribute to its satisfaction potential.

5. Concurrent anxiety. Finally, as in the case of initial satisfaction, it was assumed that the greater the concurrent anxiety from other sources the greater the generalized drive-reduction obtained through the progressive response and, hence, the greater its learned reward value. Here, the time when the progressive habit was most definitely being learned was concentrated on so far as the data permitted.

Our judges evaluated progressive satisfaction for each system of behavior in two ways, just as in the case of initial satisfaction and socialization anxiety: an absolute rating on a seven-point scale, and a ranking of the five systems of behavior from highest to lowest in progressive satisfaction for the particular society.

We have determined the relation of performance therapies to the *progressive* satisfaction potential of each system of behavior in precisely the same way that we determined in the previous section of this chapter the relation of these same therapeutic practices to the *initial* satisfaction potential of each system. Since we are dealing with exactly the same sets of therapeutic practices, we can make a direct comparison between the results obtained with the two measures of satisfaction potential. Since we are interested in the contrast between positive and negative fixation, we have made the calculations which permit a comparison also with the effects of socialization anxiety on these therapeutic techniques.

Table 14, then, presents the relationship between each set of performance therapies (as defined earlier in this chapter) and the measures of initial satisfaction, socialization anxiety, and progressive satisfaction for the corresponding system of behavior. Each relationship is expressed by a t ratio. A positive t (indicated by a +) means that societies having the given type of therapy have a higher degree of the corresponding variable in child training than do societies which lack this type of therapy. Each relationship has been tested both by use of the ratings of child training and by use of the rankings of child training, and

TABLE 14. The Relation of Performance Therapies to Three Aspects of Child Training Practices

The entries in this table are values of t, representing the consistency with which societies having the therapeutic techniques defined as performance therapy corresponding to a particular system of behavior differ from societies lacking it in their rating or ranking on a measured aspect of child training practice. The number of societies varies from 30 to 61. Coefficients marked with an asterisk meet a 5% significance criterion; those marked with two asterisks meet a 1% criterion. (A one-tailed criterion is applied only for initial satisfaction, where the direction of difference was predicted.)

MEASURED ASPECT OF CHILD TRAINING PRACTICE IN A
PARTICULAR SYSTEM OF BEHAVIOR

	Initial satisfaction		Socialization anxiety		Progressive satisfaction	
	Rating	Ranking	Rating	Ranking	Rating	Ranking
Oral	+0.9	+0.5	+0.4	+0.1	+2.4 *	+1.1
Anal	+0.1	+0.7	+0.4	−0.9	−2.4 *	−2.2 *
Sexual	+2.7 **	+2.5 **	−1.1	−2.4 *	+1.6	+1.8
Dependence	−0.9	−0.6	+0.6	+0.3	+0.2	−0.8
Aggression	+0.7	−0.3	+0.1	−1.8	+1.6	+1.6

the ranking scale has been inverted so that the direction of difference has the same meaning for both scales. The t is the ratio of the difference between the two groups of societies (those having and those lacking a particular therapy) to the standard error of this difference.

It will be seen from Table 11 that for the oral and anal systems of behavior clearly significant results were obtained. For the oral system the relationship is in the expected direction. Oral therapies such as the ingestion of medicines are found to occur most frequently in societies which have a high rating on progressive oral satisfaction.

In the case of the anal system there is a relationship opposite in direction. In other words those societies which have the belief that defecation or urination has therapeutic value are the ones which tend to have *low* progressive anal satisfaction. This finding might be considered contradictory to predictions that would be made from the notion of progressive satisfaction. The prediction that should be made is, however, not clear; satisfaction might be attached primarily to the act of defecating in an approved manner, or to the restraints involved in learning to do this. In any event, unless this is a chance result, it is clear that the ratings of progressive satisfaction have a closer relation to adult behavior than do the ratings of initial satisfaction, even though the relation is not of a character clearly predictable from the concept of satisfaction.

In two of the other three systems of behavior—sex and aggression, but not dependence—there is evidence of some consistency in relationship between therapeutic techniques and progressive satisfaction, even though in these cases the progressive habit may be of highly variable character. There is some tendency for high progressive satisfaction in sexual behavior to be associated with the occurrence of sexual intercourse as a therapeutic technique. Similarly, there is some tendency for high progressive satisfaction in the aggressive system to be associated with the occurrence of aggressive therapeutic techniques. These tendencies do not reach ordinarily accepted standards of statistical significance; the four t's involved are significant at or about the 10% level only. Some degree of confidence can perhaps be attached to them because of the general tendency for reasonably high values of t to be found in testing these various relationships between therapeutic techniques and progressive satisfaction. It is only in the case of dependence that there is no evidence of a relationship which merits any attention.

Finally, we should note that the therapeutic practices which we have picked out as likely to grow out of high satisfaction potential in each of these systems of behavior do not show any very consistent relationship to socialization anxiety. There is some evidence of a negative relationship to socialization anxiety in the case of sexual and aggressive behavior; with these exceptions the values of t are very small. But these negative relationships provide no evidence that the *same* effects may follow from either positive or negative fixation; they add to the evidence presented in Chapter 8 that these two kinds of influence have opposite effects, and thus tend to confirm the value of our distinction between two types of fixation.

The analysis reported in this section was prompted by a question we posed at the end of the previous section. We asked whether positive fixation might be intrinsically as real and lasting a process as negative fixation, but early-established satisfactions are found generally lacking in permanent effect simply because later conditions of learning lead to their being supplanted by later learning of new satisfactions. The evidence presented in this section tends to provide an affirmative answer to this question. The later-established or progressive satisfactions show some consistency of relationship to the therapeutic practices we had predicted to be symptomatic of the satisfaction potential of each of the five systems of behavior. Hence it may be simply the later intrusion of these progressive satisfactions that prevents any lasting effect of the initial satisfactions.[2] At the same time we must note that even this evidence is not very marked. We have no such high relationships as we found in the case of socialization anxieties and explanations of illness. Positive fixation would appear to be somehow a less conspicuous or influential process than negative fixation, insofar as reactions to illness can provide a proper and comparable test in the two cases. Before drawing any such definite comparative conclusion, however, we should stop to consider critically the question of the adequacy of therapeutic practices as an index of the personality characteristics for which we have used them.

2. It can now be seen, too, that the one significant finding for initial satisfaction in the sexual system may be attributable to progressive satisfaction. The few societies which have sexual performance therapies tend to be high in both initial and progressive satisfaction in the sexual system.

The Adequacy of Therapy as an Index

We had at the outset of our study greater doubts about the adequacy of therapeutic practices as an index of personality characteristics than we had about explanations of illness. It seemed to us likely that therapeutic practices would be more strongly influenced by other factors than the personality variables we were studying than would be the case with explanations of illness. Hence the influence of personality variables might be too small to be apparent except in a very large body of data such as we could not hope to obtain at present. It is appropriate to review here some of the notions we had about other variables likely to influence therapeutic practices, and in particular about two kinds of variables on which we were able to obtain some evidence.

THE INFLUENCE OF EXPLANATIONS OF ILLNESS

First of all, it seems likely that therapeutic practices would be directly influenced by explanations of illness. The customs relating to illness can be considered as a custom complex in which the components are related to one another in the manner described in Chapter 2. In this instance the explanations for illness are a type of *belief* which should contribute to specifying the stimuli and responses of the *practice* of therapy. Since we have judgments on both the beliefs and the practices of this type of custom complex, we are enabled to test this hypothesis.

First we may consider what types of belief (explanations of illness) might be presumed to directly influence the therapeutic practices which were used previously in this chapter as indices of positive fixation. Of these, perhaps the most likely relationship is between an oral explanation and an anal therapy. If a society has the belief that illness is brought about by swallowing something harmful, it might well hit upon the practice of inducing defecation as a means of getting rid of what had been swallowed. A second instance where one of our indices of positive fixation might be dependent upon an explanation of illness is provided by the practice of prayer. This practice seems most likely to be found in societies where spirits or gods are believed to play an important part in causing illness. A third instance is ingestion therapy, which might in some cases grow out of a belief that illness comes from not eating. Sexual behavior as therapy might be brought about by a belief that illness is due to sexual abstinence. Finally, the likelihood that therapy would take the form of aggressive action toward a person or spirit might depend upon the custom potential of the belief that a person or spirit is responsible for causing illness. A test of these five hypotheses yields correlations which are all in the predicted direction, though only one of them, that between prayer and the importance of spirits or gods, even approaches statistical significance.

In addition to the therapeutic practices we have used as indices of positive fixation, there are a number of other therapeutic techniques which may similarly be influenced by the explanations of illness current in a society. To the extent that some of these other therapies are adopted because of their consonance with explanations of illness, there is less chance for the adoption of the particular therapies we have chosen as indices.

We picked out six other instances where it seemed likely that the presence of a particular explanation of illness would lead to the adoption of a corresponding item of therapeutic practice. These instances are as follows:

1. A belief that illness is produced by ingestion of something might lead to vomiting as a means of getting rid of the noxious substance.

2. The same belief also seems likely to lead to the therapeutic observance of food taboos as a means of preventing worsening or recurrence of the illness through repeated ingestion of the dangerous material.

3. Attribution of illness to sexual behavior should favor sexual abstinence as a therapeutic practice.

4. Similarly, attribution of illness to sexual behavior should favor observance of specific sexual taboos as a therapeutic practice.

5. Where illness is blamed on the patient's having lost something or having had something removed from his body, therapy might be expected to be directed at restoring or replacing whatever has been lost or removed.

6. Where illness is believed to be brought about by the magical introduction of some object or spirit into the patient's body, therapy might be expected to involve an effort to remove this alien object or spirit.

In each of these six cases we have tested whether societies which have the specified explanation of illness are thereby more likely to have the therapeutic practice which seemed to correspond. In every one of the six cases we found a positive relationship. It is surprising that only one of the six relationships is large enough to be statistically significant. With respect to the general point that therapeutic practices are influenced by explanations of illness, however, the uniform direction of these six associations and the five previously reported is an impressive finding (though the fact that several of the associations involve the same measures prevents a statistical evaluation of this over-all finding).[3]

We cannot, of course, be sure that the therapeutic practices are influenced by the explanations of illness. It is possible that the influence underlying these relationships is the reverse of what we suspected—that is, that the therapeutic practices give rise to explanations which make the practices seem reasonable. Inasmuch as we have for explanations of illness found striking

3. The lack of statistical significance in several of these relationships is attributable to the very small number of societies in which one of the beliefs or practices is present, rather than to a definite appearance of a low relationship.

evidence of origins outside this culture complex, and for therapeutic practices have found no such striking evidence of independent origins, it seems proper to stress the direction of influence that we have.

THE INFLUENCE OF SOCIALIZATION ANXIETY

A second possible difficulty with the use of the therapeutic practices which we have chosen as indices of positive fixation is that there are other therapeutic practices with which they must compete which seemed likely to reflect negative fixation instead. This is a suggestion on which we are able to offer some evidence. For each system of behavior we could distinguish certain therapeutic practices as possible outgrowths of socialization anxiety attached to the particular system. These are practices which seem to represent quite directly the avoidance or the undoing of responses in that system. It would appear that severe anxiety about a given system of behavior might, when coupled with the added anxiety of illness, lead a person to attempt such avoidance or undoing as a means of reducing anxiety. For convenience we will call such practices *avoidance therapies* in contrast to the *performance therapies* in which the doing of a response in the system appears to be the source of security. The practices which we distinguished as likely to constitute avoidance therapies are as follows:

Oral avoidance therapies—spitting, vomiting, and adherence to food taboos.

Anal avoidance therapies—retention of feces, washing or cleansing, and adherence to cleanliness taboos.

Sexual avoidance therapies—general sexual abstention, or adherence to specific sexual taboos.

Dependence avoidance therapies—therapeutic practices which involve isolating the patient or removing him from his home for the duration of his illness.

Aggression avoidance therapies—the sacrifice of property as a therapeutic device, or therapeutic practices which take the form of attempts to placate the agent responsible for the illness.

We have dealt with these five sets of avoidance therapies in a way exactly parallel to that described earlier in this chapter for the five sets of performance therapies which we used as indices of positive fixation.[4] For purposes of comparison we have determined the relationship to each of three measures of child training practices—initial satisfaction, socialization anxiety, and progressive satisfaction—just as was ultimately done for the performance therapies. Table 15 presents these relationships in the same form that Table 14 did for the performance therapies.

TABLE 15. The Relation of Avoidance Therapies to Three Aspects of Child Training Practice

> The entries in this table are values of t, representing the consistency with which societies having the therapeutic techniques defined as avoidance therapy corresponding to a particular system of behavior differ from societies lacking it in their rating or ranking on a measured aspect of child training practice. The number of societies varies from 30 to 61. Coefficients marked with an asterisk meet a 5% significance criterion; the one marked with two asterisks meets a 1% criterion. (A one-tailed criterion is applied only for socialization anxiety, where the direction of difference was predicted.)

MEASURED ASPECT OF CHILD TRAINING PRACTICE IN A
PARTICULAR SYSTEM OF BEHAVIOR

	Initial satisfaction		Socialization anxiety		Progressive satisfaction	
	Rating	Ranking	Rating	Ranking	Rating	Ranking
Oral	+1.0	+0.9	+0.3	−0.7	+0.3	−0.4
Anal	−1.2	−0.6	+2.0 *	+0.6	−1.8	+0.8
Sexual	−1.3	−1.9	+1.3	+1.7 *	+0.8	−0.5
Dependence	−0.2	+0.5	+2.1 *	+2.9 **	−0.2	−1.3
Aggressive	+0.1	+1.6	−0.5	+0.1	−0.2	−0.5

4. In accordance with the rule stated previously, instances of disagreement between the two judges are classified as "absent" for aggression avoidance therapies, and as "present" for the other four categories.

The results tend to confirm our prediction that these therapeutic practices would be related to socialization anxieties, though the confirmation is not very striking. Of the ten t's measuring relationship between socialization anxieties and the corresponding sets of avoidance therapies, eight are in the predicted direction (positive). Four of the eight reach significance at approximately the 5% point, and one of these four is significant at the 1% point. For the relation of avoidance therapies to initial satisfaction and progressive satisfaction, on the other hand, there are only two t's which are as large as the smallest of these four, and there is less consistency of direction.

We have some tentative evidence, then, that certain kinds of therapeutic practice grow out of a people's anxieties rather than out of their satisfactions. These are therapeutic practices which are of essentially a negative character—avoiding or undoing responses in the system with which anxiety is associated. Insofar as the therapeutic practices of a society are brought about through this sort of influence and are of this negative character, one would expect therapeutic practices to provide a less sensitive test than otherwise of the influence of childhood satisfactions on adult personality.

OTHER CONSIDERATIONS

There are other considerations which should be kept in mind in evaluating therapy as an index of personality characteristics, even though we have no evidence to offer from cross-cultural correlations.

One of these additional considerations is the probability that therapeutic practices, more than explanations of illness, have in many instances a thoroughly realistic effect and have come to be adopted for this reason. Setting broken bones has an obvious reward value of a realistic character; particular beliefs about how bones come to be broken, even if they may be instrumental in allowing people to avoid accidents, do not provide such immediate relief from states of similarly intense pain and alarm. Quinine has a dramatic effect on malarial fever; no particular explanation of malaria is likely, under conditions of primitive life, to have such dramatic effect in the only way possible, that is, by leading to the discovery and use of this specific. The ingestion of warm liquids may have a quite realistic effect of increasing general bodily comfort. Poultices or skin-pricking, in a similar fashion, may have a definite reward value because of distracting attention from the more serious and alarming source of pain. Such properties are not in general likely to be shared by explanations of illness. To the extent that therapeutic practices are influenced by such realistic effects of their use, there is less room for them to be also simultaneously influenced by the personality characteristics of the patient.

Another general consideration lies in the probability that therapeutic techniques are generally more under the control of specialists than are explanations of illness. In community studies in modern nations we have had opportunity to observe that this appears to be true of the transition from folk customs to scientific medicine. In a Latin American village one of us found that residents who could afford to consult doctors did so and followed their therapeutic regimens with enthusiasm; but the explanations these same people would offer for being sick obviously came from the folk culture and not from the physicians. Again, one of us observed among second-generation Italians in New England that ascription of headaches to the Evil Eye seemed to persist long after the magical practices for getting rid of such headaches had given way to aspirin and other remedies prescribed by physicians. It seems likely that in primitive communities, as well, medical specialists are more concerned with and more respected for their therapeutic practices than their explanations of illness. If this is true, it means that therapeutic practices would be more susceptible of being influenced by the personality characteristics of the individual specialists, and explanations of illness would be more susceptible of being influenced by the typical personality characteristics of members of the community as a whole.

Two Types of Fixation: Conclusions

We began our discussion of fixation in Chapter 6 with a discussion of the psychoanalytic concept of fixation, and with modifications in it suggested by modern behavior theory. We suggested, in particular, that behavior theory suggests that the concept of fixation should be analyzed into two separate concepts—positive fixation and negative fixation. These two terms point to two processes which behavior theory suggests should be quite distinct theoretically, and not necessarily occurring together, whereas in psychoanalytic theory they tend not to be distinguished from each other or to be pictured as leading to identical results.

For the process of negative fixation we have found ample evidence. The principal evidence is that presented in Chapter 7. There we show that the custom potential of the anxiety developed in any of five systems of behavior, as a result of the socialization practices in a society, is related to the tendency for adults in that society to show continued concern about that system of behavior, which is evidenced by their explaining illness by attributing it to acts or materials relevant to that particular system. We found significant evidence for this general relationship in the case of three systems of behavior—oral, dependent, and aggressive; for two other systems of behavior—anal and sexual—we found only smaller tendencies in the same direction. This major evidence for negative fixation has, of course, been further strengthened by the analysis of various alternative interpretations in Chapter 8; we were able to show evidence against various interpretations which would suggest that our findings might be mere artifacts or errors, and to conclude that our findings do give evidence of genuine natural processes, among which negative fixation seems very likely to be an important component.

This major evidence for negative fixation, deriving from study of explanations of illness as the major index we selected for this purpose, is supplemented to some degree by a secondary sort of evidence which has been presented somewhat incidentally in the present chapter. We have shown in this chapter that there is some evidence that custom potential of socialization anxiety in each system of behavior is related to the tendency to select, as a therapeutic practice, behavior or procedures which seem to reflect by undoing or avoidance an anxiety about that system. Our main object in presenting this evidence in the present chapter was to illustrate the fact that therapeutic practices appear to be determined by a number of motivational factors, rather than to an overwhelming extent by some one kind of motivational factor. But at this point we would like also to call to the reader's attention the fact that this evidence has another function, too—that of confirming the connection between severity of child training, and content of adult anxiety, which we have more decisively demonstrated in Chapter 7.

The evidence from our study has led to further clarification, in one respect, of our hypothesis of negative fixation. We proposed to test this hypothesis primarily by relating indices of adult personality to measures of socialization anxiety which have to do with the practices used in training children out of their initial habits in each system of behavior. Our strongest general evidence for negative fixation came from our making this test. But we have also reported (in the final section of Chapter 7) tentative evidence that the same indices of adult personality are related in a negative way to measures of initial satisfaction in each of the five systems we have considered. The drive-producing responses which a child learns through initial deprivation in a given system of behavior, then, have in this respect an effect similar to that of the drive-producing responses which the child learns when he is being systematically trained out of an infantile behavior which may have been formerly permitted to him but which he is now expected to renounce in favor of more mature behavior.

Our findings about the second type of fixation process, that of positive fixation, are much less sharp than those about negative fixation. We found no consistent evidence that high initial satisfaction potential of a given system of behavior in infancy and early childhood would lead to a lasting reliance upon that system as a source of security, as in the selection of therapeutic practices. We did, however, find some tentative evidence that high satisfaction potential in a given system of behavior, established later in connection with the progression of socialization toward more mature behavior, has such a lasting effect.

These results suggest that the process of positive fixation is a real phenomenon, although our evidence for it is not nearly as strong as in the case of negative fixation. At the same time they suggest very strongly that the role of early training is less important, as establishing lifelong personality tendencies, in positive fixation than in negative fixation. We have already suggested that this difference may be due in part to cultural factors. The social conditions responsible for the development of anxiety in a given system of behavior may, in general, be cultural characteristics which exert pressures upon the individual fairly uniformly at different periods of his life, so that the early learned anxiety is reinforced later by a continuation, in the behavior of other people, of essentially the same attitudes and overt behavior which were responsible for the development of the anxiety originally in the crucial period of socialization. The social conditions responsible for the development of an initial satisfaction for a given system of behavior may, in general, have to do with the behavior of other people specifically in their role as caretakers of very young children; to the extent that this is true, the social conditions would change as the child progressed to a stage of maturity where he was no longer to be treated as a very young child. Thus, positive fixations would be more subject than negative fixations to unlearning and being replaced by new habits, simply because the social conditions relevant to the learning are more subject to change.

It is possible, however, that there would be this difference between the permanency of negative and positive fixation even without a greater change in the relevant social conditions in the one case than in the other. Assume that the relevant social conditions change radically in both cases. Then we might expect less change in the learned behavior in the case of negative fixation than in the case of positive fixation, simply because of the greater resistance to unlearning which appears to characterize learning based on punishment. There is a variety of evidence from experimental studies in psychology suggesting that there may be a general difference of this sort. Our evidence is, unfortunately, not competent for reaching a decision as to the extent to which such a basic difference between two kinds of habit, and to what extent social conditions, may underlie the difference in our findings for negative fixation and for positive fixation.

We have seen, moreover, that negative conclusions about positive fixation on the basis of our evidence must be accepted only tentatively and with caution. For it is quite likely that at least some of the difference may be due to the fortunate chance of our having hit upon a highly suitable index of adult personality in the case of negative fixation, and a less suitable and less pure index of adult personality in the case of positive fixation.

But the most important and definite conclusion in comparing the two types of fixation is that the two are not the same process and do not have the same result. We found highly significant evidence that frustration and punishment in socialization produce fixation. We found tentative evidence that indulgence of certain interests in connection with socialization produces fixation. But "fixation" in these two cases refers to quite different consequences—in the first case, evidence of anxiety about certain acts and materials; in the second case, evidence that certain acts or materials are a source of satisfaction or drive-reduction. Moreover, the indices of adult personality which were found to be positively related to socialization anxiety were not positively related to initial satisfaction, as would be required by an assumption of identical effects of the two types of fixation; on the contrary, we found evidence of a negative relationship here.

It may be objected that we have not tested in an appropriate way the notion that the same sort of fixation may result from either extreme frustration or extreme indulgence. It may be felt that a comparison of correlations obtained, as between our scales of anxiety and our scales of satisfaction, does not provide an appropriate test. The other test which is possible on our data, which some readers might feel to be more appropriate, is a comparison of the two extremes on each scale separately. It could be argued that societies rating very high and societies rating very low on any one of these scales should represent a contrast between extremes of frustration and of indulgence. Then, if the two extremes tend to produce similar effects, an appropriate index of adult personality should show similar results for these two extreme groups when they are compared with the rest of the societies which fall nearer the center of the scale.

We have tested this line of reasoning against our data. We have done it in two separate ways—first, by dealing with the 25% of societies highest on a scale and the 25% lowest, and comparing each with the middle 50%; second, by dealing with the 10% of societies highest on a scale and the 10% lowest, and comparing each with the middle 80%. We have not felt that interest in this specific question justifies lengthy presentation of the results of this analysis. But we may summarize them fairly by reporting that in neither case do we find any consistent evidence of a tendency for the two extremes to resemble each other. This method of analysis too, then, leaves us with the feeling that negative fixation and positive fixation are distinct processes which need to be understood separately and which will occur together not consistently but only when the conditions of learning are such as to set in motion both of these distinct processes.

CHAPTER 11. *Origins of Guilt*

Now WE turn to certain aspects of our study which are of much more exploratory character than those presented thus far. The study was conceived primarily to study fixation as a set of processes mediating the personality integration of culture. Here and in the following chapter we will instead be dealing with topics on which we did less satisfactory advance planning but on which the analysis by our judges of the ethnographic data—centered though it was around the concept of fixation—yet permits us to make some contribution. In this chapter we propose to explore the problem of the origins of guilt feelings, and will begin with an example or two which will help make clear what we mean by feelings of guilt.

Occasionally a newspaper reports that someone has anonymously made restitution for a minor theft many years in the past. A railroad company, for example, is reported to receive $1.50 with an accompanying letter explaining that this is payment for a ride the writer took ten years ago without having bought a ticket. Here it is clear that the person who stole a free ride is being driven to make restitution by some state of discomfort which is repeatedly evoked by recollection of his action, and which he hopes to get rid of by making the restitution. There is clearly no fear of punishment; there is no chance that the minor theft could be discovered at this late date, no chance that any legal action could be taken against the transgressor, and in many cases not even any expectation of serious disapproval by his friends and associates if they should learn of the matter. Some feelings not obviously connected with expectation of punishment motivate the person to try to undo his misdeed.

Another example may be used to illustrate another frequent

outcome of guilt feelings, the outcome of self-punishment. In a number of personality studies of American Negroes recently reported by Kardiner and Ovesey (1951), a recurrent theme is guilt about the individual's competitive striving for status and financial success, where the individual feels this striving to have the character of an aggressive act against fellow Negroes who are denied these advantages. Thus, one of the women they studied said in an interview, "I'm supposed to be a superior dancer. I could have had the dancing scholarship, but during the tryouts I couldn't handle myself well and I was suddenly self-conscious because I was being watched. I didn't want to be good and so I fell down. This failure, at the point of success, is a pattern with me. I used to do this in tests at school. I want to give but I can't. I'm afraid I will do well." (Kardiner and Ovesey, 1951, p. 288).

What we mean by guilt, then, is painful feelings of self-blame, self-criticism, or remorse which result from deviation (real or imagined) from proper behavior.[1] Feelings of guilt typically motivate either a quest for self-punishment, as in the second example we have cited, or an effort at restitution or undoing of the deviation, as in the first example. This usage of the term *guilt* corresponds in the main with generally accepted usage in psychoanalytic writings.[2]

People differ greatly from one another in the extent to which, having deviated from some cultural rule, they feel guilty. This is an important kind of personality difference, a conspicuous sort of variation between one adult and another. Special interest is attached to individual differences in guilt, however, because of the role played by guilt in the process of socialization, and this role we would like to consider next.

1. For our purposes here, proper behavior may be understood to mean for the most part conformity to cultural rules. Guilt may in special cases, however, also be evoked by deviation from purely idiosyncratic standards of behavior.

2. See, for example, Alexander (1948, p. 118), Fenichel (1945, p. 134), and Horney (1939, p. 237).

The Role of Guilt in Socialization

The end result of socialization is the conformity of the individual to the rules of his culture. Conformity to the rules may, however, be achieved in several different ways; guilt feelings play an essential role in one of these ways of producing conformity.

Conformity to cultural rules may, first of all, be produced to a limited extent by making transgression impossible or at least exceedingly difficult. This is a method of ensuring conformity which does not depend on socialization; it prevents a person from transgressing successfully regardless of his training. In our society this method is used with respect to certain rules about property, where the property is of great value. The government and private individuals who have large holdings of precious metal or currency commonly keep such property in vaults which, when properly guarded, practically exclude the possibility of theft. Less dependable devices are of course in common use, but their use varies among individuals and segments of our society. In American cities, for example, it is common practice for people to keep their houses locked and thus place certain difficulties in the way of potential burglars. In the country, on the other hand, it is much more common for people to leave their houses unlocked and depend on the socialized habits of all their neighbors for protection against loss of property.

This reliance upon physical prevention of transgression of property rules varies markedly from one culture to another. One of us had this brought clearly to mind in traveling through Central America. In one Central American country, our local friends repeatedly warned us to guard our property carefully and keep our quarters safely locked. Moving on to a nearby country of very different culture origins, we found that our hotel rooms were not even provided with any means of being locked; it was apparently not conceivable in this community that there could be any need for preventing a person from entering where he had no right to go.

Physical prevention as a means of ensuring conformity is obviously very limited in application. Most cultural rules can be violated by a word or an action against which there can be no physical barrier. Physical prevention none the less plays an important role in combination with socialized habits. This is particularly true of the enforcement of sexual mores. In many societies such a combination is seen in the enforcement of rules against premarital and extramarital intercourse on the part of women. Where women are kept always in the home or in the presence of other members of their family, forbidden sexual relations can be prevented merely by training men to avoid entering others' dwellings or to avoid public sexual approaches without, however, the necessity of training men to avoid sexual approaches under other conditions. Incest rules may be enforced by a different sort of combination of physical barrier and socialized habit; where a man is stringently trained not to touch or look at his sister, he does not have to learn to struggle against a mobilized tendency to approach her sexually, for his habits of avoidance create a physical barrier which prevents such a mobilization.

Conformity to rules is then, with the exception of special cases, ensured primarily by the process of socialization—that is, by the development in each individual of habits which lead him to make responses which conform to the rules instead of transgressing them. But what is involved in the process of socialization? We would suggest that there are several processes of learning involved which it is important to distinguish. Methods of attaining conformity are not to be classified simply into external prevention and dependence upon socialization. Socialization itself needs to be analyzed.

First of all, much of socialization involves simply the development of positive habits on the basis of reinforcement through reward. A child learns the language of his society because of the many rewards he receives through the communications he can make as he acquires it. A person develops a taste for the foods used in his society, because these have satisfied his hunger. He acquires many of the values of his society because of the obvious or subtle approval with which his elders greet his expression or acceptance of them.

This process of positive learning through reward may itself be rather a complex and variable matter, but we do not propose to attempt further analysis of it here, as it is not the main object of our inquiry in this chapter. We would simply point out that it appears to be of importance in producing conformity primarily where there are a number of ways in which a given drive could be satisfied, where the way favored by the culture is a fairly satisfactory one, and where there are no special conditions creating a tendency to adopt some deviant way. Under ordinary circumstances this is true of the examples we have given; the language, the foods, and the sentiments characteristic of a culture are routinely acquired and held to by practically all members of a stable society, and there is little temptation to deviate from them. But under certain conditions, such as those of culture change under the impact of an alien culture, this may no longer be true. The ambitious member of a conquered society may be strongly tempted to adopt the language, the food, and the sentiments of its conquerors. Under these conditions, if the conquered society is still continuing to function and keep its own identity, its members may no longer rely simply on rewarding their children for adherence to the old customs but impose definite negative sanctions for deviation in the direction of alien temptation.

But what is true for certain aspects of culture only under very special conditions is true under typical conditions for certain other aspects of culture. These other aspects of culture involve drives for which human societies seem unable to make any provision so fully adequate as to eliminate temptation to seek gratification in other than the approved ways. Hence conformity to the cultural rules requires more than just a positive habit of following the approved way; it requires also the development of negative habits which will produce avoidance of the disapproved ways of reducing the drive. This is perhaps most uniformly true of the sexual and aggressive drives.

In the case of the sexual drive, provision is commonly made for an adult to obtain sexual gratification through intercourse with either one or some limited group of members of the opposite sex, with certain restrictions as to time, place, or other circumstances. These restrictions commonly include a requirement of privacy of the sexual act itself and, in the case of extramarital relations, often include concealment of the occurrence of the relationship. Moreover, sexual relations even between husband and wife are usually forbidden during certain periods, such as menstruation and part or all of pregnancy and lactation (cf. Ford and Beach, 1951). It is clear that in general, and perhaps universally, allowable sexual behavior does not result in eliminating temptation to engage in forbidden sexual behavior. An adult in any society is likely to become sexually aroused under conditions which do not permit immediate gratification, or in relation to another person with whom sexual relations are forbidden. How then is transgression of the mores prevented? To some extent physical prevention of transgression by separation of forbidden partners is used, as has already been indicated. But for the most part human societies rely upon the development, in the course of socialization, of habits which will be in conflict with tendencies toward forbidden sexual responses, and which will be strong enough to prevent those tendencies from being carried out into overt behavior.

This is even more obviously true in the case of aggressive drive. The arousal of aggressive tendencies as a response to the frustrations of human life appears to be a universal phenomenon. Also universal is the outlawing of much of the most direct and adequate expression of these aggressive tendencies in overt behavior. Here again physical prevention may play some minor part in preventing transgressions. In a Costa Rican village, for example, the policeman takes the *machetes* of all participants in a drinking bout, to be returned after the party is over; if one of the participants becomes so violent as to be dangerous even without this weapon, he is put in jail until he has recovered from his drunkenness. In South Italian culture the custom of enemies isolating themselves from each other by refusing to speak may have a similar value in preventing murderous quarrels. But the normal life of a community requires that most of its members be willing to speak and act together, and be available for work and recreation. So the main dependence for the prevention of aggression, too, must be on the development in each individual of habits which will conflict with the forbidden tendencies and prevent them from reaching overt expression.

What is so clearly true of sexual and aggressive tendencies is also true for many other forms of behavior such as failing to take responsibility, laziness, overdependence, or lack of courage. Transgression of cultural rules in these behavior systems is prevented by the presence in each individual of certain habits built up in the course of socialization.

What, then, are these habits?

Freud, in his accounts of personality development, made some valuable suggestions about the character of the internal habits which are responsible for preventing transgression of cultural rules. To these suggestions, which have been couched in the terminology of Freud's theoretical system, we will return a little later. Meanwhile we would like to review briefly the efforts that have been made to deal with this problem in recent years with the concepts of general behavior theory.

The behavioristic attack on this problem has focused attention primarily on what we may call the fear of punishment. A child who breaks a cultural rule, if his transgression is known to his elders, is punished in some way. As a result of such experience he learns to anticipate similar punishment whenever he breaks a cultural rule. The transgression of a rule thus brings to a child one or both of two unpleasant consequences: punishment by his elders, and fearful anticipation of such punishment. Finally, by further consequences of the learning process, the fear comes earlier. Now the thought of possible transgression, or presence in the situation in which he committed a transgression, is sufficient to arouse the uncomfortable anticipation of being punished or of giving himself grounds to fear imminent punishment. This anticipatory state of fear, like other emotional states, serves as a drive to motivate behavior which may lead to elimination of the drive. The behavior that is most effective from this point of view is avoidance of the transgression. If the child moves away from temptation, gets out of the situation, or decisively makes a response in accordance with the cultural rule, he no longer has occasion to fear punishment. Thus conformity with cultural rules is rewarded by the reduction of fear of punishment.[3]

In applying this sort of theoretical interpretation to the problems of socialization, there seems to have been an assumption that probably the process of learning to fear external punishment adequately accounts for the acquisition of negative habits which serve to inhibit transgression of cultural rules. Freud, on the other hand, has suggested that this process is not the only one. He suggests a distinction between two kinds of internal responses which serve to inhibit transgressions. One, which he calls "objective anxiety" corresponds to fear of punishment in our terminology. (We have not used Freud's term because we believe it is likely to be confusing as suggesting that the fear of punishment is objectively justified or realistic, as of course it is very often not.) The other, which he calls "moral anxiety" represents a fear, not of external punishment but of guilt. Freud makes this distinction in discussing the concept of the superego, and as will be seen in the following passage he regards moral anxiety as a distinctive function of the superego:

> The role, which the super-ego undertakes later in life, is at
> first played by an external power, by parental authority.
> The influence of the parents dominates the child by grant-

3. Substantially this theoretical account of the role of punishment in socialization is given, for example, by Whiting (1941) and by Dollard and Miller (1950, Ch. 10). In planning our present research we shared this emphasis, as may be seen from the way we measured socialization anxiety (pp. 52–55).

ing proofs of affection and by threats of punishment, which, to the child, mean loss of love, and which must also be feared on their own account. This objective anxiety is the forerunner of the later moral anxiety; so long as the former is dominant one need not speak of super-ego or of conscience. It is only later that the secondary situation arises, which we are far too ready to regard as the normal state of affairs; the external restrictions are introjected, so that the super-ego takes the place of the parental function, and thenceforward observes, guides and threatens the ego in just the same way as the parents acted to the child before. . . . The basis of the process is what we call an identification, that is to say, that one ego becomes like another, one which results in the first ego behaving itself in certain respects in the same way as the second; it imitates it, and as it were takes it into itself. This identification has been not inappropriately compared with the oral cannibalistic incorporation of another person (Freud, 1933, pp. 89–90).

Let us try to recast Freud's suggestions into terms of general behavior theory. In the early socialization of the child, avoidance of transgression is achieved solely by the development of fear of external punishment. This fear presumably continues throughout life to make an important contribution to the maintenance of conformity. But in addition a more complicated process supervenes. The child comes to respond with guilt when he has transgressed. He then learns to anticipate this guilt, and the fear of guilt plays the same inhibitory role in ensuring conformity as the fear of external punishment.

Whence, then, arise the internal responses called guilt to which Freud attributes this important role in producing conformity to cultural rules? Freud traces their origin to a process which he calls identification. Identification is supposed to involve the child's imitating the evaluative responses of his parents, and thus punishing himself (by guilt feelings and other punishment to which they may lead) whenever he has done something for which he believes his parents would feel he should be punished.[4]

Freud's account of the development of the superego, and hence of guilt feelings, is expressed primarily in terms of supposed universals. The same process of identification occurs in everyone and leads to essentially the same result, the superego (which then differs in content according to the content of the parental evaluations). Freud and other psychoanalysts do, however, speak of variations in the effectiveness or punitiveness of the superego. From such discussions and from the account of the supposedly universal process of superego development it is possible to formulate certain hypotheses about the correlates of variations in strength of guilt tendencies, hypotheses which it is possible to test in a preliminary way from the cross-cultural data of our study. We will attempt to test three such hypotheses drawn from Freudian theory of superego development. In addition we will present evidence bearing on two other hypotheses which are of interest in relation to this theory. But before we present and test these hypotheses, we must consider the problem of how we have tried to measure the degree of guilt characterizing the members of each society in our world-wide sample.

A Cultural Index of Guilt

As a cultural index of the degree to which guilt feelings characterize the members of a society we have used a measure of the extent to which a person who gets sick blames himself for having gotten sick. Self-recrimination, as a response to illness, seemed to us a probably useful index of the degree to which guilt feelings are strong and widely generalized.

At first glance the idea of self-blame as a major reaction to illness may seem absurd to some of our readers. Samuel Butler, in his *Erewhon,* presents a picture of an imaginary society in which people who get sick are punished in much the same way

4. Identification is given a similar role in a recent behavioristic account by Mowrer (1950, pp. 573–616).

that criminals are punished in our society. But he uses this picture simply as a means of satirizing our treatment of criminals, whose transgressions are presumably due to causal laws just as much as is the occurrence of a disease. Apart from its satirical meaning, the idea of strong guilt feelings and punishment as a way to deal with a sick person probably appears rather ludicrous to readers of *Erewhon.*

The fact is, however, that even in our society some degree of guilt is a frequent reaction to one's getting sick. Even with our scientific knowledge about the causes of many diseases, we are perfectly capable of making use of this knowledge to justify (perhaps quite rationally) feelings of guilt about having gotten sick. One person may blame his illness on his having so imprudently overeaten the night before, another on a long drinking bout, and another on his carelessness in exposing himself to contagion from his relatives or acquaintances.

In primitive societies self-blame is generally more conspicuous as a reaction to illness, although it still shows a great deal of variation from one society to another.

A strong tendency to react to illness with guilt feelings may be illustrated by the Harney Valley Paiute. According to the beliefs of this group, as reported by Beatrice Whiting (1950, p. 34),

> a common cause of sickness is one's own power, for it is believed that if a person fails to obey his spirit helper he will become ill. To avoid such sickness one must perform in every detail the rituals taught by the spirit helper. During my stay at Burns, Sarah became ill, and Dr. Thomas diagnosed the illness as follows: Jerry J. had a sty in his eye and came to her for treatment; although he did not have seventy-five cents to pay, Sarah took pity on him and scraped his eye. According to Dr. Thomas, she became ill because, contrary to the dictate of her spirit helper, she worked without pay. . . . Another case concerned J. Smith, a bullet-proof man, who had power in guns. He was killed by his own power for disobeying instructions about

rituals he was to perform. "He grew thinner and thinner as his power got the best of him, and just before he died, an unloaded gun standing in the corner of his house fired by itself." This event gave evidence of the cause of his death.

By contrast Gorer's description (1938, p. 231) of a Lepcha belief shows a relatively low degree of patient responsibility.

> When a Mun is called in to exorcise a devil the most usual situation is as follows: After the specific devil has been divined the Mun spends a night in his own home *munthen-ing*—that is summoning and communing with his possessing spirit—to discover the reason for that particular devil having attacked that particular person, and to learn what sacrifices or ritual are necessary to exorcise it. The question of causation is bound up with the conception of *tawitoom*—the necessary consequence of an earlier act; *often this act was not committed by the sufferer, but by fairly remote ancestors.* [Italics ours.]

The belief that sickness is caused by malicious witches who act whimsically and without regard to their victims' behavior indicates even less patient responsibility. Junod (1927, pp. 475 ff.) reports of the Thonga that the *baloyi,* a secret society of witches, act in this manner. He says of them, ". . . the great crime of the baloyi is that of killing . . . two motives inspire this crime, hatred and jealousy."

It should be pointed out that even in the case of the Thonga, who received a low score for guilt by our measure, some degree of patient responsibility is indicated, i.e., making a witch angry or jealous. In fact in no society in our sample do we find clear evidence that patient responsibility is completely absent. This is not surprising, since it is probable that some degree of guilt is necessary for social living, and that it generalizes to the explanation of illness. Our index of patient responsibility, then, is not a categorical, all-or-none measure, but rather a motivational potential which varies along a dimension from more to less, from strong to weak.

The most direct measure of this motivational potential would be a rating of the extent to which, in each society, people who fall sick are tortured by really painful feelings of guilt. We do not have such a direct measure. It is quite doubtful, moreover, that it would be possible to obtain it from most of the ethnographic reports available. The usual accounts of customary reactions to illness in a primitive society do not give any very direct evidence of the extent to which a person is made really uncomfortable by the self-blame associated with the explanation of illness.

It is possible, however, to make a somewhat more indirect approach, and this we have done. Such an approach involves the assumption that the custom potential of beliefs which attribute illness to the actions of the patient himself will give an indirect index of the extent to which guilt feelings appear as a reaction to illness. Assuming that generally the purely cognitive reactions to illness—on which information is available—will be correlated with appropriate emotional reactions, a society in which illness is attributed primarily to the actions of the patient will be one in which people who are sick feel guilty. While we have no direct evidence as to whether this assumption is justified, it appears to us to be reasonable.[5]

In the analysis of explanations of illness made by our judges, three points appeared to be relevant to our purpose here, as contributing information about the custom potential of the belief

5. We are aware, however, that the index we arrive at by this reasoning is fallible in particular cases, as is illustrated by the Navaho. The Navaho are well above average on our index, yet Kluckhohn (1943, p. 225) says of them, "As a matter of fact, it may be questioned whether minimally acculturated Navahos ever feel 'guilt'—in the sense of anxiety or self-punishment for undetected acts which are, however, known to bring disapproval or punishment if observed by others. 'Shame' as opposed to 'guilt' is a striking Navaho configuration. 'Conscience' is hardly an important deterrent of action for Navahos—only anticipation of actual overt punishment."

that the patient himself is responsible for becoming ill. They are as follows:

1. THE NUMBER OF SPECIFIC ACTS OF A PERSON WHICH ARE BELIEVED CAPABLE OF MAKING HIM SICK. On the rating sheet used for the analysis of explanations of illness, as has been indicated in Chapter 6, appeared a list of specific acts on the part of the patient which might be believed to lead to his becoming sick. The rater was to make a rating of the custom potential of each of these for which there was any evidence. The number of different acts of the patient, contained in this list, to which illness was reported to be attributed was an item which we considered relevant to the strength of the tendency for the patient himself to be blamed for his illness.

2. THE MAXIMUM IMPORTANCE OF THE BELIEF THAT ANY SPECIFIC ACT OF A PERSON COULD LEAD TO HIS BEING SICK. This item was drawn from the same set of ratings as the preceding item. It is possible for illness to be ascribed occasionally to a variety of acts of the patient, and yet for all these explanations to be of slight importance. We chose, therefore, as a second item the maximum rating assigned to any one of these specific explanations which attribute illness to acts of the patient.

3. RATING OF THE IMPORTANCE OF PATIENT RESPONSI- BILITY FOR ILLNESS. The judge was instructed to make a rating on a seven-point scale of the importance, for each society, of attribution of illness to acts of the patient. This was an abso- lute rating in the sense that it was to be made for all societies for which evidence was available on a single scale of comparison which the rater would keep in mind. It is thus comparable to the ratings of child training practices, in contrast to the rank- ings. In arriving at this rating, of course, the judge used in part the information which he had already analyzed about the im- portance of various specific acts of the patient. In addition, however, he could draw upon any more general information contained in the account of the society's reaction to illness.

The last of these three items was, of course, intended to be by itself a direct measure of patient responsibility for illness.

Unfortunately, it turned out that each judge's ratings on this item were almost entirely concentrated in a narrow range from 3 to 5 on a seven-point scale; hence the societies were not very widely spread out on this measure, and it did not yield as sensitive or reliable an index as would be desirable. For this reason we decided to pool it with the first two items to obtain the index of patient responsibility we would use in testing the hypotheses to be presented here.

The three items which were to be pooled could not reasonably be simply added to each other, because they had very different distributions and hence would contribute very unequally to determining the final pooled index. What we decided to do was to convert the ratings on each of the three items into a standardized normal distribution, thus approximately equalizing the spread and shape of each distribution.[6] We then added for each society the three scores so obtained, and the result was our pooled index of patient responsibility. While a somewhat complicated statistical procedure was used, the meaning of what was done is not complex. Our pooled index of patient responsibility is simply an average of the three relevant items from our analysis of explanations of illness, and this average is determined by a procedure which ensures that each of the three items will contribute about equally to the index.

Certain of the measures of child training practices with which we intended to correlate this index (the measures of type of punishment and agent of socialization, which we will describe later in this chapter) were ones which are probably influenced by adequacy of information. Therefore, to reduce the chances of similar influence on the measure of customs about illness, we decided to select a group of societies for which there seemed to be a reasonable uniformity of coverage. The criterion we chose was based primarily on a set of entries in the rating sheet which called for the judge to rank the relative custom potential

6. For an account of how a set of scores may be converted into a standardized normal distribution, see for example Walker (1943, pp. 181–193).

of explanations which blamed the patient, blamed others, and blamed no one for the illness. We felt that where both the judges had been able to make these rankings, we had assurance of especially good coverage of beliefs about responsibility for illness. In addition, we set up the criterion that at least one judge must have a definite rating (rather than a judgment of no evidence) on each of the three items which were to contribute to our index. By using these two criteria we selected, on grounds of adequacy of coverage, 35 societies on which our index of patient responsibility was calculated. Since the number of societies available was thus reduced at the outset, we arbitrarily decided to make all tests in this chapter on as many of these societies as possible—that is, by including societies where judgments on the child training variables met only an intermediate criterion of confidence.

THE ROLE OF SOCIALIZATION ANXIETY

The first hypothesis we will test about the origins of guilt feelings is one which grows out of the behavioristic treatment of socialization that we have mentioned earlier. This theoretical treatment has emphasized the role of severity of punishment as responsible for the restraint of socially disapproved behavior, and this emphasis suggests the possibility that severity of punishment is the sole factor that contributes to this restraint and to the development of guilt feelings. Guilt feelings, according to this hypothesis, are just one form that anxiety about punishment may take, so that there would be no very important distinction between fear of external punishment and fear of guilt. The fear of guilt is merely one of a variety of specific types of behavior that may be elicited by a broadly generalized fear of external punishment.

From this hypothesis there would be predicted a positive correlation between our index of patient responsibility and the average socialization anxiety in the five systems of child behavior we have dealt with. The relation between these two variables is shown in Table 16. It will be seen that the relation is indeed a positive one. Societies with a high average socialization anxiety tend to be higher on the index of patient responsibility than do societies which are low in average socialization anxiety.

TABLE 16. Relation Between Patient Responsibility for Illness and Average Socialization Anxiety

(The name of each society is preceded by the value obtained for it on the index of patient responsibility, and followed by the value obtained for it on average socialization anxiety.)

	Societies below the median on average socialization anxiety		Societies above the median on average socialization anxiety	
			21 Maori	12
			17 Dobuans	16
			17 Navaho	13
			16 Alorese	13
Societies above the median on patient responsibility			15 Hopi	12
			14 Kwoma	13
	18 Pukapukans	11	14 Manus	12
	14 Lakher	11	13 Chamorro	14
	12 Yakut	10	12 Dahomeans	13
	10 Lepcha	11	11 Arapesh	12
	10 Papago	11	11 Chiricahua	14
	9 Marquesans	10	9 Azande	13
	9 Siriono	9	9 Samoans	12
	9 Teton	11	8 Kwakiutl	12
Societies below the median on patient responsibility	9 Tikopia	8	6 Tanala	13
	8 Bena	9	5 Lesu	12
	8 Wogeo	11	4 Rwala	14
	7 Ainu	11	4 Thonga	13
	6 Kurtatchi	11	2 Chagga	13
	5 Comanche	9		
	5 Trobrianders	11		
	1 Chenchu	9		

In order to test whether this relationship is statistically significant, a correlation coefficient seems appropriate, as both variables are fairly symmetrical in distribution. The correlation coefficient takes account of the exact numerical values of both variables. The coefficient has been calculated and found to be $+0.29$. For the number of our cases, the probability that a positive correlation of this magnitude would arise purely through random error is less than 5%, and we may conclude that we have significant evidence of the existence of the predicted relationship.

The absolute value of the correlation found here is low. Since the measure of socialization anxiety is an average of separate measures for the five systems of behavior, it is worth inquiring into the relation of patient responsibility to each of those five measures separately. Perhaps the modest correlation coefficient obtained for the average covers up a very high relationship with some one or two of those measures and a complete lack of relationship with the others. Another reason for doing this is that two of the specific anxieties have been specified in Freudian theory as particularly relevant to the development of the superego and to guilt. The final conversion of external to internalized or superego controls has been said to come at the time of the resolution of the Oedipus dilemma, when the child consolidates his identification with a parent of the same sex. If it can be said that the resolution of the Oedipus dilemma is accentuated by the severity of sex training, then the severity of socialization of this system of behavior should be correlated positively with our index of guilt. Aggression is a second system which might be particularly relevant to another possible source of guilt feelings —that of self aggression or aggression turned inward. The authors of *Frustration and Aggression* (Dollard, Doob, Miller, Mowrer, and Sears, 1939, p. 48) suggest that this form of aggression should be related to the degree of inhibition of more direct forms of aggression. Thus guilt, if this hypothesis is correct, should be related to socialization anxiety with respect to aggression. For the above reasons we have calculated the relation between patient responsibility and socialization anxiety for each of the five systems of behavior. We will not present the full tables identifying the various societies for each of these relationships, but do present in Table 17 the correlation coefficients which summarize the relationships.

TABLE 17. Relation Between Patient Responsibility for Illness and Socialization Anxiety in Each of Five Systems of Behavior, as Expressed in Correlation Coefficients (each coefficient is based on 35 cases)

System of behavior	Correlation of socialization anxiety with patient responsibility
Oral	+0.25
Anal	+0.06
Sexual	+0.02
Dependence	+0.18
Aggression	+0.28

The effects of the separate socialization anxieties on our index of guilt suggest in the first place that there is indeed a general or uniform effect of socialization anxiety in any system of behavior, since all five relationships are positive in direction and no one of them is outstandingly high. As far as the hypotheses with respect to the sexual and aggression systems are concerned, it will be seen that there is some confirmation of the latter, the correlation just attaining the 5% level of confidence, but no confirmation for the former, the relationship being barely in the positive direction and indeed the lowest for any of the five systems. The relatively strong though not significant relationship between oral socialization anxiety and patient responsibility might suggest a relevance of the psychoanalytic notion of a relation between oral incorporation and the superego. We are not at all clear, however, about just what prediction about our measures ought properly to be drawn out of this notion.

The results, then, offer confirmation of the prediction made from the first hypothesis, and for the particular influence of socialization anxiety in the aggressive system. There seems to be some positive relationship between these two antecedents and the tendency for the patient to blame himself for having gotten ill. But the evidence does not suggest a very close relationship between these variables. To the extent that we can place faith in our indices to measure the theoretical variables they are intended to measure, we may conclude that an interpretation of guilt feelings as reflecting almost solely the strength of either over-all socialization anxiety or aggression anxiety is not satisfactory, and are encouraged to look for other variables that may also have an important influence on the tendency for people to feel guilt.

THE ROLE OF INITIAL NURTURANCE

We come now to the first of the three hypotheses which have been most directly suggested to us by psychoanalytic theory about the development of the superego. Psychoanalytic theory stresses the role of the child's concern about the love of its parents and about the possibility of losing this love. This suggests to us the hypothesis that the strength of the superego might vary with the strength of this concern, that is with the strength of the child's drive for dependence upon his parents. A strong drive for maintenance of an affectionate dependent relationship to the parents could provide the background out of which further parent-child interaction could develop a strong superego; a weak drive for maintenance of affectionate dependent relationship to the parents would mean that the child lacked the necessary structure of internal habits from which a strong superego could subsequently be developed in further interaction with the parents.

To test this hypothesis, some sort of direct measure of the strength of the dependence drive would be most desirable. Unfortunately, we do not have such a direct measure on the societies in our sample, and are doubtful that it could be obtained from the ethnographic data at present available. It is possible, however, that the hypothesis might still be tested more indirectly. This can be done if we have a measure of the antecedents pertinent to the development of the dependence drive. One possibility is that the strength of the dependence drive is a direct function of the initial nurturance of the child by its parents— that where the child is very well and indulgently cared for it will develop a strong drive for dependence on its parents, and where it is neglected it will develop only a weak drive for dependence. We do have a measure of this possible antecedent of the dependence drive. It is the measure of initial indulgence of the child's dependence upon its parents, and of the consequent satisfaction potential of dependence. To the extent that dependence drive is built up simply by the parents' gratification of the child's basic needs for care by adults, we may test the present hypothesis by testing the relationship between patient responsibility and the degree of initial indulgence of dependence in the child training practices of various societies.

This relationship is presented in Table 18. If the hypothesis were confirmed, there should be a positive relationship—that is, societies high in initial nurturance of the child should tend more strongly to blame illness on the patient himself than societies which are low in initial nurturance of the child. As far as the evidence goes, it is against this hypothesis, for the indication is in fact slightly in the direction of a negative relationship. This indication is not at all dependable. The correlation coefficient expressing the closeness of relationship between the two variables is only -0.06, a negligible quantity from the point of view both of its absolute magnitude and of the confidence that may be placed in its giving evidence of any relationship at all. All we can safely conclude, then, is that our hypothesis, as tested in this particular way, is not confirmed at all. There is no acceptable evidence of any kind of relationship between degree of initial nurturance and our index of patient responsibility for illness.[7]

7. Two recent studies of individual differences (Faigin and Hollenberg, 1953; Levin, 1952) do find marked positive relations between initial

TABLE 18. Relation Between Patient Responsibility for Illness and Initial Indulgence of the Child's Dependence

(The name of each society is preceded by the value obtained for it on the index of patient responsibility, and followed by the value obtained for it on initial indulgence of dependence.)

	Societies below the median on initial indulgence of dependence		Societies above the median on initial indulgence of dependence	
	18 Pukapukans	15		
	17 Dobuans	11		
	16 Alorese	12		
Societies above	15 Hopi	14		
the median	14 Lakher	14	21 Maori	16
on patient	14 Manus	12	17 Navaho	16
responsibility	12 Dahomeans	15	14 Kwoma	19
	12 Yakut	11	13 Chamorro	17
	11 Chiricahua	13	11 Arapesh	18
	10 Lepcha	14	10 Papago	18
	9 Marquesans	12	9 Azande	18
	9 Samoans	12	9 Siriono	17
	9 Tikopia	12	9 Teton	17
Societies below	8 Bena	15	8 Wogeo	17
the median	8 Kwakiutl	14	6 Kurtatchi	16
on patient	7 Ainu	9	6 Tanala	16
responsibility	5 Trobrianders	15	5 Comanche	16
	4 Rwala	13	5 Lesu	16
	4 Thonga	14	2 Chagga	16
	1 Chenchu	15		

There are two reasons for which we believe this negative finding should not be regarded as very conclusive evidence against the fruitfulness and validity of the hypothesis we are testing here. One is that the range of variation in degree of

nurturance and degree of identification; if the relation between identification and guilt is what we have assumed, these findings give reason for continued exploration of the hypothesis we have stated here.

nurturance with respect to the customary child training practices of various societies may not be great enough to have this particular effect. It may be that in the customs of all societies children are treated indulgently enough to develop a dependence drive of sufficient strength for subsequent parent-child interaction to lead to the development of guilt feelings, and that additional indulgence does not increase the strength of guilt feelings. It is possible, in short, that this variable is significant only up to a certain point and beyond that has no further effect. The deviant families in any society, then, who are unusually neglectful of their children may tend to develop little guilt feeling in their children, but there may be little difference from one society to another in this respect.

A second reason, and in our opinion a more important one, is that we have great doubt about the validity of the indirect index we are using here. It is possible that the strength of the dependence drive is a direct function of degree of nurturance; obviously, we consider this a sufficiently plausible assumption in the present state of scientific knowledge to have warranted testing our hypothesis by way of this assumption. On the other hand, this assumption may well be wrong. There is some evidence, for example, which suggests that conflicting expectations in the child are a much more important determiner of dependence drive, that inconsistency of nurturance rather than degree of nurturance is the antecedent variable relevant to the strength of acquired drive for dependence (Carl, 1949). Inconsistency of nurturance is a variable, unfortunately, for which we have no index in our analysis of child training practices in these primitive societies.

ROLE OF TYPE OF PUNISHMENT

The second hypothesis which was suggested to us by psychoanalytic theory of superego development has to do with the techniques of punishment customarily used by parents in socializing their children. Psychoanalysts speak of the role of threat-

ened loss of the love of the parents in giving rise to the superego. This feeling of potential loss of parental love, insofar as it
has an objective basis, must grow largely out of the meaning for
the child of the punishments he receives from his parents for
transgressions of cultural rules.

Now it might be that all punishment of a child by its parents
has about equally the meaning of potential loss of the parents'
love. Freud may have had such a notion in speaking, in a passage
we have quoted earlier in this chapter, of "threats of punishment,
which, to the child, mean loss of love."

We suspect, however, that different techniques of punishment
may differ from each other quite strikingly in what they mean
for the child with respect to his relation to his parents. In order
to make distinctions relevant to the problem we are discussing,
however, it is necessary to consider a little further the role that
this threatened loss of love might have in leading to the development of guilt feelings. It appears to us that this role involves
keeping the child strongly oriented toward seeking the love
of his parents, while at the same time arousing uncertainties
about his attaining this goal. Out of this continued striving for
love, and conflicting expectations about achieving it, an imitation of the parents' evaluative responses might be expected to
develop because of two functions that such imitation would have
for the child: (1) Insofar as the child is deprived of the still
valued love of his parents, self-love or self-admiration may have
the function of a substitute goal; where the parents refuse adequate recognition of the child's good behavior, he is able to
reward himself by his own internal self-praise which has been
modeled on their earlier praise of him. (2) The imitation of
the parents' evaluative responses would have a further, and perhaps more important, function as instrumental responses which
are conducive to the final attainment of either the original goal
of the parents' love or the substitute goal of self-praise. The
child's chiding of himself for his bad behavior (self-chiding
which is modeled after the parents' earlier evaluations of the
child's behavior) serves to inhibit repetition of bad behavior,

and thus facilitates the occurrence of good behavior and the consequent obtaining of rewards from his parents and from himself.

This analysis suggests that the crucial thing about the techniques of punishment used by the parents is whether they are likely to have the dual effect of keeping the child oriented toward the goal of parental affection and at the same time arousing uncertainty about the attainment of this goal. It appears to us that all punishment of the child by its parents is likely to have the second of these two effects. But it also appears that techniques of punishment differ in the extent to which they at the same time contribute to maintaining the child's orientation toward this goal. We sought to distinguish on just this basis among the techniques of punishment by parents on which our judges made ratings of custom potential for the societies in our sample.

There were three techniques of punishment in our analysis which seemed likely to have this double effect: punishment by denial of love, punishment by threats of denial of reward, and punishment by threats of ostracism. These may be called *love-oriented techniques* of discipline.

On the other hand, there were three techniques which seemed likely to tend on the whole to interfere with the child's orientation toward seeking the love of his parents. They are physical punishment, threats of physical punishment, and punishment by ridicule. Each of these seems likely, when used by parents, to have to a considerable degree the effect of setting up a tendency for the child to avoid the parents. Avoidance of the parents, because of anticipated pain or humiliation, should interfere to some extent with continued pursuit of the positive goal of obtaining parental affection.

There were other techniques of punishment included in our analysis sheet about which we did not feel we could make any tentative generalization with respect to these effects. Punishment by actual denial of reward, and punishment by actual ostracism, are examples. Here we felt there was some reason to expect continued maintenance of strivings for parental affection and also some reason to expect the development of avoidances, and we could see no basis for making any *a priori* judgment about the balance of these two. It should be noted, finally, that the same thing is to some extent true of the two groups of punishment techniques singled out above for attention in connection with the hypothesis to be tested here. We do not argue that denial of love has no tendency to produce avoidance of the parents; we do not argue that physical punishment is completely inconsistent with maintenance of strivings for parental affection. We would suppose that the effects of either of these would vary a great deal according to the detailed character of the punishment and according to the cultural setting in which it occurred. We are only suggesting that on the average it is reasonable to expect the difference we have described between these two groups of disciplinary techniques.

In order to test the relation of guilt feelings to this difference, it is necessary to decide how to obtain a suitable measure of the importance of these punishment techniques. Our judges made a rating of the custom potential of each of these six techniques of punishment by parents. There were a great many disagreements among judges, and a great many omissions. The disagreements arose in part out of failure of the judges to distinguish consistently among the three techniques placed together in the first group (denial of love, threats of denial of reward, and threats of ostracism), and among two of the three techniques placed together in the second group (physical punishment and threats of physical punishment). As our first step, therefore, we decided to consider for each judge simply the highest rating he gave to any of the three techniques which we have placed together in a single group. A second step was a decision about how to treat the instances of omissions, that is, absence of a rating by a judge for one group of techniques in a given society. There were enough omissions so that to have included in our sample only societies for which all judges made all the relevant ratings would have left us with too few societies to have made any test. We decided to assume, therefore, that the absence of a rating could be taken as evidence of absence or low importance of the given technique and that we could therefore give it a value of zero. This did not seem to be as safe an assumption as it was in the case of explanations of illness, because on the whole the information on disciplinary techniques was not nearly as full as the information on explanations of illness. To counter this difficulty, we decided that only the relative rating of the two groups of punishment techniques should be considered, not the absolute rating of a single group (for it seemed likely that low ratings arising from inadequate information might affect about equally, on the whole, the ratings on the two groups of techniques). Accordingly, we added together the ratings of the three judges for each group of techniques of punishment, and then took the difference between the two measures so obtained. This provided us with a measure of the relative importance of love-oriented techniques, in comparison with non-love-oriented techniques of punishment by parents, for each society in our sample.

We may now state the hypothesis to be tested in this section, in the form in which it became possible to test it. The hypothesis is that relative importance of love-oriented techniques of punishment by parents will be positively correlated with the importance of patient responsibility in the explanation of illness. In Table 19 we present the data that are pertinent to the test of this hypothesis. It is clear that for the 35 societies available for this test there is a positive relationship as predicted.

When a correlation coefficient is calculated from these data, its value is found to be only $+0.10$, which is a negligible outcome. It is noteworthy, however, that there are a few societies which have very deviant scores on the relative importance of love-oriented techniques. This fact suggests to us that this is a case where it is proper to place greater reliance on a method of statistical analysis which does not take account of the exact scores on this variable, but merely considers the difference (in patient responsibility) between societies above and below the

TABLE 19. Relation Between Patient Responsibility for Illness and Relative Importance of Love-oriented Techniques of Punishment by Parents

(The name of each society is preceded by the value obtained for it on the index of patient responsibility, and followed by the value obtained for it on the relative importance of love-oriented techniques.)

	Societies below *the median on relative importance of love-oriented techniques of punishment*		Societies above *the median on relative importance of love-oriented techniques of punishment*	
			21 Maori	0
			17 Navaho	−6
			16 Alorese	−3
Societies above			15 Hopi	−3
the median	18 Pukapukans	−8	14 Kwoma	−5
on patient	17 Dobuans	−16	14 Manus	−3
responsibility	14 Lakher	−13	12 Yakut	−6
	13 Chamorro	−14	11 Arapesh	−3
	12 Dahomeans	−14	10 Lepcha	−3
	11 Chiricahua	−16	10 Papago	−6
	9 Azande	−18	9 Marquesans	−6
	9 Tikopia	−15	9 Samoans	2
	8 Bena	−12	9 Siriono	4
Societies below	7 Ainu	−11	9 Teton	−6
the median	6 Kurtatchi	−9	8 Kwakiutl	−3
on patient	5 Comanche	−16	8 Wogeo	0
responsibility	5 Lesu	−7	6 Tanala	14
	4 Rwala	−20	5 Trobrianders	−2
	4 Thonga	−11		
	2 Chagga	−11		
	1 Chenchu	−9		

median on the relative importance of love-oriented techniques. This is the t technique, which we have also employed in earlier chapters where one variable was treated as simply varying between presence and absence, or high and low. When t is calculated for these data, it is found to have the value of 1.77, which is significant at the 5% point. We believe it is proper to conclude that we have some dependable evidence of the predicted relationship, that guilt feelings as measured by patient responsibility for illness are related to the relative importance of love-oriented techniques in the punishment of children by their parents. But certainly there is no evidence to suggest a very close relationship here.[8]

The Role of the Agent of Socialization

Psychoanalytic theory assigns to the parents a critical role in the development of the child's superego and hence guilt feelings. Since parents generally play the major caretaking and nurturant role with respect to their children, they are the primary models for the identification on which the superego is based according to psychoanalytic theory. So far as we know, psychoanalysts have not systematically discussed the question of the effects on superego development of variation from one family to another in the relative importance of the parents' role in the socialization of the child. One might draw from psychoanalytic theory, however, the tentative hypothesis that where the parents play a less important role in the socialization of their children, the children will tend to develop weaker superegos than where the parents play a more important role.

If we are to test this hypothesis in more specific form for our cross-cultural data, we need an index of the relative importance of the parents' role in socialization in the customary practices of the societies in our sample. We did not have our judges make a direct rating of the importance of the parents. They did, however, make some more detailed ratings from which a usable index can be derived. In the part of our analysis sheet which dealt with techniques of punishment used in socialization, rat-

8. The plausibility of the hypothesis we are testing here is also increased by the fact that Faigin and Hollenberg (1953) and MacKinnon (1938) have obtained evidence in confirmation of it in studies of individual differences.

ings were made separately for each technique as employed by each of the following categories of person: parents, relatives, nonrelatives in the community at large, and socialization specialists (i.e., teachers, priests, chief, or any other person whose role called for him to take a formal and distinctive part in the socialization of children who were not his relatives). We thus had ratings of the importance of each technique of punishment as practiced (if at all) by each kind of agent of socialization. The maximum importance of any technique of punishment as practiced by a given agent could then be used as a rough index of the importance of that agent in the socialization process.[9]

These ratings are thus essentially the same ones that we have dealt with in the preceding section, where we were concerned only with the techniques of punishment used by a single agent, the parents. The use of the ratings is hampered by the same difficulties described there, and we have attempted to deal with the difficulties in exactly the same way. Since we felt that a measure which compared two sets of categories on the analysis sheet was essential, as in the previous section, we decided in this case to compare the importance of parents as socializing agents with the importance of specialists or nonrelatives in general (whichever of these two had the higher rating for a given society). The measure with which we emerge, then, is one of the relative importance of parents in comparison with agents of socialization who are unrelated to the child. Relatives other

9. It might be argued that some agent (e.g., specialists) might make important use of some one technique of punishment and yet play a relatively unimportant role in the total socialization process. With this difficulty in mind we also tried as another index the sum of the ratings for all techniques of punishment as used by a given agent of socialization. While this index gives specific values which are very different from those given by the simpler index we actually used, the outcome of the test of the hypotheses, as determined by the t test, turns out to be identical with that obtained through the simpler index. It is unfortunate, however, that we have to depend on either of these indirect indices instead of having obtained the direct rating by our judges which would be more clearly pertinent to the hypothesis.

than parents have been left out of consideration on the grounds that the effects of punishment by them should be intermediate between the effects of punishment by parents, on the one hand, and punishment by unrelated individuals on the other hand.

The specific hypothesis to be tested in this section, then, is as follows: The strength of guilt feelings characterizing a society, as measured by the custom potential of patient responsibility for illness, will be positively related to the relative importance of parents, as contrasted with nonrelatives and specialists, as agents of socialization. In Table 20 we present the data relevant to a test of this hypothesis. Again, the results are slightly in the predicted direction. Societies in which the index of relative importance of parents in socialization is above the median tend to have a greater degree of patient responsibility than do societies in which the index of relative importance of parents in socialization is below the median.

This finding, however, is not statistically significant. The correlation coefficient calculated from these data is only $+0.08$, an entirely insignificant figure. For the same reason as in the previous section, we believe the t test is more appropriate here; the value of t, however, is only 0.92, also to be considered as not even approaching statistical significance. We therefore can place no confidence in this positive relationship as a genuine and stable phenomenon which would continue to be found if we had larger or different samples of societies available to test the same hypothesis.

There are other ways in which essentially this same hypothesis might be tested, and we will cite the results obtained by these methods for their confirmatory value, even though they also are for the most part not statistically significant.

It might be supposed that the comparison between the importance of parents and of unrelated persons as agents of socialization would not be particularly relevant on the grounds that the parents always have so much the more important role that slight variations in this comparison would not be expected to have a great deal of significance. So far as we can judge, the

TABLE 20. Relation Between Patient Responsibility for Illness and Relative Importance of Parents, in Comparison with Unrelated Persons, as Agents of Socialization

(The name of each society is preceded by the value obtained for it on the index of patient responsibility, and followed by the value obtained for it on the index of relative importance of parents.)

	Societies below *the median on relative importance of parents as agents of socialization*		Societies above *the median on relative importance of parents as agents of socialization*	
			21 Maori	9
			18 Pukapukans	13
	17 Navaho	−4	17 Dobuans	16
Societies above	16 Alorese	7	14 Lakher	13
the median	15 Hopi	7	14 Manus	10
on patient	14 Kwoma	5	13 Chamorro	12
responsibility	11 Arapesh	3	12 Dahomeans	13
	11 Chiricahua	0	12 Yakut	9
	10 Papago	4	10 Lepcha	10
	9 Marquesans	6	9 Azande	18
	9 Samoans	4	9 Siriono	13
	9 Teton	2	9 Tikopia	9
Societies below	8 Bena	8	7 Ainu	11
the median	8 Kwakiutl	5	6 Tanala	12
on patient	8 Wogeo	7	5 Comanche	13
responsibility	6 Kurtatchi	2	5 Lesu	11
	5 Trobrianders	7	1 Chenchu	9
	4 Rwala	5		
	4 Thonga	3		
	2 Chagga	6		

parents certainly do have the more important role in all of the 35 societies in our sample; yet there was one society (the Navaho) for which by our particular index the importance of unrelated persons turns out to have a higher rating than the importance of relatives, but we suspect this is attributable to the peculiarities of our index and does not really mean that in this society the over-all role of parents in socialization is less important than the over-all role of unrelated persons.

From this criticism one might proceed to the suggestion that in comparing agents of socialization in various societies, the dominant role of the parents should be taken for granted. The relevant question might be then concerned with what agents of socialization play the most important secondary role. Other relatives of the child are likely to have a relationship to him somewhat akin to the relationship of his parents; to the extent that the secondary place in socialization is taken by other relatives, then, rather than by unrelated persons, a tendency toward a relatively strong superego might be predicted. On the other hand, to the extent that the more important secondary role is played by unrelated persons rather than by relatives, one might predict a tendency toward a somewhat weaker superego on the average. To be sure, in view of the likely assumption that the role of the parents is typically much greater than either of these, this difference might not be very large or consistent.

With little expectation of great consistency we have none the less tested this relation with our data, employing for relatives an index exactly parallel to the ones we have already described for parents and for unrelated persons and then obtaining for each society the difference between this index and that for unrelated persons. This difference we have then related to our index of patient responsibility for illness. The results are presented in Table 21. The tabulated data do indicate a positive relationship, as predicted from the general hypothesis we are testing. But the relationship here also is one in which little confidence may be placed. The correlation coefficient calculated from these data is only $+0.18$, and the value of t is only 0.64. We can draw no definite conclusion here either.

This comparison between the importance of the secondary roles in socialization of relatives and unrelated persons suggested to us one final test of the hypothesis we are considering in this section. Granted that the role of the parents is in general the

TABLE 21. Relation Between Patient Responsibility for Illness and Relative Importance of Relatives (Other than Parents), in Comparison with Unrelated Persons, as Agents of Socialization

(The name of each society is preceded by the value obtained for it on the index of patient responsibility, and followed by the value obtained for it on the index of relative importance of relatives.)

	Societies below the median on relative importance of relatives as secondary agents of socialization		Societies above the median on relative importance of relatives as secondary agents of socialization	
			18 Pukapukans	12
			17 Dobuans	13
Societies above			16 Alorese	4
the median	21 Maori	0	15 Hopi	8
on patient	17 Navaho	−7	14 Manus	4
responsibility	14 Kwoma	−1	13 Chamorro	3
	14 Lakher	0	12 Dahomeans	10
	11 Arapesh	−8	10 Lepcha	2
	11 Chiricahua	−12	10 Papago	2
	9 Azande	0	9 Samoans	5
	9 Marquesans	0	9 Tikopia	5
	9 Siriono	−3	8 Bena	7
	9 Teton	−6	5 Comanche	7
Societies below	8 Kwakiutl	1	5 Trobrianders	5
the median	8 Wogeo	−1	4 Rwala	3
on patient	7 Ainu	0	1 Chenchu	3
responsibility	6 Kurtatchi	−2		
	6 Tanala	−3		
	5 Lesu	0		
	4 Thonga	−2		
	2 Chagga	−2		

principal one, certain variations among primitive societies in rules of residence might be expected to have an effect on the relative importance of other relatives and nonrelatives as secondary socializers. At one extreme, in 22 societies in our sample a married couple takes up residence in close proximity to the immediate family of one of them, and which family is specified by custom (matrilocal or patrilocal rule of residence). This custom implies the availability of other relatives as fellow householders or immediate neighbors, and in general the institutionalization of their role as secondary socializers of the couple's children. At the other extreme, in 4 societies with a neolocal rule of residence it is not customary for a married couple to reside in immediate proximity to any specified relative, and not necessarily to any relative at all. Hence it appears likely that relatives other than parents will on the average have a more important secondary role in socialization in the former group of societies, and nonrelatives a more important secondary role in the latter group of societies. It would be predicted, then, from our hypothesis, that a weaker superego and hence lower degree of patient responsibility for illness would be found in the societies with a neolocal rule of residence than in the societies with a matrilocal or patrilocal rule. This does indeed turn out to be the case. The mean index of patient responsibility for illness is 11.4 for the matrilocal and patrilocal societies, and is only 6.0 for the neolocal societies. This difference is so large that it is highly significant statistically despite the small number of cases on one side of the comparison ($t = 2.59$).[10]

There is a third group of societies for which the rules of residence seem likely to be intermediate between these first two groups in their implications for the role of relatives and nonrelatives as secondary socializers. This group includes six societies in which a couple may choose whether to live in proximity to the husband's family or to the wife's family and one society in which a couple lives at different times with each of the two families; these rules would seem to make for a less well-estab-

10. We are greatly indebted to Dr. G. P. Murdock for supplying us with information about rules of residence on several societies in addition to those for which he had already given this information in his book, *Social Structure* (1949). For one society out of the 35 the information was not available.

lished role of the relatives in the rearing of the couple's children. This group also includes one society in which a couple lives in proximity to the husband's maternal uncle—that is, with relatives who are not the relatives by whom either husband or wife was reared. This group of societies does indeed turn out to be intermediate in the mean index of patient responsibility, with a mean of 8.8. The difference between this group and either of the extreme groups is not statistically significant.[11]

The outcome of this indirect test of the effect of the agent of socialization upon the development of guilt, then, is to provide stronger support for the hypothesis than was obtained by the more direct tests.

We feel that the unsystematic evidence of casual observation within our society offers some tentative evidence in favor of this hypothesis. It is consistent with what we would guess to be the facts about social class differences in typical personality as related to class differences in child rearing. The middle class in our society (and in Western European civilization more generally) is commonly believed to have a stronger average tendency toward guilt feelings than either the lower or the upper class; and it also appears to be true that the parents have a much more predominant role in socialization in the customary practices of the middle class than in either the lower or the upper class.

We should point out, finally, that this hypothesis is not entirely independent of the one we have considered in the previous section of this chapter. If a predominant role of the parents, and secondarily of other relatives, in the socialization of the child makes for a strong superego, this may be partly because the love-oriented techniques of discipline are more likely to be used by them than by unrelated individuals. It is clear to common-sense consideration that the love-oriented techniques are better suited

---

11. It might be argued that the avunculocal society should have been classified, for our purposes, with the neolocal societies. The effect of this would be to make the difference between the two extreme groups even more significant.

to the role of parent or relative in our society; this is confirmed as a more general phenomenon by the results of our analysis of child training practices in primitive societies, for our judges rarely found evidence of the use of the love-oriented techniques by persons unrelated to the child.

THE ROLE OF AGE OF SOCIALIZATION

The final hypothesis we propose to test in this chapter is that the development of strong tendencies toward guilt feelings is favored by early socialization. There are three distinct lines of reasoning that all suggest this hypothesis. We will indicate these lines of reasoning, present the results relevant to the hypothesis in general, and then see whether any of the detailed results offer any evidence to support one rather than another of these lines of reasoning as the correct explanation of the findings.

The three arguments which might lead to this hypothesis are as follows:

1. If, as has been suggested in the preceding sections of this chapter, denial of love plays an important role in the development of the superego, then the timing of socialization might be expected to be a relevant variable. This implication follows from the fact that a child's need for love, or in other words the strength of his dependence drive, should vary with age. When the child is still relatively helpless, withdrawal of love should be considerably more effective as a disciplinary technique than when he is older and has developed habits of self-reliance and can cope with the environment by himself. Thus, if early socialization does increase the efficacy of denial of love, it should produce a stronger superego than late socialization.

2. It might be surmised that early socialization is on the whole more severe than late socialization. At an early age the child, because of his greater biological immaturity and lesser learning, may be able to learn a given restraint only at the expense of stronger anxiety than would be necessary at a later age. In Chapter 5 we have shown that our cross-cultural evidence indicates

that this appears to be the fact; societies with early socialization in any system of behavior tend to socialize more severely than do societies which attempt it only at a later age. Hence the hypothesis (the first one tested in this chapter) that strength of superego is a function of general severity of socialization should lead to a prediction of the present hypothesis as well.

3. The third line of reasoning proceeds from the observation that our index of guilt feeling is one which depends upon a broad generalization of guilt feelings acquired in socialization. The child is originally made to feel guilty about actual transgressions of cultural rules. Our index has to do, however, with the point whether in the face of illness a person is led to suppose that he *must* have done something wrong even if he was not aware of it at the time. Such a broad generalization may well be seen as an inappropriate or unrealistic generalization. Now here again, the lesser maturity and learning attainment of the very young child would lead one to expect this consequence to a greater degree than would be found in the older child or adult. Dollard and Miller have made this point very effectively with respect to the fear of punishment acquired in the course of socialization,[12] stressing in their account the role of the child's changing capacity for making appropriate discriminations (particularly in view of his increasing command of language). What is true for anxiety acquired simply through fear of punishment should be equally true for anxiety acquired through a more complex process of identification—that inappropriate generalization is more likely if the anxiety is established at an early age than if it is established at a later age.

All three of these lines of reasoning, then, lead to a general prediction that the age of socialization in any system of behavior should be negatively correlated with the resulting strength of superego and hence with our index of patient responsibility. In order to test this prediction we have made use of the estimated ages of onset of training which we have already referred

12. Cf., for example, their discussion of the effects of early vs. late toilet training (Dollard and Miller, 1950, pp. 138–140).

to in Chapters 3, 4, and 5. These estimates are available for five aspects of socialization—weaning, toilet training, modesty training, control of heterosexual play, and independence training—and in Table 22 we present the results for each of these aspects in turn.

TABLE 22. Relation Between Patient Responsibility for Illness and Estimated Age at Onset of Various Aspects of Socialization

The upper part of the table shows the mean index of patient responsibility for societies with various estimated ages at onset of each aspect of socialization; in parentheses after each mean is shown the number of societies on which it is based. The age intervals are not of uniform size, having been selected to avoid excessive bunching or spreading of cases in any of the five distributions. In the last line of the table are correlation coefficients expressing the closeness of relation between the index of patient responsibility and estimated age at onset of each aspect of socialization. Coefficients marked with an asterisk are significant at the 5% point; those marked with two asterisks are significant at the 1% point.

	ASPECT OF SOCIALIZATION				
Age at onset	Weaning	Toilet training	Modesty training	Training in heterosexual inhibition	Independence training
Below 1.0	11.0(2)	4.0(2)			
1.0 to 1.9	11.6(5)	11.9(8)			
2.0 to 2.4	11.0(10)	11.7(7)			15.8(4)
2.5 to 2.9	9.1(9)	9.0(1)			9.9(8)
3.0 to 3.9	9.5(4)	14.0(1)	13.8(4)		9.0(9)
4.0 to 5.9	4.0(2)	8.0(1)	10.5(3)		9.2(11)
6.0 to 7.9			9.2(5)	12.1(7)	6.0(1)
8.0 to 9.9				9.0(3)	
10.0 and above			9.0(1)	5.5(4)	
Correlation coefficient	−0.42**	+0.21	−0.50*	−0.74**	−0.34*

There is a marked consistency in the results presented in this table. In general, the mean index of patient responsibility shows a steady decline with increasing age of socialization. Exceptions of appreciable magnitude to this generalization occur only in instances where the mean for a given age span depends upon a very small number of societies. Tests of statistical significance for each of the five relationships may be made by use of the coefficient of correlation. The relationship is on the whole quite significantly confirmed. For two aspects of socialization—weaning and training in heterosexual inhibition—the specific relationship is highly significant. For two other aspects—modesty training and independence training—the relationship reaches the 5% significance point. For anal training, finally, the relationship is not at all significant and in fact reversed in direction.

Thus we may conclude that the hypothesis of a negative relationship between age of socialization and strength of guilt feelings is strikingly confirmed by our cross-cultural data.

Now is there any evidence to argue for a choice among the three lines of reasoning which each suggested this hypothesis? We cannot hope for decisive evidence from our meager data, but there are some suggestive indications.

First of all, the interpretation of this finding as due to the negative correlation between age of socialization and severity of socialization may be tentatively rejected. We have found a much closer relationship of patient responsibility to age of socialization than to severity of socialization. As far as our present evidence goes, then, it would be more reasonable to interpret the latter relationship as a by-product of the former, than to do the reverse.

Second, there is suggestive evidence that interpretation of these findings in terms of the child's increasing capacity for making appropriate discriminations is not entirely adequate. This suggestive evidence has to do with the breakdown of the relationship between age and patient responsibility at the earliest ages. For two aspects of socialization—weaning and anal training—there are instances where a society is judged to start socialization before the age of one year. These societies tend to have lower indices of patient responsibility than would be expected by extrapolation from the rest of the data. In the case of toilet training, the two societies with this very early socialization have such low indices of patient responsibility that their presence leads to a negative correlation for the data as a whole, whereas the relationship otherwise is slightly positive. This breakdown at an early age cannot confidently be considered to be valid in view of the very small number of cases involved. Should it be confirmed, however, it appears to be inconsistent with interpreting these relationships entirely in terms of the child's capacity for discrimination, for this capacity should certainly be much lower still at this early age than in successive years.

The apparent breakdown of this relationship at very early ages does, on the other hand, appear to be consistent with an interpretation of the relation in terms of identification growing out of concern over possible loss of parental love. In the first place very early socialization may interfere with the development of the dependence drive upon which this hypothesis depends; and secondly, the imitation of evaluative responses may require a degree of verbal facility which the one-year-old child does not yet have.

Of the three lines of reasoning which we introduced in this section, then, the interpretation first offered, of age of socialization as relevant to superego development because of its implications in relation to the child's need for a satisfactory love relationship with its parents, seems on the present evidence to offer the most satisfactory explanation of the facts. We must, however, point out that better evidence about more societies is needed before we can be certain that the facts to be explained are in detail what they appear to be from the data we have been able to present.

Summary and Discussion

We began this chapter by considering the sources of the internal responses which, by winning out in a conflict with the tendency to make overt responses which are unacceptable in the person's cultural setting, serve to prevent transgressions of cultural rules. We saw that one important internal response which has this function is the fear of external punishment, which originates in the experience of external punishment and the threat of it, though it may be generalized to many situations in which there is little realistic likelihood of incurring punishment. We then saw that psychoanalytic theory suggests another important internal response which serves the same function but is believed to have a different origin. This response is the fear of future feelings of guilt, and the origin offered for this fear by psychoanalytic theory is a process of identification with the parents. Our aim in this chapter has been to review the relevant cross-cultural evidence to see whether it offers any support for the psychoanalytic view that inhibition of transgression is in part dependent upon this second, more complex process rather than being basically dependent upon simple fear of external punishment even where the person's conscious fear is of his own guilt feelings.

We have made this exploration by use of an index of the extent to which the patient himself is blamed for his becoming ill. This appears to be a useful, though not the best possible, index of the extent to which members of a society experience the conscious feelings of guilt and fear of guilt to which psychoanalysis calls attention in its account of this supposed second process by which possible transgressions are inhibited.

We first tested the relation of our index of patient responsibility to the over-all severity of socialization, in order to see whether there is such a high relation here as to suggest that feelings of guilt are just a by-product of strong anticipation of external punishment. We found that this relationship, while statistically significant, is not very high; the same is true of severity of socialization in the aggressive system alone. We were encouraged to test the further hypotheses that were suggested to us by the psychoanalytic account of the origins of guilt feelings.

The outcome of the rest of the chapter is to offer some tentative evidence in support of the importance of a process of social-ization through identification, with origins akin to those ascribed to it in psychoanalytic theory. One of the specific hypotheses concerned with the role of degree of initial nurturance was not confirmed at all by the cross-cultural evidence. For all the other hypotheses there was some positive evidence. Only in the case of hypotheses about techniques of socialization and about the age of socialization was the major evidence statistically signifi-cant. The consistency of confirmation however, not only of several hypotheses but with several distinct tests in the case of two of the hypotheses, leads us to the conclusion that we have strong tentative evidence for the importance, as a variable in socialization, of a distinct process of socialization through identi-fication.

We will conclude this chapter, then, with an attempt at a coherent interpretation of socialization through identification. We have thus far introduced specific hypotheses in somewhat scattered fashion, drawing upon various elements in the rather loosely organized theoretical statements of psychoanalysis. Let us see whether these various hypotheses can be fitted together into a coherent account in terms of general behavior theory.

We suggest that the basic process responsible for socialization through identification is one of the child's learning to substitute self-love for love from others when and if the latter is withheld at a time when the child strongly needs to be loved. The reward of self-love is obtained by imitating the evaluative behavior of the parents, and is provided by the child to itself in situations similar to those in which the parents have provided special in-dications of love. Under these conditions self-love is thus tied to conformity with cultural rules, for it is conformity rather than non-conformity which has previously led to parental love. Self-blame thus serves an instrumental role in inhibiting the child's transgressions of cultural rules and facilitating the con-formity which will provide the cue for his self-love.

At the same time self-blame can serve the same instrumental role in relation to the child's striving still in actuality for the love of the parents. Like the striving for self-love, this striving too would be expected to be more intense when parental love is withheld at a time when the child strongly needs to be loved. Reinforcement of self-blame through renewed parental love may be a powerful influence on the initial development of feelings of guilt, though we would suspect that their continued maintenance throughout life is dependent upon the taking over of the parent's role by the person's own imitation of their evaluative responses.

In the light of this general interpretation of the process of identification we find that our hypothesis about the role of initial strength of dependence drive is relevant because it has to do with the strength of the drive for parental reward whose frustration leads to the substitution of self-reward. In the form in which we tested this hypothesis, by making use of a measure of degree of initial nurturance of the young child, we failed to confirm it; but for reasons which we have already indicated we feel this hypothesis merits continued consideration.

Our hypothesis about the role of techniques of punishment is relevant for much the same reason. The techniques which we have termed *love-oriented* techniques favor the development of guilt feelings because they threaten the child's attainment of the goal of parental love yet keep him oriented toward that goal rather than encouraging primarily avoidance of the parents.

It is interesting to note that clinical evidence suggests that loss of love may have a similar effect even when it is brought about, not by discipline, but by the death of a loved person. It has frequently been observed that a bereaved wife, for example, will adopt characteristics of her deceased husband, as though she were attempting to make up for the loss of a loved person by attempting to be that person (see, for example, Lindemann, 1944). In other words, identification here too becomes a means of retaining love in a substitute form by playing the nurturant and loving role of the lost person.

Our hypothesis about the role of the agent of socialization is more diverse in its possible relations to the general interpretation we are offering. In the first place, as we indicated earlier, the suggested relationship here may just be a special case of the dependence of guilt feelings upon love-oriented techniques of punishment, since these techniques are used primarily by parents and other relatives and not by unrelated persons. In the second place, an important role in socialization assigned to nonrelatives and especially to specialists may interfere with the development of guilt feelings because the child is then being disciplined by people with whom he does not have the intimate contact and knowledge out of which a widespread imitation of their evaluative responses could develop. Finally, where an important role in negative discipline is assigned to people outside the family, the parents may be able to maintain a consistently nurturant attitude toward the child. Thus, if our hypothesis about the effects of denial of love upon identification is correct, the child will not be motivated to adopt the parental role in evaluation of his own behavior and will instead retain the dependent role of infancy, expecting and presumably receiving love from his parents no matter what he does.

Our hypothesis and findings about the age of socialization, lastly, are relevant to our general interpretation because they have to do with whether threats of loss of parental love occur at a time when the child greatly needs parental love, or whether they instead occur at a time when the child has attained a degree of independent mastery of his world which makes it easier for him simply to abandon pursuit of parental love or of an internal substitute for it. Suggestive evidence indicated, however, that if the threat comes at a very early age it may also not be conducive to the development of guilt feelings, because the child has not developed a strong dependence drive and is not yet capable of the complex symbolic behavior of imitating the parents' evaluative responses.

WHY DO some people fear that their fellow human beings wish to do them harm? Why do some people imagine the world to be filled with supernatural beings who wish them ill? And why do others confidently expect that their fellows and the supernatural will be either indifferent or positively benevolent toward them?

In this chapter we will test certain hypotheses that may be offered in explanation of why people vary in these respects. First it seems desirable to give a more precise notion of how we propose to measure fear of others.

THE MEASURE OF FEAR OF OTHERS

Here, as in preceding chapters, our measure of typical personality characteristics in the members of a society is based on the customs with respect to illness found in that society. Beliefs about the causes of illness are here made use of again. Certain beliefs about the agent responsible for causing illness appear to provide a suitable index of the custom potential of fear of others. These beliefs fall into two general groups: the belief that the agents are living persons (other than the patient), and the belief that they are supernatural beings. We assume here that the custom potential of a belief that illness is caused by a particular category of beings may be used as an index of the degree to which that category of beings is feared by the members of a society.

Fear of other human beings was represented primarily by three items on the analysis sheet used by our judges. One is the belief that illness is due to the agency of a specialist in sorcery;

a second is the belief that illness is due to the agency of a non-specialist—that is, any member of the society is likely to act as a sorcerer to produce illness; the third is the belief that sorcerers are responsible for illness, but without clear evidence as to whether they are specialists or ordinary members of the society. The judge's aim was, first of all, to rate the custom potential of each of the first two more clearly defined beliefs; only if the evidence was too vague to permit this precision was he then to rate the third and more vaguely defined belief.

Fear of supernatural beings, or spirits, was represented by four items on the analysis sheet. Three of these were clearly defined items whose custom potential was to be rated if the evidence permitted. One of these is the belief that illness is brought about by spirits of the dead; a second is the belief that illness is brought about by other spirits of human form; the third is the belief that it is brought about by spirits of animal form. A fourth item to be used where the evidence was either partly or entirely vague is the belief that illness is brought about by unspecified spirits—that is, spirits which could not with confidence be classified under one of the first three items.

Within each of these two groups of beliefs there was considerable room for disagreement between the two judges in assigning a belief to a particular one of the several items. On the other hand, there did not appear to be much likelihood of disagreement about whether a belief referred to a human being or to a spirit. We attempted to take account of these considerations in deciding on the measures with which we would start our exploration of the origins of fear of others. For each judge we took the highest rating of custom potential made for any one of the three items under human beings; the ratings so obtained for each of the two judges were then added together to provide an estimate of the custom potential of attribution of the agency of illness to other human beings. The same procedure was followed for the four items under spirits, yielding an estimate of the custom potential of attribution of the agency of illness to spirits. These two estimates, one for human beings and one for spirits, could then be added together to give an over-all measure of the custom potential of fear of others.[1] The first results we will present are based on these three measures: the custom potential of fear of human beings, of fear of spirits, and of these two together.

The two judges who rated the ethnographic material on explanations of illness were both able to make these judgments rather uniformly. We have considered the rare instances where no entry was made as providing evidence of a low degree of attribution of illness to the kind of causal agent involved, and have treated them as ratings of zero (on a scale which otherwise went from 1 to 6 for each judge). Since ratings were thus available for all societies, we have generally used in this chapter only those societies for which confident judgments were made for the variables of child training, as this restriction leaves us with a workable number of societies for testing most hypotheses. Where the hypothesis requires the use of an average of several childhood measures, however, the number of societies for which all those measures are confident is very small; in those instances we have also cited results obtained by using all societies for which all those measures reach at least our intermediate criterion of confidence.

FEAR OF OTHERS AS GENERALIZED FEAR

The first hypothesis we will consider is that unrealistic fear of others arises by generalization from the objects of realistic fears. Since this generalization is, more or less by definition, inappropriate or unrealistic, it may be spoken of as overgeneralization. But this term does not imply any special mechanism. The familiar psychological principle of generalization may be adequate to explain why this should occur, the principle that re-

1. Since the two measures that were added together to yield this over-all measure had similar distributions, we saw no need here (as we did in the case of an over-all measure of guilt in the previous chapter) to transform the separate measures into normalized scales before adding them together.

sponses first learned in the presence of certain stimuli may then be evoked by stimuli which have some similarity to those original stimuli. In the present instance, fear learned as a response to parents as stimuli generalizes to sorcerers and spirits by virtue of their similarity to parents. The habit potential of these generalized tendencies is assumed by Hull, in his statement of this principle (1943, p. 199), to be a function of two factors. First, with increasing strength of the originally learned habit, there will be increasing potential of the generalized habits. Second, with increasing dissimilarity between the original stimuli and the new stimuli, there will be decreasing potential of the generalized habits. In this section of the present chapter we will not be concerned with this second factor, and will treat the several kinds of fear as though the degree of similarity to the originally feared objects might remain essentially constant. We will, however, be concerned with the first factor, the dependence of the potential of the generalized habit upon the strength of the original habit.

As was suggested above, the habits with which we are dealing here are habits of fear or anxiety. There are many situations in which a person is injured or punished by others. A person acquires a habit of fearing others in these situations. The fear which he has thus learned may then be evoked, through generalization, in situations where there is no realistic basis for fearing others. The potential of this generalized habit is, as we have said, assumed to be a positive function of the potential of the original habit of fear in the situation in which it was learned.

One important situation in which fear of others is learned is that of socialization. The child is necessarily deprived, frustrated, punished by his parents as he is discouraged in his initial habits and is made to replace them with more mature habits. As a result some degree of fear of the parents should be learned, but the potential of the fear learned in this way is variable. For the consistent differences among societies we have tried to measure essentially this kind of variation in our ratings of socialization anxiety in each of five systems of behavior. High socialization anxiety corresponds to parental behavior which is likely to teach the child to fear frustration and active punishment by his parents; low socialization anxiety is not likely to have this effect.

If fear of others is based on overgeneralization of anxiety, then, the custom potential of fear of others should be correlated positively with average socialization anxiety in all systems of behavior.

The test of this hypothesis makes use of the same judgments about personality effects of child training practices that were used earlier in testing the hypothesis of negative fixation. It should be noted, however, that a different assumption is being made here about the generalization of these personality effects. In testing negative fixation we assumed that anxiety acquired in childhood might be generalized to objects, impulses, and acts which are similar to those involved in the initial acts which the child is trained to inhibit. In the present chapter we are assuming instead that anxiety acquired in childhood might be generalized to other people (or spirits) because of their similarity to the persons responsible for the frustration and punishment of the child—their similarity, above all, to the child's parents. These two assumptions about generalization are not at all incompatible. We would make the assumption commonly made in behavior theory that a learned response may be generalized to a variety of stimuli which differ from the original stimuli in a variety of ways.

A notion closely akin to this hypothesis of overgeneralization of fear has been suggested by Kluckhohn (1944, pp. 60–61) in his theoretical interpretation of sorcery among the Navaho. He points out that

> . . . man not only craves reasons and explanations, but in most cases these reasons involve some form of personification, some human-like agency either natural or supernatural. It seems that only a small minority among highly sophisticated people can fairly face impersonal forces and the phenomena of chance. Doubtless the explanation for this attitude is that during the years of dawning conscious-

ness practically everything that happens is mediated by human agents—the parents or their substitutes.

While Kluckhohn makes here an additional assumption of a need for explanation, he uses implicitly the same central idea we are considering here, that is, of the generalization to other objects of a response first learned in relation to the parents. It is worth noting, however, that the fears which according to Kluckhohn may then be assimilated to this generalized fear are much more inclusive than those growing out of the restrictions imposed by socialization; they include also, for example, those growing out of the uncertain food supply and out of acculturative pressures from whites. Here there is certainly no fundamental difference between our hypothesis and his. We have phrased ours in terms of fears growing out of socialization, because that is the only source of fears with which we are equipped to deal in this study. The same mechanism which might lead to overgeneralization of these fears, however, could also lead to overgeneralization of fears deriving from other sources.

TABLE 23. Fear of Others: Relation to Average Socialization Anxiety in the Five Systems of Behavior

For each of three measures of fear of others (explained in the text) the table shows the correlation coefficient (r) expressing its relationship with average socialization anxiety, and the probability (p) that so large a coefficient in the predicted direction could have arisen through sampling error alone, for two samples of societies.

	For 10 societies where all the childhood ratings used are confident		For 47 societies where all the childhood ratings used meet at least intermediate criterion of confidence	
	r	p	r	p
Fear of human beings	+0.50	—	+0.26	<0.05
Fear of spirits	−0.15	—	+0.03	—
Over-all fear of others	+0.60	<0.05	+0.25	<0.05

In Table 23 we present the correlation coefficients which are pertinent to an evaluation of the hypothesis that fear of others arises by generalization from fear of the parents acquired as a result of severity of socialization. The results provide some confirmation of the hypothesis. With the over-all measure of fear both of human beings and of spirits the correlations are significant at the 5% point both for the restricted group of societies with confident judgments and for the larger group of societies for some of which the data are less adequate. For fear of human beings the confirmation is somewhat less satisfactory; for the restricted group of societies the correlation here falls a little short of being significant at the 5% point, but for the larger group of societies it too is significant at the 5% point. For fear of spirits, finally, one of the correlations is actually in the reverse direction from that predicted, though neither of the coefficients is large enough to give any dependable evidence of a true relationship.

Before attempting to assess the adequacy of this hypothesis we will turn to consider other hypotheses which might be able to account more adequately for the origins of fear of others.

Fear of Others as a Defense Against Sexual Anxiety

A second hypothesis which we will consider is that fear of others arises as a defense against sexual anxiety. This hypothesis has been suggested to us by Freud's analysis of paranoia as a defense against homosexual tendencies.

Paranoia is a type of psychosis which is generally characterized by a pathologically exaggerated fear of others. At an extreme the paranoid patient may view the world around him as united in a malignant conspiracy against him. In a famous interpretation of a case of paranoia Freud (1911) traced the origins of this psychosis to fears of homosexual temptation. The patient is bothered by homosexual temptations which arouse strong anxiety in him. He attempts to resolve this conflict by reacting aggressively, instead of erotically, toward the object of temptation. He is acting at this stage, Freud suggests, as though he were saying to himself, "I do not *love* him; I *hate* him." But the hate also arouses anxiety, and this new conflict he attempts to resolve by seeing the other person as the locus of aggression; here it is as if the patient were saying to himself, "*He hates* (persecutes) *me,* which will justify me in hating him." Thus the fear of others is seen as an ultimate resolution of the conflicts to which homosexual temptation gives rise.

This theoretical suggestion of Freud's would appear to be capable of being tested in its application to cross-cultural data. One would only need to add the assumption that what is said to be true of paranoia is true in lesser degree of the less extreme tendency to fear others that is found to characterize members of certain societies. This does not seem a far-fetched assumption. The extent of general fear of others that characterizes members of certain societies has a sufficient superficial resemblance to paranoia so that the term "paranoid" has sometimes been considered appropriate as a descriptive term. If there is this much similarity in behavior, there might well be a similarity of origin. We would, then, set up the hypothesis that the custom potential of fear of others in various societies will be correlated with the severity of anxiety about homosexuality. Unfortunately, the lack of good enough data on reactions to homosexuality in a sufficient number of societies seems to prevent any adequate test of this hypothesis at present.

Freud's interpretation of paranoia does, however, suggest to us the possibility of the more general hypothesis, which can be tested from our data, that fear of others arises as a defense against general sexual anxiety. This represents a considerable modification of Freud's suggestion. For homosexual, rather than heterosexual, temptation plays a definite role in the interpretation he offers for paranoia. This point is again stressed by Freud in another paper (1915) devoted to a case where the temptation appears superficially to be heterosexual. A possible reason for the special importance of homosexual impulses, though it does not seem to be suggested by Freud, is that the impulses represent a temptation toward passive homosexual submission, and gratification of this temptation may be partially obtained in symbolic form in the delusions of persecution. Thus the fear of others may play the dual function of defending the patient against realistic sexual submission and permitting some fantasy gratification. This would presumably not be so often the case if heterosexual temptation were the original locus of conflict.

We have felt that our more general hypothesis might none the less have sufficient plausibility to be worth testing with our data. This feeling proceeds from two considerations. First, homosexual temptation is itself likely to be a function of heterosexual anxiety. That is, the more a normal heterosexual gratification is hindered by fear of it, as a result of the customs of a society, the more frequent and intense is likely to be the temptation toward homosexual behavior as a substitute. Thus the severity of the inhibition of heterosexual behavior might provide an index of the likelihood that the very chain of events described by Freud, centering around homosexual conflicts, would be set into motion. Second, while heterosexual impulses might not so frequently find partial gratification in fantasies of persecution as would homosexual impulses, they might still do so in a sufficient proportion of cases so that this more general hypothesis would have on the average some degree of validity.

We have, accordingly, considered it appropriate to test the more general hypothesis that fear of other human beings plays a defensive function in relation to sexual temptation, and will hence be found to be correlated with the severity of interference with free sexual gratification. The specific prediction to be tested is that fear of other human beings will be positively correlated with socialization anxiety in the sexual system.[2]

2. Perhaps, indeed this hypothesis should be extended to the fear of spirits; this depends upon a conjecture about the extent to which sexual inhibition is likely to give rise to fantasies of sexual temptation from supernatural creatures. Such fantasies do of course occur in primitive societies

TABLE 24. Fear of Others: Relation to Socialization Anxiety in the Sexual System

> For each of three measures of fear of others the table shows the correlation coefficient (r) expressing its relationship to social-ization anxiety in the sexual system, as determined from 28 societies with confident ratings, and the probability (p) that so large a coefficient in the predicted direction could have occurred by chance in the absence of a true relationship.

	r	p
Fear of human beings	+0.37	<0.05
Fear of spirits	+0.14	—
Over-all fear of others	+0.30	<0.06

The results of a test of this hypothesis are presented in Table 24. It will be seen that the prediction that sexual anxiety will be correlated positively with fear of other human beings is con-firmed at the 5% confidence point. Fear of human spirits, also included in the table for the sake of comparison, shows a very low correlation in the same direction. The correlation with over-all fear of others is large enough to be on the borderline of the 5% criterion of significance.[3]

as well as in the religious traditions and folk tales of Western Europe. If it were supposed that this generalization of sexual temptation from human objects to supernatural objects commonly occurred, then from the hypoth-esis we are now considering a correlation between sexual anxiety and fear of spirits might also be predicted. Such a prediction receives no signif-icant confirmation from the findings reported in Table 24. This interpreta-tion of fear of spirits as a defense against sexual temptation also seems to receive no support from a detailed analysis of fear of different categories of spirit such as we will report later in this chapter.

3. It might be felt that for the hypothesis as we have phrased it a more appropriate test would be provided by ratings of socialization anxiety in connection with heterosexual play alone rather than for sexual behavior in general as a single system. When this measure is used instead, the cor-relation for fear of human beings falls to +0.13, an insignificant value; the correlation for fear of spirits is approximately the same (+0.18). These correlations are based on 27 societies.

Fear of Others as Projection of Aggression

A hypothesis quite different from those we have so far considered is also suggested by psychoanalytic theory—the hypothesis of projection of aggression. According to this hypothesis a person tends to fear others because he attributes to them his own aggressive impulses. Having thus, so to speak, created a world of Frankenstein monsters, he both fears his creations and considers his own ailments to result from their aggressive actions.

But under what conditions does the projection of aggression occur, and under what conditions will it not occur? Are there any events in the process of child training which should predispose an individual or the typical members of a society to project their aggressive motives to others and, as a consequence, fear them? Psychoanalytic theory suggests a prediction that projection of aggression will be favored by the development during socialization of a high degree of anxiety in the aggressive system.

This prediction is a more specific form of a general prediction that high anxiety about aggression will favor indirect expressions of aggression. There are of course a number of ways in which aggression may be expressed indirectly, may be diverted or disguised as a result of anxiety about its direct expression. In this section we consider *projection* from the self to other agents as one form of indirection; in the following section we will consider *displacement* from one object to another as a second form of indirection. The general account that follows is pertinent to both these forms.

Psychoanalytic theory tends to conceive of aggressive drive, like many other drives, as an energy source which a person has in some given amount and which requires a given amount of reduction by appropriate responses. If the most appropriate direct aggression against the original objects of hostility is prevented from occurring, then, this drive will motivate other and less direct aggressive responses. If the most direct aggression is prevented because of fear of its consequences, the individual will instead make some indirect aggressive response whose consequences he does not fear so much. The effect of inhibition of direct aggression will thus be not to decrease the total amount of aggression expressed but to deflect its expression to more indirect forms. Indeed, since the inhibition of direct aggression is in itself frustrating, the total amount expressed may even be increased.

Now it is not necessary to conceive of aggressive drive as literally existing in a unitary amount in a given individual and demanding reduction, in order to agree with this general line of reasoning. Even if aggressive drive is a product of internal responses to stimulation largely from outside, and therefore contingent upon the external situation, it still follows that so long as some degree of aggressive drive is present and is not reduced by direct aggression it can motivate indirect aggression. This principle has been commonly assumed in discussions of aggression outside the specific psychoanalytic tradition and in a context of general behavior theory. Dollard, Doob, Miller, Mowrer and Sears (1939, p. 40) expressed the principle as follows: ". . . *the greater the degree of inhibition specific to a more direct act of aggression, the more probable will be the occurrence of less direct acts of aggression.*" [4]

Since the form of indirect aggression we are considering in this section is aggression projected onto another person or spirit, we must now consider specifically how the mechanism of projection might operate to produce results which could be tested with our data. For this purpose it must be assumed that aggressive fantasies are satisfying or rewarding.[5] Thus a person who

4. It will be noted that this formulation is a rather guarded one; the use of the word *specific* indicates that the authors had in mind (perhaps because of awareness of the principle of generalization) the possibility that if the inhibition were not entirely specific the consequences might be rather different. To this point we will turn later in the chapter.

5. This assumption is so commonly made by psychiatrists and psychologists that to many it may seem a truism; direct evidence in favor of this

has been frustrated by someone should get some satisfaction through imagining a situation in which he meets his frustrator and gives vent to his anger by insulting him, physically attacking him or even killing him. If, however, such a person's anxiety about aggression is so strong that he cannot enjoy or even have such fantasies, the hypothesis we are proposing here would predict that he will attribute his hostile feelings to someone else, human or supernatural, and imagine that this person or spirit is committing aggressive acts. Such a fantasy of aggression performed by some other agent, although less satisfying than the more direct fantasy, nevertheless would yield considerable satisfaction and would be the kind of fantasy produced by a person who is strongly inhibited from the more direct fantasy. Such a person, then, whenever he becomes aggressive will tend to have fantasies about aggressive action by other persons or spirits. On the assumption that occasions frequently arise in any person's life when he feels aggressive, these fantasies will probably be frequent enough to have a conspicuous influence on his general perception of the world around him. That is, he will tend to see it as including a number of people or spirits who are rather dangerously aggressive.

Applying this hypothesis of the projection of aggressive fantasies to our data, we would predict that those societies whose members have strong anxiety about aggression trained into them in the course of socialization would tend to attribute aggression to others rather than admit it in themselves. The general perception of the social and supernatural world developed in such a society should be one of a world in which a number of potentially very aggressive agents reside. Hence when illness occurs in such a society, the ready explanation is that it was caused by one of these aggressors. The prediction that we can test with our data, then, is as follows: The custom potential of socialization anxiety in the aggressive system will be positively cor-

assumption was, however, lacking until Feshbach (1951) obtained direct experimental evidence in support of it.

related with the custom potential of the belief that illness is caused by some human being or spirit, and hence with our indices of fear of others.

TABLE 25. Fear of Others: Relation to Socialization Anxiety in the Aggressive System

> For each of three measures of fear of others the table shows the correlation coefficient (r) expressing its relationship to socialization anxiety in the aggressive system, as determined from 32 societies with confident ratings, and the probability (p) that so large a coefficient in the predicted direction could have occurred by chance in the absence of a true relationship.

	r	p
Fear of human beings	+0.43	<0.01
Fear of spirits	+0.13	—
Over-all fear of others	+0.58	<0.0005

A test of this prediction is presented in Table 25. It will be seen that each of the three relationships presented is in the predicted direction, and that the relationship of aggression anxiety to fear of human beings and to over-all fear of others is of considerable magnitude and highly significant. We will show later in the chapter that when the implications of this hypothesis are more fully developed, the low value of the correlation with fear of spirits is not necessarily evidence against this hypothesis in a more fully elaborated form. Apart from this difficulty with this hypothesis as we have so far developed it, we can conclude that the hypothesis of projection of aggression as a result of severe socialization seems to be strongly confirmed.

FEAR OF OTHERS AS JUSTIFICATION FOR THE
DISPLACEMENT OF AGGRESSION

As we have stated in the previous section, projection is not the only form of indirect expression of aggression. Another form of indirection is that referred to as object displacement. A person who fears to express his aggression directly against the original social objects responsible for his frustration may express his aggression instead against some other object. Since the aggressive attack may in this case be thought of as shifted in social space from one object to another, the term *displacement* has come to be used for this sort of indirection.

The general reasoning about the origins of indirect aggression, which we have outlined in the previous section of this chapter, applies to object displacement in the same way that it does to projection. The reasoning presented there would suggest that the tendency to express aggression against irrelevant objects would increase with increasing anxiety about expressing aggression against the actual sources of frustration. Our measure of socialization anxiety in the aggressive system provides us with what we can hope to be a measure of the extent to which anxiety is developed about the expression of aggression toward parents and other close relatives. The remaining question then is, do we have any sort of index of the tendency to express aggression against irrelevant objects?

The answer to this question is that we do have a possible index of this sort if it be assumed that displaced expression of aggression is generally accompanied by a belief that justifies it. We believe this is a very reasonable assumption, both in general and for the particular phenomena we are concerned with. If this assumption is made, then the tendency to attribute undesirable characteristics to others may be seen as a product of displaced aggression against them and may be taken as an index of the potential of such displaced aggression.

The notion that displaced aggression generally is accompanied by beliefs that justify it is perhaps most familiar already to students of prejudice against minority groups. Aggression against Negroes is often justified on the grounds that they are like children or like animals, against other minority groups on the grounds that they are stupid, dirty, or covetous. Dollard (1938, p. 21) gives an explicit statement of the role of the justifying belief in permitting the displaced aggression in such cases as these.

Either rivalry or traditional patterning creates a stereotyped image in the minds of current members of society of a class of individuals who may be more or less painlessly detested. These images usually denote men who are to some degree released from the moral order which binds us and who are feared because "anything" may be expected of them; because they do not accept our mores, they are also regarded as inhuman beings to whom "anything" may be done. It is an effect of this stereotyping to produce the categorical treatment which is given those against whom prejudice is felt; individual discriminations tend to drop out and the differential treatment accorded to ingroupers is omitted. Within our own group we judge people according to their deserts and not according to standard classifications, but not so with the group against whom prejudiced stereotypes exist.

In the material we are considering here, we are concerned with sorcerers and spirits as possible objects of displaced aggression. In both cases the evidence from various ethnographic reports suggests that one function of the belief that this kind of agent causes sickness is to justify aggression against that kind of agent. Such evidence is perhaps clearest for the belief in sorcery.

Beatrice Whiting reports that capital punishment was not permitted by the Paiute except for the one offense of sorcery. The maximally aggressive act against a person, in other words that of killing him, was permitted only if the other members of the community agreed that the person was a sorcerer. The killing of a supposed sorcerer, however, was rare in comparison with the less violent aggressive behavior which was, and still is, repeatedly directed against such persons. "Accusations of sorcery are still rife and gossip is still the main pastime among the Paiute. This seems to be one of the best ways for venting aggression, part of which is probably displaced from the family" (Beatrice Whiting, 1950, p. 76). Kluckhohn, in his interpretation of sorcery among the Navaho, makes even more explicit the view that one important function of the belief in sorcery is to justify feeling or acting aggressive toward those individuals who are accused of being sorcerers. In this society, too, supposed sorcerers have on occasion been killed. And again, belief in sorcery repeatedly justifies less violent aggression. Kluckhohn writes,

> The witch [i.e., in our terms, sorcerer] is the person whom the ideal patterns of the culture say it is not only proper but necessary to hate. Instead of saying all the bitter things one has felt against one's stingy and repressive father-in-law (which would threaten one's own economic security as well as bring down upon one's head unpleasant social disapproval), one can obtain some relief by venting one's spleen against a totally unrelated witch in the community. This displaced aggression does not expose one to punishment so long as one is discreet in the choice of the intimates to whom one talks. And if one rages against a witch who isn't even in the locality but lives over the mountain a safe hundred miles away one is perfectly assured against reprisals (1944, p. 55).

But aggression against spirits also may be justified by attributing evil characteristics to them. The Kwoma shake their fists and spit at the *Marsalai* spirits, but only after they first blame them for causing a rainstorm or a high wind. And in the days when belief in the Devil was more vigorous in our society than it is now, a feeling of the religious man that he was waging an aggressive spiritual warfare against the Devil could apparently be a source of genuine gratification.

The belief that spirits or sorcerers cause illness thus can be satisfying, according to the present hypothesis, because it justifies and permits the occurrence of displaced aggression.[6] Pre-

6. A belief in sorcery could in some instances be used to justify direct aggression. (Cf. Kluckhohn, 1944, pp. 56–57.) If A is frustrated by B, he may accuse B of sorcery and use this accusation to justify direct retaliation; indeed the accusation itself is a direct aggressive act. If the motive

sumably, therefore, the greater the need for displaced aggression, the more likely will it be that such justifications will occur.

From this reasoning we arrive at exactly the same predictions for our data to which the previous hypothesis, that of projection, led. A positive relation between fear of others and socialization anxiety in the aggressive system would be predicted equally from the hypothesis of displacement or the hypothesis of projection. The two hypotheses therefore share in the confirmation we reported in the previous section. We are unable to make predictions for our data which will differentiate the two hypotheses. It seems to us most probable that both of the two mechanisms may indeed be operating jointly.[7]

---

for the accusation is so obvious, however, and not shared by other members of the community, A is not likely to be able to get his accusation accepted by others. We would suspect that on the whole displaced aggression plays a more important part.

7. We must recognize the possibility of still a third explanation for the close connection between aggression anxiety and fear of others. This is the possibility that the custom potential of belief in sorcery is strongly influenced by the custom potential of the practice of sorcery, and that the latter is directly influenced by aggression anxiety. There is some reason to doubt each of the two propositions upon which this interpretation rests. That the practice of sorcery influences the belief in some instances is no doubt true. But in some societies where the belief in sorcery has a high potential, the ethnographer has been unable to find convincing evidence that the practice is present at all; in any event, if fewness of assumptions is an advantage, it is pertinent that in general, as Kluckhohn (1944, p. 48) remarks of the Navaho, "most of the data evidence belief in witchcraft rather than practice of witchcraft." That the custom potential of the practice of sorcery would be positively related to aggression anxiety is also doubtful. The practice of sorcery is less directly aggressive than murder, but since the conscious intent is the same as in murder, it is very much more directly aggressive than the other kinds of indirect aggression we have been considering. It is interesting to note that Kluckhohn (1944, pp. 47–48) suggests that sorcerers among the Navaho are likely to be individuals with unusually strong drive for aggression—not individuals with unusually strong anxiety about aggression. Finally, a third disadvantage of this interpretation is that it is confined to fear of human beings alone and would have to be accompanied by some independent explanation of fear of spirits.

RELATIVE MERIT OF VARIOUS HYPOTHESES

We have discussed four hypotheses which might account for the occurrence of the belief that agents such as spirits and sorcerers have the power to cause illness. In this section we will consider in comparative fashion the evidence relevant to these several hypotheses.

In order to make this comparison of the several hypotheses more graphic, we present in Table 26 some of the relationships already presented in previous tables in this chapter along with the relationship between our measures of fear of others and socialization anxiety in the systems of behavior which have not yet been separately considered.

TABLE 26. Fear of Others: Relationship to All Measures of Socialization Anxiety

The table shows, for socialization anxiety in each system of behavior and in the five systems averaged, the number of societies available and the correlation coefficient expressing the relationship between the anxiety and each of three measures of fear of others. Coefficients marked with an asterisk are significant at the 5% point; coefficients marked with a double asterisk are significant at the 1% point.

| | | MEASURE OF FEAR OF OTHERS | | |
System of behavior	Number of societies	Fear of human beings	Fear of spirits	Over-all fear of others
Oral	39	+0.29*	+0.04	+0.27*
Anal	20	+0.18	−0.02	+0.18
Sexual	28	+0.37*	+0.14	+0.30
Dependence	30	−0.01	−0.12	−0.06
Aggression	32	+0.43**	+0.13	+0.58**
Average (all judgments confident)	10	+0.50	−0.15	+0.60*
Average (including judgments of intermediate confidence)	47	+0.26*	+0.03	+0.25*

It will be seen from Table 26 that the strongest support from our data seems to come for the two hypotheses which derive the fear of others from aggression anxiety—the hypotheses of projection and displacement. Two of the three correlations for aggression anxiety are both of considerable magnitude and of greater statistical significance than any of the other correlations presented in the table.

There is also support for the hypothesis of generalization of fear of parents. In addition to the correlations we have presented before, based on average socialization anxiety in all five systems, we also see now explicitly that there is some evidence of a consistent tendency for socialization anxiety in each separate system to be positively correlated with fear of others. The only system that provides a complete exception is that of dependence, where the correlations are all negative though very low.

There is also some significant confirmation of the hypothesis of defense against sexual anxiety, and also some significant evidence of a positive correlation of fear of others with oral socialization anxiety—a correlation that is predicted only by the generalization hypothesis among the several hypotheses we have considered.

While we have used socialization anxiety as the measure of child training most clearly pertinent to these hypotheses, there is another measure of child training which may usefully be considered in a comparative evaluation of these several hypotheses. In Chapter 8 (pp. 166–171) we found some reason to believe that our scale of initial satisfaction in each system of behavior, if inverted in direction, would provide a measure of initial anxiety acquired before the period of major socialization. This measure is for most systems highly correlated with the measure of socialization anxiety (see above, pp. 106–110). But to the extent that it is independent, results obtained with it might provide a useful check on results obtained with socialization anxiety. The socialization anxiety, being the later learned, might be more likely to be continuous into adult life. But the hypotheses we have used in predicting fear of others from socialization anxiety should apply also to initial anxiety to the extent that it too continues into adult life. Accordingly, we present in Table 27 results directly comparable to those summarized in Table 26 except that they are based on initial anxiety instead of socialization anxiety.

TABLE 27. Fear of Others: Relationship to All Measures of Initial Anxiety

The table shows, for initial anxiety in each system of behavior and in the five systems averaged, the number of societies available and the correlation coefficient expressing the relationship between the anxiety and each of three measures of fear of others. Coefficients marked with an asterisk are significant at the 5% point; coefficients marked with a double asterisk are significant at the 1% point.

| | | MEASURE OF FEAR OF OTHERS | | |
System of behavior	Number of societies	Fear of human beings	Fear of spirits	Over-all fear of others
Oral	51	+0.04	+0.06	+0.09
Anal	22	+0.18	+0.15	+0.34
Sexual	31	+0.0004	+0.20	+0.17
Dependence	38	−0.15	+0.27	+0.10
Aggression	31	+0.54**	−0.02	+0.51**
Average (all judgments confident)	15	+0.39	+0.19	+0.68**
Average (including judgments of intermediate confidence)	47	+0.11	+0.18	+0.25*

The outcome of this supplementary evidence is to leave unchanged the substantial evidence for the role played by aggression anxiety, to leave the evidence for the generalization hypothesis about as strong as before, but to cast doubt on the strength of the specific evidence for a positive relationship between fear of others and either sexual or oral anxiety. We are inclined, therefore, to feel that the significant positive correlations obtained for socialization anxiety in the sexual and oral systems should be tentatively interpreted as special instances of the generalization hypothesis, rather than as distinctive evidence of a special role of these systems of behavior in the development of fear of others. We would conclude, however, that, aggression anxiety does appear to have a special importance and that the evidence most strongly supports the two hypotheses of projection and displacement of aggression.[8]

The difficulty with these two most satisfactory hypotheses— so far as we have till now developed their implications—is that they seem to be inconsistent with the finding of little relationship between aggression anxiety and the fear of spirits. In this respect they have no advantage over the hypothesis of generalization of fear. It is now time to tackle this problem directly.

CONFLICT THEORY AND THE ORIGINS OF FEAR OF OTHERS

The two hypotheses which we have thus far found most satisfactory—the hypothesis of projection of aggression and the hypothesis of displacement of aggression—have a very important point in common. They both ascribe to the beliefs which occasion fear of others an important role in allowing the individual to gratify his aggressive needs, and since there is anxiety about these aggressive needs they both ascribe to these beliefs an important role in the resolution of conflict. Now modern psychology has seen a considerable effort toward the systematic formulation of principles about conflict (see, for example, Lewin, 1935; Miller, 1944 and 1948; Brown and Farber, 1951). From some of these efforts it is possible to draw out suggestions which can contribute to understanding the origins of fear of

8. If we thus separate out the aggressive system as a special case, it becomes pertinent to ask whether average anxiety in the other four systems, with aggression excluded, is still significantly related to fear of others. Socialization anxiety does still yield a significant relationship with overall fear of others ($r = +0.52$) for the restricted group of 10 societies with all judgments confident; so does initial anxiety ($r = +0.60$) for a restricted group of 16 societies with all judgments confident. The other correlations that are significant when aggression is included in the average are no longer statistically significant.

others. The pertinent aspects of conflict theory unfortunately depend upon quantitative assumptions which make their application to a problem like this depend upon a number of ad hoc assumptions. Our interpretations hence must have a tentative and speculative character of a sort which we believe is not shared by the rest of the work reported in this volume. But we see no reason why this should discourage us from making interpretations which though tentative in character may play a useful part in a larger body of developing knowledge about psychological conflict.

The central point, suggested particularly by Miller's treatment of displacement in terms of conflict theory (1948), is this: Where indirect expression of a drive such as aggression occurs, because direct expression is prevented by incompatible habits of anxiety, the habit potential of this indirect expression will not be a simple function either of the strength of the positive habit of aggression or the strength of the inhibiting (negative) habit of anxiety, but may be some complicated function of both, and of the "degree of indirectness" of the behavior. This degree of indirectness has been dealt with in conflict theory primarily in terms of degree of similarity to elements in the original situation in which the positive and negative habits were learned. The possibility of using suggestions from conflict theory depends upon whether we do have a dependable basis for judging differences in degree of similarity to the original situation among the various specific forms that fear of others takes.

This question of similarity must be considered separately for the two hypotheses we propose to explore further. First we will consider the hypothesis of displacement of aggression. Here the conflict is assumed to be concerned with the expression of aggression by the person himself *toward* the agent named as responsible for illness. The habit of being aggressive would appear to arise primarily in the context of the person's normal daily life, especially in the formative years of childhood, so that the most direct objects would in general be his parents and other close relatives who on the whole would seem to be the major source of frustration. In the child we would assume that the parents or other major socializers are of necessity the principal source of frustration. In adulthood much the same would appear to be rather generally true of the people with whom an individual lives in intimate contact; that they are thus necessarily the principal source of frustration. This assumption is not related to any pessimistic view of life, for the same persons are also the principal source of gratification, and our argument does not depend upon any kind of judgment about the balance between frustration and gratification. The habit of anxiety about being aggressive seems likely also to be determined primarily by learning with these same persons: in childhood as a result of socialization by the parents, and in adulthood by the continuing inhibitory pressures from immediate relatives and other intimate associates.

The question of similarity for the displacement hypothesis, then, has to do with the degree of similarity between these close relatives and the persons or spirits specified in a belief about the responsibility for illness. The differences among the various living human beings who might be specified as agents should represent differences in similarity here; a belief that one's relatives are the potential sorcerers to be feared should represent greater similarity to the relatives who are perceived as frustrators than a belief that only nonrelatives are to be feared. Unfortunately our data have not been analyzed in this way, and we are not able to make use of any distinctions among living human agents. In the case of spirits there are two categories in our analysis that seem to be clearly different in degree of similarity to the patient's relatives. Spirits of the dead, or ghosts, should be much more similar to a person's relatives than should animal spirits. For the displacement hypothesis, then, the only information we have on differing degrees of similarity to the original situation will be provided by differences between the custom potential of belief in ghosts [9] and in animal spirits as the agents responsible for illness.

9. For convenience we will hereafter use the term "ghosts" to mean spirits of dead persons.

In the hypothesis of projection of aggression the role of the agent specified in the belief is quite different. He is the aggressor in a person's fantasy, and the person is supposed to gratify his aggressive needs by having this fantasy. The fantasy is presumed to be a symbolic expression of behavior which the person himself is tempted to carry out overtly. The dimension of similarity in this case has to do with the effect of the agent upon the extent to which the fantasy resembles aggressive acts of the person himself. Again, though for different reasons, it seems reasonable to suppose that the difference between ghosts and animal spirits will be relevant. It seems likely that on the whole a fantasy about aggression committed by a ghost will more closely resemble one's own aggression, because of the greater similarity of the agent to oneself, than will a fantasy about aggression committed by an animal spirit. And again, no distinctions can be made among the living human agents as we have analyzed them.[10]

Having established that ghosts and animal spirits can provide us with two distinguishable points along a dimension of similarity, we are now ready to consider what ideas may be adapted from conflict theory to apply to the present problem. We present in Figure 1 a schematic, hypothetical diagram around which we will center our account, and we will give our account first in terms of the displacement hypothesis.

The base line of Figure 1 represents a dimension of dissimilar-

10. It might be argued that human agents should, for either hypothesis, have a closer similarity to the original situation than should either category of spirits. In our opinion the nature of the beliefs involved is too variable to justify this assumption, and indeed it is probable that ghosts ordinarily represent greater similarity to the original situation, with respect to both these hypotheses. People feared as sorcerers are sometimes foreigners, and often are regarded as set apart from the rest of the society. Illustrative of this conception is the frequent tendency to associate sorcerers with animals and to believe them to assume animal form. Ghosts, on the other hand, often are spirits of immediate ancestors—that is, in a sense, close relatives who are ordinary members of the society but are now living in the other world.

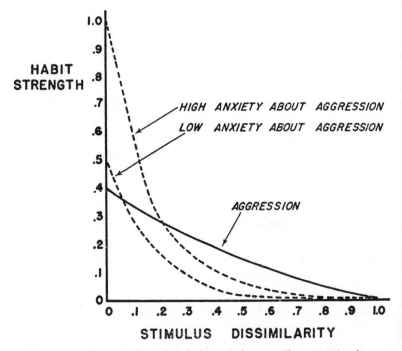

FIGURE 1. Theoretical model (adapted from Miller, 1948), showing different rates of generalization decrement for aggression and for high and low anxiety about aggression. The habit strength of each of these three habits is plotted separately, as a function of dissimilarity to the original stimulus.

ity to the original object of aggression, i.e., the parents and other relatives against whom, as the prime sources of frustration, the person first learns to be aggressive. At the extreme left of the base line, represented by 0, would be the original object of aggression. At the extreme right, represented by 1, would be objects completely dissimilar to the original object of aggression. Between these two extremes are a series of points which represent various cultural categories of potential objects of displaced aggression; these points may be thought of as forming a scale of degree of dissimilarity. For example, other relatives who stand in a position to the person somewhat similar to that of the original objects of aggression, but who are not actually major sources of frustration for him, might fall somewhere between 0 and .1. Near .2 might fall nonrelatives who are ordinary members of the local community, and so on with increasing degrees of dissimilarity. We are in a position, as we have said, to deal systematically only with the relative position of two such points, which we will specify after explaining the vertical dimension in the figure.

The vertical dimension represents the habit "strength" [11] of the two response tendencies which will be considered—the tendency to be aggressive toward a particular object, and the tendency to be anxious about such aggression and hence avoid it. The solid line represents the first of these tendencies as a function of degree of dissimilarity from the original object. The broken lines represent, for the two different conditions which we will describe, the habit strength of the tendency to be anxious about aggression toward an object as a function of the dissimilarity between that object and the original object of aggression. The condition represented by the lower of the broken lines is one of fairly low habit strength of the tendency to be anxious

11. We use here for the first time the term habit *strength,* as distinct from habit *potential.* We did not introduce this term in Chapter 2, because the distinction is relevant only at this one point. Habit strength is the strength of a behavior tendency as influenced only by the effects of previous learning which is directly relevant (as involving the same or similar stimuli and responses). Habit potential is the strength of a behavior tendency as influenced both by its habit strength and by other factors such as the momentary strength of relevant drives. Here the distinction becomes important because we will want to consider separately the effects of directly relevant learning and the effects of drive strength. Elsewhere we have used the single term *potential* regardless of the particular route of influence we were considering. To avoid introduction of still another technical term which would be used only in this one place (*custom strength* as distinguished from *custom potential*) the theoretical discussion here is phrased in terms of habit rather than custom. The distinction we are making here is taken from Hull's *Principles of Behavior* (1943), though as noted in Chapter 2 we have used the term *habit potential* instead of his term *reaction potential.*

about aggression. The condition represented by the upper of the broken lines is one of fairly high habit strength of the tendency to be anxious about aggression. The assumptions which are involved in representing these tendencies the way we have in this figure are as follows:

1. We assume that the habit strength of the tendency to be aggressive toward other social objects, arising by generalization from the tendency to be aggressive toward the originally frustrating objects, falls off with increasing dissimilarity to those original objects. This assumption is taken directly from the principle of generalization. In referring earlier in this chapter (p. 266) to the principle of generalization as formulated by Hull, we pointed out that it postulates two factors as influencing the strength of a generalized habit tendency. One of these factors, the strength of the original tendency, we have already used in this chapter and will use again shortly. The other factor, that of degree of similarity to the original stimulus, is the basis of the present assumption.

2. We assume that the habit strength of the tendency to be anxious about aggression toward other social objects, arising largely by generalization from the same tendency as learned in connection with aggression toward the originally frustrating objects, also falls off with increasing dissimilarity to those original objects. This assumption has the same origin as the preceding one.

3. We assume that the habit strength of the positive tendency to be aggressive falls off less rapidly than does the habit strength of the negative tendency to be anxious about aggression. This assumption does not come directly from anything which we regard as a useful general principle of behavior, and we would follow Miller (1948, pp. 172–173) in supposing that this assumption does not always hold true. Direct conjecture about whether it is likely to hold true for the particular phenomena we are dealing with would be so highly speculative that we prefer to offer as justification for this assumption only the fact that predictions made indirectly with its help, in the analysis

of individual response to conflict, have thus far on the whole been confirmed.[12]

4. We assume, in accordance with Hull's formulation of the principle of generalization, that variations in the habit strength of the original tendency (the tendency to be anxious, in the case of Figure 1) will produce more or less proportional variations in the strength of all the generalized tendencies, and hence a shift of the entire curve up or down.

5. Because we have no adequate basis for assuming the curves represented in Figure 1 to have any exact shape, we are representing them in the form of negative growth curves. The predictions we will make on the basis of the assumptions we are using would hold true, however, for any of a great variety of exact shapes of the curves. Miller has made this point in some detail in his theoretical treatment of displacement (1948) from which we have adapted our first four assumptions.

6. We assume that in any society the customary habit strength of anxiety about aggression toward the original objects of aggression will be somewhat greater than the habit strength of the aggression toward them. We base this assumption on the supposition that the main function of inhibitory training with respect to aggression is to prevent the overt aggression within the nuclear social group which would be fatal to the integrity of a society, and that in all successful societies this function

12. Speculation about this assumption can of course become very profitable when data are available to check on the outcome. We will cite one example. Miller suggests that one factor perhaps responsible for a usually greater steepness of the negative gradient in comparison with the positive is the frequently greater dependence of the negative tendency upon the presence of certain external cues. In the case of aggression anxiety it would appear that dependence upon external cues should be much greater in societies where this anxiety is based primarily upon fear of external punishment than in societies where it is based primarily upon fear of guilt. Hence displacement or projection (to anticipate our subsequent argument) should occur much more in the former group of societies than in the latter. We have not at present the information needed for testing this prediction.

is by and large successfully served.[13] What is represented in Figure 1 is a general tendency to be aggressive toward various social objects, in covert as well as overt ways, and this consideration of social function does not apply so strongly to covert aggression against the original object; but it has still seemed reasonable to represent, even for this average aggressive tendency toward the original objects, the anxiety as on the whole higher than the positive tendency, even for societies with relatively low anxiety about aggression.

For the original objects of aggression, then, and for objects only slightly dissimilar to them, the habit strength of anxiety is higher than the habit strength of the positive response of aggression. The result should be a general inhibition of aggression toward those objects. For objects of increasing dissimilarity to the original ones, however, the habit strength of the positive response of aggression becomes higher than that of the anxiety. The extent of the difference between these two habit strengths varies for different points along the base line. Following Hull and Miller, we assume that the net or effective habit strength of the positive response for any given point is given by the magnitude of this difference.[14] A diagrammatic representation of the curves that result under the two conditions of high anxiety and low anxiety is given in Figure 2. This figure is derived from Figure 1 by subtracting, for each point along the dimension of dissimilarity, the habit strength of anxiety from the habit strength of the positive response.

At this point we must introduce a final assumption not used by Miller in his analysis of displacement, which seems to be essential for explaining certain aspects of our results. This new assumption is that the effective habit potential of these generalized tendencies will be directly influenced not only by their

13. Cf. Dollard, Doob, Miller, Mowrer and Sears (1939, pp. 76–90).

14. A probability model involving a somewhat different method of calculating net effects of conflicting habits is described by Bush and Whiting (1952). The general conclusions from this model are the same as those proposed here.

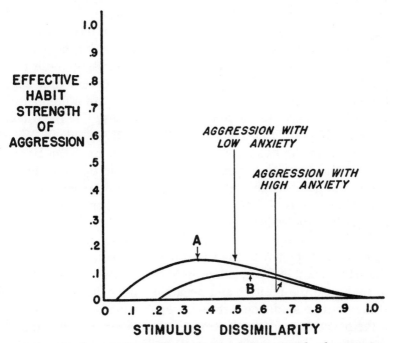

FIGURE 2. Theoretical model of effective habit strength of aggression, with high and low anxiety about aggression. (This figure is obtained by subtracting the appropriate anxiety curve of Figure 1 from the aggression curve of Figure 1.)

effective habit strength derived from relevant learning, but also by the amount of relevant drive present, with the effective habit strength and the drive interacting in a multiplicative fashion (as postulated by Hull, 1943).[15] But what will be the effect of a heightened anxiety gradient upon the strength of relevant drives? We suggest that the heightened anxiety gradient will bring about an increase in the strength of relevant drives for two reasons to which we have briefly alluded earlier in this chapter:

1. The greater the number of aggressive responses the individual is able to make (because for those points the positive

15. For an explanation of the terminology used here, see footnote 11 above.

tendency is greater than the negative tendency), the more will aggressive drive be reduced by making other responses than the two we are considering, and the lower will be the general level of aggressive drive available for motivating these two particular responses. It will be seen from Figure 1 that with the lower of the two anxiety gradients, there are a number of possible responses to the left of 0.2 on the base line for which the positive gradient is higher than the negative gradient. With the higher of the two anxiety gradients, there are none. Hence the general level of aggressive drive available to motivate responses at points to the right of 0.2 should be somewhat higher under conditions of high aggression anxiety than under conditions of low aggression anxiety.

2. We assume that the individual continues in any case to come into contact with the social objects which are at or near the extreme left of the base line, or to think about them, and that in such case the positive and negative tendencies are aroused. If the positive tendency is stronger, aggression is expressed. But if the negative tendency is stronger, aggression is inhibited and the individual remains in a state of conflict since he cannot altogether escape from the situation. This state of conflict, we assume, is itself drive-producing, and the drive it produces is one which will among other things summate with other aggressive drive to motivate a response of aggression. Such an assumption has been used by Whiting and his associates in an interpretation of aggressive responses of children in doll play (cf. Hollenberg and Sperry, 1951). It has also been proposed by Brown and Farber (1951) in a more general theoretical treatment of conflict and emotion, and Lowell (1952) has obtained experimental evidence to support it. Since many more points along the base line will give rise to conflict, and to conflict-produced drive, with a high anxiety gradient than with a low anxiety gradient, these considerations would also lead to the prediction that the drive available to motivate aggressive responses at points to the right of 0.2 would be stronger with a high anxiety gradient than with a low anxiety gradient.

For purposes of exposition we must assume some arbitrary values for the drive strength which arises in this way under varying conditions of anxiety. We have chosen for convenience of graphic representation the value of 3 for drive strength under the condition of low anxiety, and the value of 6 for drive strength under the condition of high anxiety. That the value should be greater for high anxiety than for low follows, of course, from the assumptions we have just stated. The precise values we choose are arbitrary, but substantially the same conclusions would follow with quite a variation in the precise values.

Following Hull's postulate that effective habit potential is a multiplicative function of effective habit strength and drive strength, we obtain the theoretical model represented in Figure 3. The curves in this figure were obtained simply by multiplying the low anxiety curve of Figure 2 by a factor of 3, and the high anxiety curve by a factor of 6. This figure, when compared with Figure 2, illustrates the implications of combining Miller's interpretation of displacement with our hypothesis about drive factors resulting from conflict. We will return later to some of the general implications, but are now ready to consider directly its implications for our specific problem here—that arising from the comparison of fear of human spirits and of animal spirits.

We have already indicated that ghosts clearly must fall to the left of animal spirits along the base line of our graphs, as being less dissimilar to the original objects of aggression. In order to apply our theoretical reasoning, it is now necessary to assign ghosts and animal spirits to more definite locations, and at the present stage of our knowledge this assignment must be largely arbitrary and largely *ex post facto*. We will suppose that ghosts fall approximately at the point of maximum habit potential for the low anxiety curve (at about 0.36, as marked by the letter A in Figure 3), and that animal spirits fall approximately at the point of maximum habit potential for the high anxiety curve (at about 0.57, as marked by the letter B in Figure 3). The inferences we will draw would hold true despite consider-

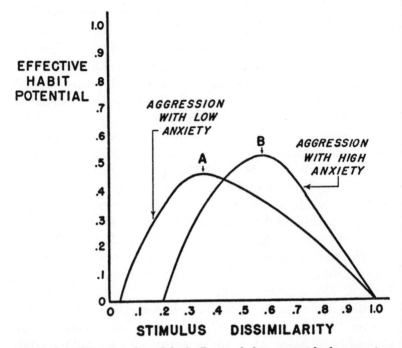

FIGURE 3. Theoretical model of effective habit potential of aggression, with high and low anxiety about aggression. (This figure is obtained by multiplying each curve of Figure 2 by a drive factor, as explained in the text.)

able departure from these locations, but not for all possible locations.

From these assumptions there follow two major implications which are consistent with our data:

1. DIFFERENT SLOPES FOR HIGH ANXIETY AND LOW ANXIETY. If points A and B alone in Figure 3 are considered, it will be seen that from A to B the habit potential decreases for the low anxiety group, whereas for the high anxiety group it increases. For some considerable range of points near A and near B the same thing will be true. For a somewhat wider range of points it will remain true that the slopes differ in the same direction, even though not so radically different; that is, a

straight line connecting the two points on the low anxiety curve might be approximately horizontal, while that for the high anxiety curve would rise, or else the latter might be horizontal and the former falling. These theoretical observations may be put into a single generalized statement as follows: Our theoretical model predicts for a considerable range of exact locations of ghosts and animal spirits on the generalization continuum that between these two points the curve for the high anxiety group will have a more positive slope than the curve for the low anxiety group.

In Figure 4 we present the empirical findings which cor-

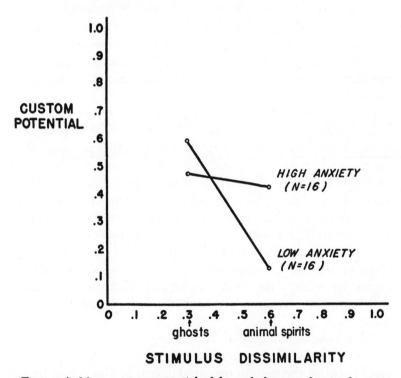

FIGURE 4. Mean custom potential of fear of ghosts and animal spirits, for societies with high and with low anxiety about aggression. (For each group of societies the two empirical points are connected by a straight line to facilitate comparison with the theoretical curves of Figure 3.)

respond to this prediction. This figure differs from the earlier ones in that the vertical axis no longer represents a hypothetical dimension but represents now our actual ratings of custom potential of fear of ghosts or of animal spirits. The horizontal dimension is still a hypothetical one, and we have placed ghosts and animal spirits at arbitrary points on it which correspond to points A and B in Figure 3. There are 32 societies for which confident ratings are available on socialization anxiety for aggression. We divided these societies into two groups of equal numbers, according to the potential of this anxiety. There are 16 societies with anxiety ratings of 13 or less; these we will term the *low anxiety* group. There are 16 societies with ratings of 14 or higher, which we will call the *high anxiety* group. In Figure 4 we present separately, for each of these two groups, the mean custom potential of fear of ghosts and of animal spirits as the agents of illness, with a straight line connecting the two points for each group.

It will be seen that the two lines presented in Figure 4 do indeed differ in slope in the stated direction. For the low anxiety group, animal spirits have a much lower custom potential than do ghosts. For the high anxiety group, the custom potential of animal spirits and of ghosts is about equal. For the sake of simplicity we have dealt here only with two groups of societies, those above and below the median in aggression anxiety. If we make the high anxiety group more extreme by selecting only the upper quarter instead of the upper half of our societies, the slope of the line actually rises; for these societies of highest aggression anxiety the mean custom potential of fear of ghosts is 3.9 and the corresponding value for fear of animal spirits is 5.7.

To test the significance of this finding, the appropriate datum with which to work appears to be the difference for a given society between the custom potential of fear of ghosts and fear of animal spirits. For each of the two groups of societies—high anxiety and low anxiety—we may determine the mean value of this difference; this mean corresponds to the slope of the line in

Figure 4 for each of the two groups. The significance of the difference between the two groups in this mean may then be tested by the t technique. The value of t is 1.71, which is significant only at the 10% level. If for a test of significance more extreme groups are chosen—the upper and lower quarter in anxiety instead of the upper and lower half—the value of t rises to 2.34, which is significant at the 5% level. The t technique neglects the exact values of the anxiety variable, and it may be more appropriate to calculate the correlation of aggression anxiety with the difference between the custom potential of fear of ghosts and of animal spirits. The value of the correlation coefficient obtained in this way is -0.41, which is significant at the 2% level. We may conclude that there is very clear evidence that the custom potential of fear of animal spirits, in comparison with ghosts, tends to increase with increasing anxiety about being aggressive.

2. HIGH ANXIETY AS INCREASING THE POTENTIAL OF EXTREMELY DISPLACED RESPONSES. The theoretical model we have presented predicts that the habit potential of extremely displaced responses will be greater with high anxiety than with low anxiety. In Figure 3, for example, it will be seen that for the particular conditions represented there, high anxiety leads to a greater potential than does low anxiety for every point on the base line beyond 0.44, where the two curves cross. This represents a major difference between Miller's analysis of displacement and ours, as a result of our including consideration of drive strength. Miller's model predicts that for every point along the base line the effective habit strength of the aggressive response will be greater with low anxiety than with high anxiety (as shown in Figure 2 by the fact that the one curve remains always higher than the other). Our model predicts that this relationship may be reversed with a sufficient degree of displacement (as shown in Figure 3 by the fact that the two curves cross).

Our empirical data shown in Figure 4 are consistent in this respect also with the theoretical model we have presented. The custom potential of fear of animal spirits is markedly higher in the high anxiety group than in the low anxiety group. This difference is significant at the 2% level, according to the t test (t = 2.68). Since the distributions here are highly skewed, a chi-square test may be more appropriate; when this test is done by dichotomizing the total sample at the median, the value of chi-square (3.12) is significant only at the 8% level.

This second outcome of our theoretical model is even more strikingly confirmed by the findings we have reported earlier in this chapter about the relation of fear of sorcerers to aggression anxiety. We found highly significant evidence that the custom potential of fear of sorcerers is positively correlated with aggression anxiety. Now if we are to predict custom potential directly from the height of the curve for effective habit strength or habit potential, as shown in Figures 2 and 3 respectively, such a result is compatible only with the model shown in Figure 3 and not with the model shown in Figure 2. For when habit strengths only are considered, as in Figure 2, the effective habit strength is at all points greater with low anxiety than with high anxiety, so that custom potential of the fear of any agent should be negatively related to aggression anxiety. It is only when drive is also taken into account, as in Figure 3, that effective habit potential for high anxiety rises above that for low anxiety for agents sufficiently dissimilar to the original objects of aggression; under these conditions, then, the custom potential of the fear of such an agent should be positively related to aggression anxiety, as we found to be true for fear of sorcerers.

There are difficulties which prevent this from being an altogether conclusive argument for the necessity of incorporating a drive factor into conflict theory. Our argument depends upon taking our measure of custom potential of fear of a given agent as an absolute function of the effective habit potential of aggression toward that agent. It could, on the other hand, be interpreted as reflecting rather its relative strength in relation to the strength of competing tendencies to be aggressive toward other agents. With such an interpretation it might be possible to predict essentially our findings from Miller's analysis without including the drive factor. We feel that this is a less economical and less plausible interpretation, but it is a possible one in the present state of knowledge. A final resolution of the issue could only be attained by research in which better control of the meaning of variables is attained than has been possible in the present study.

Our interpretation of our findings by conflict theory has thus far been expressed in terms of the mechanism of displacement; as we have already indicated, the same conclusions could be reached by an argument referring instead to the mechanism of projection. We have chosen to use displacement in presenting our reasoning in detail, because the assumptions which have been used before (by Miller) have been used in a discussion of displacement, so that a part of the argument is already familiar to readers of his article.

The application of these assumptions to the mechanism of projection is more novel, and for this reason we will summarize it here, even though briefly. The base line of Figure 1 still represents a dimension of dissimilarity, but it is now dissimilarity to the person himself. The extreme left of the base line represents the self as the agent of aggression. The other points represent other persons or spirits as the agents imagined in the fantasies of the self as performing aggressive acts. It is assumed that the positive tendency to have such aggressive fantasies decreases with greater dissimilarity of the agent to the self. It is also assumed that the tendency to be anxious about such fantasies (and hence to avoid having them) decreases with greater dissimilarity of the agent to the self, and that this negative gradient is steeper than the positive gradient. It is assumed that the effective habit strength of the tendency to have aggressive fantasies of the kind represented by any particular point along the base line of our graphs is a summative effect of the height of the two gradients at that point; the outcome of these assumptions is represented by Figure 2, just as it was for the displacement mechanism. Finally, drive remaining through inhibition or resulting from conflict (where the negative gradient is higher than the positive gradient) is assumed to have a multiplicative interaction with this effective habit strength, to produce the effective habit potential of the tendency to have aggressive fantasies involving any particular kind of agent. Figure 3 represents the outcome of this added assumption, for projection as well as for displacement.

From this reasoning, then, there follow the same conclusions that we arrived at in applying conflict theory to the displacement hypothesis. As in previous sections of this chapter, we are unable to make differential predictions from the two hypotheses of projection and displacement of aggression. It may well be that both mechanisms are involved in producing the consistent relationships we find in our data.

SUMMARY AND DISCUSSION

In the preceding section we have considered the implications of conflict theory for the hypotheses that fear of others grows out of displacement or projection of aggression. Conflict theory as we present it makes use of Miller's analysis of displacement, phrasing that portion of the analysis in terms of habit strength. By adding consideration of the role played by drive strength, as influenced by the inhibition of more direct responses and by the presence of conflict, we arrive at two somewhat distinctive predictions. One is that high aggression anxiety, in comparison with low aggression anxiety, will make for increasing custom potential of fear of animal spirits relative to fear of ghosts. The other is that for fear of animal spirits, as the response which is further displaced (or projected), the custom potential may be higher under high anxiety than under low anxiety. The data show a significant agreement with both of these predictions. Because *ex post facto* assumptions are to some extent involved in making these predictions, and because of difficulties in being certain of the exact theoretical meaning to be assigned to our variables, these findings should not be taken as very conclusive. However, their general tendency is in our opinion to offer some substantial evidence for the validity of the conflict theory we have presented.

This support for the hypotheses of displacement and projection, as modified in the light of conflict theory, has implications for the outcome of previous sections of this chapter. We see now that the finding of a low correlation between aggression anxiety and fear of spirits in general is not negative evidence against the projection and displacement hypotheses. Conflict theory suggests that aggression anxiety might well be related differently to the potential of indirect aggressive responses which lie at different points along the dimension of similarity to the original locus of aggression and aggression anxiety. The low correlation of aggression anxiety with fear of spirits in general is an outcome of differing correlations between aggression anxiety and fear of various specific kinds of spirits. Aggression anxiety tends to be correlated positively with fear of animal spirits and negatively with fear of ghosts (this general tendency may be noticed by inspection of Figure 4, though the skewed distribution of these specific measures leads us to feel that a correlation coefficient might not be a suitable general measure of the tendency).

It also follows that predictions from the projection and displacement hypotheses made without consideration of conflict theory—predictions which we ventured in earlier sections of this chapter and which are paralleled in the interpretative use of these hypotheses by other writers—are not very adequate predictions. The marked confirmation obtained for the prediction that fear of sorcerers would be positively correlated with aggression anxiety suggests, in the light of conflict theory, that the position of sorcerers along the similarity dimension is for most societies closer to that of animal spirits than to that of ghosts, for the outcome for fear of sorcerers was more like that obtained for animal spirits than like the outcome for ghosts.

We would conclude that, of the several hypotheses we have considered in this chapter to account for the origins of fear of others, the hypotheses that trace fear of others to the projection and displacement of aggression are much the most consistent with the whole range of findings we have been able to present. We would also conclude, however, that these hypotheses need to be set in a context of conflict theory and cannot be adequate in the simple, isolated form in which we first presented them.

CHAPTER 13. *Conclusion*

WE HAVE asked in this study two distinct but related questions. First, do early experiences in the life of an individual have a persisting effect on his personality? Second, do the personality characteristics of the typical member of a society determine in a measurable way any of the beliefs and practices in that society? The first question has to do with personality development, the second with culture integration. Although these two questions can be considered and tested independently of one another, this was not possible in the present study. The evidence we have adduced for certain hypotheses about personality development has been equally relevant to hypotheses concerning culture integration.

From our general interpretation of personality development and of culture integration, together with more specific hypotheses about each, we have made a number of predictions about cross-cultural relationships. Some of our predictions have not been confirmed. We cannot tell from the evidence of our study whether this failure of confirmation is due to errors in our theory of personality development, to errors in our theory of culture integration, or to the inadequacy and unreliability of the measures we have had to use. On the other hand, a number of our predictions have been confirmed. The confirmation has been sufficient, we feel, to suggest strongly that there are some principles of personality development which hold true for mankind in general and not just for Western culture, and also to demonstrate the validity of the general notion of culture integration through personality processes. The contributions of our study, as we see them, to each of these two general questions will be reviewed in the next two sections of this chapter.

CULTURE INTEGRATION

The first problem, that of culture integration, may be divided into three aspects: first, the equivalence of habit and custom; second, the interrelation of various types of customs which we have called the custom complex; and third, the influence of personality variables on the integration of customs.

We attempted in this study to define a custom (a unit of culture) as a type of habit (a unit of individual behavior). By doing this we felt that psychological principles which have been developed to account for the learning and performance of habits could be properly applied to explain certain problems at the level of culture. To establish this bridge between the levels of individual behavior and culture we formally defined a custom as a characteristic habit of a typical member of a cultural category of persons. Thus the habits of a typical member of a society, for example, which are characteristic of his membership in the society and not idiosyncratic, represent the general, i.e. non-specialized, customs of that society.

Most of the principles of individual behavior are concerned either directly or indirectly with the determination of the strength or potential of a habit. That is, they are designed to predict the probability of occurrence, the intensity or amplitude, the latency, or the resistance to extinction of habits under various specified conditions. Our bridge definition implies then that customs will also vary in potential. The notion that customs vary in strength is not new in anthropology. Such concepts as the importance of a culture trait, the elaboration of a culture pattern, or the strength of a sanction have frequently been used in the past. Our concept of custom potential is another way of conceptualizing such variations in cultural units and one which has the advantage of permitting the application of certain principles of individual behavior.

Since all our judgments were made in terms of the concept of custom potential and we were able to demonstrate a number of relationships between customs which were both statistically significant and consistent with psychological principles, we feel that we have justified our assumption that a custom may be viewed as a special type of habit. We hope that this bridge definition will further application of psychological principles at the cultural level.

The principles developed to explain individual behavior, however, must be used with caution. They have been generally tested in the laboratory where great care is taken to exclude uncontrolled variables and to study one habit or set of habits at a time. Studies of the interaction between habits in the same individual such as the recent experiments on conflict and on acquired drives and rewards have barely begun. Psychological studies of the interaction between two individuals are even more recent (cf. Sears, 1951). In general those who have been most concerned about such problems of interaction have been those who have focused their attention on the personality of individuals and on the integration of culture. In applying principles drawn from controlled experiments in the laboratory, therefore, attention should be given to the effects of habit interaction both within a single individual and between individuals.

Although we have been primarily concerned with the integration of culture on the basis of personality variables, we have also considered another type of integration which has come primarily from the cultural rather than individual level of analysis. This type of integration is produced by what we have called the custom complex. It is derived from two major facts of social life—that of language and that of social interaction. These two factors lead to the differentiation of customs into a number of sub-types which are integrally related to one another. They are practices, beliefs, values, sanctions, rules, motives, and satisfactions. If one starts with a practice (a custom which effects a change in the environment), then associated with it are a set of beliefs about events and processes relevant to the practices; a set of values which symbolize the goodness or badness of the events involved in the practice; sanctions which are the rewarding or punishing tendencies of other members of the society in response to the proper or deviant performance of the practice; rules which specify acceptable and unacceptable variations in the performance of the practices; motives which produce whatever acquired drives are associated with the practice; and, finally, satisfactions which produce whatever acquired rewards are associated with the practice.

Since it was not the purpose of this study to test the validity of the type of culture integration implied by the above formulation of the custom complex, we have very little direct evidence bearing upon it. In Chapter 10, however, we did find that there was a consistent though not high relationship between certain beliefs about the cause of illness and certain therapeutic practices which might be logically assumed to follow from such beliefs. For example, those societies which have the belief that illness results from ingestion tend to have therapeutic practices which would cause defecation or vomiting, i.e., would get the material causing illness out of the body. Such direct tests of the implication of the custom complex, however, should not be taken too seriously since we did not devise our variables for this purpose. The indirect evidence is more convincing. If some kind of cultural integration such as that implied by the custom complex were not operating, we could not have expected to find relationships between the motives and satisfactions of adults as inferred from child training and their beliefs and practices concerning illness. In other words, our interpretation of findings with respect to the personality integration of culture presupposes the custom complex.

The personality integration of culture refers to the assumption that certain customs in a society are related to certain other customs in that same society by virtue of the personality of a typical member of the society. We are not using personality here in a precise sense but rather as a general concept referring to a set of variables which are general and persistent, and which are predictable from the so-called personality mechanisms. The particular personality variables chosen were the acquired drives and acquired rewards associated with the oral, anal, sexual, dependence, and aggressive systems of behavior, guilt, and the fear of others. The mechanisms considered have been fixation, identification, projection, and displacement.

The hypothesis that personality variables function to integrate culture, as tested in this study, is that customs relating to childhood are integrated with customs in the projective systems of a culture through personality variables. Specifically, we assumed that child training practices and their immediate effect on the child, in developing satisfactions during infancy and anxieties during the process of socialization, are integrated with particular explanations of illness and therapeutic practices. We found ample, though not uniform, verification of this general hypothesis. In a substantial number of instances child training practices were found to be correlated with customs relating to illness. Many of these correlations reached an acceptable level of statistical significance, and the relationships found were in the main consistent with one another.

Although the theoretical basis for choosing our specific hypotheses was that child training customs were the antecedents and customs relating to illness the consequents, an opposite interpretation of cause and effect could in many cases also explain our results. In Chapter 9 we have discussed this problem in the case of negative fixation, and we will return to it in the next section of this chapter. Here it is important only to point out that this problem is irrelevant to our general demonstration of the role of personality in the integration of culture. Integration may come about largely in the way we have emphasized, that is, through the influence of child training upon personality characteristics and the influence of those personality characteristics upon the projective systems of the culture. Or, conceivably, it may come about more importantly through a common influence of adult personality characteristics upon child training practices and upon the projective systems. A preference for the latter explanation has, of course, the present disadvantage of leaving unexplained the origin of the personality characteristics;

but it does not challenge our evidence for the importance of those characteristics in bringing about an integration of diverse customs in widely separated custom complexes.[1]

Another aspect of culture integration is relevant, though not crucial, to this problem of the direction of causation. We refer to the integration between maintenance systems and child training practices, where the primary direction of effect seems likely to be from maintenance systems as antecedent to child training practices as effect. By maintenance systems we mean the economic, political, and social organizations of a society—the basic customs surrounding the nourishment, sheltering, and protection of its members, which seem a likely source of influence on child training practices. The main causal sequence, we would suggest, might then be as follows:

maintenance systems → child training practices → personality variables → projective systems

We have in this study been principally concerned with the last three units in this sequence, dealing with child training practices and projective systems as observable variables and interpreting the relation between them in terms of personality

1. It is of course conceivable that the integration might be directly between the "projective systems" (which would then not merit that name) and the child training practices, personality characteristics being quite irrelevant. That such a connection may occur in some instances is suggested, for example, by a passage we have quoted (page 100) from Beatrice Whiting's account of aggression training among the Paiute; it will be seen there that among the Paiute the belief in sorcery seems to play some role in contributing to the severity of socialization of aggression. But to apply such an interpretation to the entire body of data presented in this study would require a great variety of specific and in some cases implausible assumptions. For example, it would have to be assumed that fear of animal spirits rather than of human spirits leads parents to severe socialization of aggression in their children; that for people to blame illness on acts of the patient leads them to emphasize the role of parents and relatives rather than nonrelatives in child training, etc. The combination of inefficiency and implausibility in this line of interpretation (considered as a possible sole explanation of our findings) leads us to feel that it requires no further discussion.

as a set of hypothetical intervening variables. We have used maintainence systems once in a test of an hypothesis, when in Chapter 11 (pp. 250–253) we tested the relation between residence customs and our index of guilt; the purpose there was simply to make an indirect test of a relation between guilt and an aspect of child training practices for which we did not have a dependable measure and which seemed likely to be partially dependent on residence customs. It is now pertinent, however, to consider directly the question of the effect of maintenance systems upon child training practices.

Because this question is rather apart from the main problem of our study, we have made no attempt at systematic exploration of it in this book. We will, however, summarize here certain illustrative findings which have been presented in an informal report by Murdock and Whiting (1951).

The form of marriage is one aspect of social structure which appears to be clearly related to child training practices. Most of our societies may be classified into three groups, according to form of marriage: monogamy, sororal polygyny (in which co-wives customarily are sisters), and non-sororal polygyny (in which co-wives are not sisters). The implications of marriage form for child training practices have to do primarily with a contrast between sororal polygyny and the two other forms of marriage. Societies with sororal polygyny are found in general to be more indulgent in the initial care of the young child, and less severe in subsequent socialization, than either of the other groups of societies. This finding seems quite reasonable in the light of Murdock's account of other implications of sororal polygyny. "Sisters, of course, have learned to adapt their behavior to one another in their family of procreation, and they carry their habits of cooperation and mutual tolerance with them when they move from the home of their father to that of their husband. Unlike other co-wives, they do not have to start from scratch, so to speak, in the learning of adaptive behavior" (Murdock, 1949, pp. 30–31). Murdock goes on to show that under non-sororal polygyny the co-wives often occupy separate dwellings, whereas under sororal polygyny the co-wives generally live together in the same house. It would appear, then, that sororal polygyny encourages indulgence and relatively lenient training of children because the co-wives, being cooperative and in proximity to each other, willingly share each other's burdens. In non-sororal polygyny, however, rivalry or lack of proximity often prevents such sharing. In monogamy there is less opportunity for the one wife's burden of child training and household duties to be shared with anyone else.

A second aspect of social structure which appears to be related to child training practices is the structure of the family unit. Here the significant contrast is between extended families and nonextended families. In societies with extended families a single household is occupied by members of several generations; for example, with a matrilocal extended family, a typical household may consist of an elderly couple, their daughters, and the husbands and children of their daughters. In societies with nonextended families the typical household consists only of a man, his wife or wives, and their unmarried children; when the children get married, they leave to establish new and separate family units of their own. From the point of view of child training, what is likely to be significant about this contrast is the question of whether a young child's grandparents are or are not members of the immediate household. It turns out, as reported by Murdock and Whiting, that this difference in family structure has no consistent relation to early indulgence of the child's oral and dependent needs, nor to weaning and toilet training, although societies with extended families are found to be on the average more severe in their socialization of dependent, aggressive, and sexual behavior. It would appear that with respect to these three systems of behavior, which are generally more relevant than the other two to the basic moral rules of a society, the presence of the grandparents tends to make for more stern imposition of those rules.

If customs of marriage and family organization influence child training practices, it is probable that other aspects of the main-

tenance systems of a society do likewise. We have no evidence
to present to illustrate the potential influence of the economic
and political customs on child training, but it seems probable
that such relationships could be found. In any event, the assumption of the general primacy of the maintenance systems
in the chain of cause and effect seems at present to be plausible.
The maintenance systems may of course also have a direct influence on personality variables other than by way of influencing
child training practices; investigation of this question, however,
would require another study which would have to proceed in
part from different hypotheses and with different data and techniques from those used in the present study.[2]

PERSONALITY DEVELOPMENT

Since our study of the personality integration of culture depends
upon the use of hypotheses about personality development, the
results are pertinent to the more general problem of how personality develops as well as to the more specific question of the
role played by this development in the integration of culture.
The hypotheses about personality development which we have
tested in this study are for the most part drawn from psychoanalytic theory. We have modified them, however, from the
original form in which they are expressed in psychoanalytic
writings. Our modifications derive primarily from a reinterpretation of these hypotheses in the light of general behavior theory.
We have made this reinterpretation for two reasons. One reason
proceeds from a very general consideration; we see behavior
theory as providing the possibility of integrating knowledge of

2. An example of this more direct influence is provided by Merton's
suggestion (1940) that participation in a bureaucratic organization tends
to produce certain effects on the personality of its members, regardless of
their previous background. Another example is provided by Riesman's account (1950) of changes in typical personality of members of our society
in recent generations; a part of his thesis has to do with direct effects of the
maintenance systems upon adult participants, though he also recognizes
an effect of the maintenance systems upon the child training practices.

personality development with knowledge of other behavior phenomena. The other reason is more specific to our study. What we see as a promising attack upon the problem of culture integration is one which makes use of the concepts of general behavior theory; in order to make use of this approach in our particular study, then, we needed to use the concepts of general behavior theory rather than the concepts of psychoanalytic theory.

We have, then, adapted hypotheses from psychoanalysis, expressed them in the conceptual framework of behavior theory, and applied them to the problem of culture integration. But the fact that we have thus tested them in a context of culture integration has a special implication of importance. The test has involved cross-cultural predictions which we can hope to find confirmed only to the extent that the hypotheses have validity as universal hypotheses about human behavior in all cultural settings.

The hypotheses we are testing have been developed in the effort to explain individual differences in personality among members of Western European or American society. They have, to be sure, not yet been very adequately tested even there. But even to the extent that they have been tested there, it remains possible that they may be valid only for the explanation of individual differences within our society. They may be essentially culture-bound hypotheses whose validity is dependent upon the particular social structure and customs of our society. For purposes of immediate practical application in psychiatric work it may not matter greatly whether they are thus culture-bound or whether they have a more general validity for mankind at large. But for application in other societies, and in our own society in future generations, this question of generality is highly important. For the scientist, finally, who is seeking to establish knowledge rather than to apply it, the question of generality has an obvious importance which could hardly be overlooked.

In relation to studies of personality development of individuals within our own society, then, the special contribution of our study is to test the more general validity of notions which have first been developed there. The very diversity of customs in various societies which so strikingly illustrates the variability of human behavior permits a test of the universal presence of common basic processes underlying this variability.

The problem in personality development around which our study was primarily planned is that of fixation. Psychoanalytic theory has suggested that extreme frustration or extreme indulgence of a particular form of behavior in childhood may produce a continuing fixation of interest on that particular form of behavior. We modified the original psychoanalytic formulation of this idea in several ways, of which the most important to recall in this summary are the following:

1. We split the hypothesis of fixation into two separate hypotheses suggested by an application of general behavior theory. One is that positive fixation, consisting primarily of acquired reward, would result from a high degree of indulgence of a particular form of behavior. The other is that negative fixation, consisting primarily of acquired drive, would result from a high degree of frustration of a particular form of behavior.

2. We proposed to deal with fixation in each of five systems of behavior. The psychoanalytic concept of fixation has been applied principally to the oral and anal systems and to certain components of the sexual system. Dependence and aggression have tended to be viewed, in psychoanalytic treatment of the problem, as in part an outgrowth or consequence of these other systems. We have instead treated dependence and aggression as independent systems, and have treated each of the five systems as a whole. (This latter decision was not entirely a matter of deliberate choice, but proceeded partly from the character of the data available to us.)

The general outcome of our study of fixation was to justify the separation we made between positive fixation and negative fixation and to provide clear confirmation for the hypothesis of negative fixation. For the hypothesis of positive fixation we obtained in general only some very tentative confirmation, but certainly no suggestion that it is the same process as that of negative fixation. In the case of positive fixation we obtained the strongest evidence in the case of a later period of childhood rather than an earlier period; progressive satisfaction showed more consistent relationships to our indices of positive fixation than did initial satisfaction. In the case of negative fixation our main test of the hypothesis had to do with the effects of anxiety developed during the period of socialization for each system of behavior, and it was here that we found our strongest evidence for the operation of negative fixation. But we did find some striking evidence for negative fixation as a result even of experiences during the initial period of infancy and very early childhood. It is possible that this difference between the permanence of early positive and early negative fixation may be a consequence solely of differences in the extent to which the two are reinforced later in life by a continuation of the same social pressures. It seems more likely to us, however, that this difference is also due to a more basic difference between acquired drives and acquired rewards in the ease with which they are unlearned. Finally, the difference in degree of confirmation of the two hypotheses—of positive fixation and of negative fixation—may be in considerable part due to the greater adequacy of the cultural indices we used for negative fixation in comparison with those used for positive fixation.

The outcome of our tests of fixation was not uniform for the five systems of behavior we dealt with. The most definite evidence for fixation came from analysis of the oral, dependence, and aggressive systems of behavior. There was not a complete lack of evidence of personality effects of training in the anal and sexual systems; in the chapter on positive fixation we found somewhat stronger evidence for those two systems than for the other three, and in the chapter on fear of others we presented additional evidence pointing to lasting effects of training in the sexual system. But viewed as a whole, the evidence for a lasting effect of child training practices on personality is more striking and consistent for the other three systems—oral, dependence, and aggression. This outcome certainly appears to justify our treating dependence and aggression as distinct systems of behavior. It might be tempting to go further, with other critics of Freudian theory, and argue from this outcome that Freudian theory exaggerated the importance of the biological drives associated with the anal and sexual systems of behavior, and gave too little recognition to the importance of what may well be entirely learned drives associated with dependence and aggression (and with other systems of behavior we have not dealt with). The outcome of our study alone, however, would in our opinion not justify such an argument. There are too many technical difficulties which might adequately explain each negative finding in our study.

The second problem in personality development which we have explored by the cross-cultural method is that of the origins of guilt. We showed that guilt does not appear to be entirely explicable as a simple consequence of degree of socialization anxiety. We then tested several specific hypotheses about the origins of guilt which were all derived from the general psychoanalytic interpretation of guilt as a consequence of the child's identification with his parents. The outcome here was not nearly so striking as in the case of negative fixation. Yet there is a general thread of consistency, with a few clearly significant findings, which offers some definite support for the interpretation of guilt as a consequence of identification. We presented an account of this mechanism as involving the child's rewarding himself by imitation of the parents' evaluative responses, showing that the tendency for the child to do so is especially strong if the parents' direct expression of approval is partially withdrawn at a time when the child is strongly driven to obtain that approval.

The final problem in personality development with which we have dealt is that of the origins of the unrealistic fear of other persons and of spirits. Here we have in a sense taken for granted that each aspect of child training has the long-term consequences which were confirmed in our study of fixation, and have then asked the question, Of what adult personality characteristics, resulting from socialization practices, is the fear of others an outcome? We found that the fear of others is primarily associated with anxiety about aggression. We showed that this result could be an outcome either of the mechanism of projection or of the mechanism of displacement. Consideration of either of these mechanisms in the light of modern conflict theory suggests, however, that the relative tendency to fear various objects should vary with the strength of anxiety about aggression and with the strength of the tendency to be aggressive. Insofar as we were able to test the implications of conflict theory, in the form in which we presented it, our data confirm those implications. For the aggressive system of behavior these results, depending as they do upon the assumption of fixation, further strengthen the evidence for fixation.

For each of these three major problems in personality development we feel that two main objectives are accomplished by our study. First, we have tried to take some effective steps in the direction of bringing together the valuable clinical insights deriving from the work of psychoanalysis and the fruitful constructs and generalizations deriving from the experimental work of behavior theorists. Second, having formulated hypotheses about personality development which come from this fusion of the two theoretical approaches, we have made a beginning toward testing their universal validity for the explanation of human behavior.

When our findings are considered as relevant to personality development, the direction of the cause-effect relationship becomes a more fundamental problem than when they are considered as relevant to culture integration. Let us imagine for the moment that our findings are due entirely to an effect of adult personality characteristics upon child training practices. As we have already indicated in the previous section of this chapter, in these circumstances our findings would still illustrate the personality integration of culture; the particular personality processes responsible for the integration would simply be different from those to which the integration is ascribed in the hypotheses we have formulated in this book. But under these circumstances our findings would not pertain at all to personality *development;* they would simply illustrate the manifold expression in behavior of the already developed personalities of the adult members of a society. Hence for our findings to be relevant to personality development the direction of the cause-effect relationship must be at least in part that which is presupposed in the hypotheses we have formulated: an influence of child training practices upon adult personality.

It is an unfortunate defect of the correlational method, as we have stated earlier in the book, that it can provide no conclusive evidence about the direction of causal relationships. The experimental method, which is superior in this respect, is generally not applicable to testing hypotheses about personality development. It may be possible in the future, particularly when fuller field data are available on personality in primitive societies, to improve on the methods we have used by analyzing a greater variety of variables simultaneously and attending to their interrelationships. But for greater confidence in conclusions about personality development we must also place hope in the possibility of consistent results from many studies which test the same hypotheses under a variety of particular circumstances. A position might then be reached where these hypotheses provided the only reasonable, unified, and consistent explanation of the whole body of findings, for the alternative explanations might consist largely of a special set of ad hoc hypotheses for each set of findings.

Our study makes some contribution toward such a scientific goal. For the hypotheses we have tested are based on hypotheses which have been developed primarily in one setting, that of the clinical study of individuals in our society, and which have received a good deal of informal, unsystematic confirmation in that setting; where we have obtained confirmatory evidence in this study, the confirmation has come from a radically different source. Systematic comparison of child training with later personality characteristics, for individual differences among members of one society, provides another different source of evidence which is beginning to be utilized in studies of personality development. The findings of our study add considerably, we believe, to the probable validity of the hypotheses for which we obtained positive results. They should thus encourage the attempt to test these hypotheses in other settings. In this way we see this study as playing a role in a growing system of scientific knowledge about personality development, a system in which no one item is conclusive but which may as a whole justify a high degree of confidence in the hypotheses that are most consistently confirmed.

INCIDENTAL IMPLICATIONS AND SUGGESTIONS

From our study certain implications and suggestions may be drawn which are somewhat aside from the main purposes of the study.

For one thing, of course, we have provided a better basis than was available before for setting our own child training practices in a universal perspective. We have compared the child training practices of a group of midwestern urban middle-class families with those of our sample of primitive societies. We found that this American group is generally non-indulgent during infancy, in a hurry to start the training process (especially with respect to weaning and toilet training), and quite severe in the general socialization of their children. This American group differs most markedly from our sample of primitive societies with respect to toilet training, being both exceptionally early and exceptionally severe. They are nearest the norm in the treatment of aggression, being only slightly above average in the severity with which they socialize this system of behavior.

Some readers may be inclined to use our findings in formulating practical advice about child rearing in our society. To such readers we would like to express two cautions. One is that our study has not been planned or conducted with any special attention to goodness of adjustment. Some of the terms we have used, such as fixation, identification, projection and displacement, have been commonly used in a context where goodness of adjustment is being considered. We have tried to give these terms a non-evaluative meaning, however, and would caution against any simple assumption that a high or low degree of any of our variables is necessarily desirable or undesirable in general.

A second caution is that any advice about child rearing needs to be carefully thought out in relation to the specific cultural setting to which it is to be applied, as well as in relation to general principles. The comparisons we have made between an American middle-class group and our sample of primitive societies are relevant here. In addition we would stress the evidence we have offered which shows the dependence of child training practices upon the maintenance systems of a society. Advice about child training in our society has too often been promulgated without adequate attention to this dependence, as though child training practices were an entirely independent element of culture which could be altered at will. The cultural context needs to be examined carefully, both to judge the probable difficulty of effecting a change and to judge what other effects a change might have in addition to the effects that are intended.

Other suggestions relate to our indices of personality characteristics rather than to our measures of child training practices. We used customary reactions to illness as our indices of personality characteristics, and found much evidence that this use was justified. Reactions to illness are probably much more importantly influenced by personality under primitive conditions of life than in our society at the present time. The presence, and the wide diffusion, of scientific knowledge about the causes and cures of illness undoubtedly restricts the range of variation in response to illness which might otherwise be found in our society as a result of personality differences between one person and another. Yet the diffusion of scientific knowledge about illness does not altogether exclude the possible operation of personality variables in influencing reactions to illness. The same scientific knowledge can have a different emotional meaning for different persons. Consider, for example, the fact that many diseases are known to depend upon microorganisms and upon their transmission from one person to another. Knowing that he is suffering from such a disease, one person may tend to blame others for having so callously gone about in public while sick and hence giving him the disease, while another person may blame himself for having carelessly exposed himself by contact with others rather than remaining more isolated. Still other persons suffering from the same disease may react emotionally in a way that depends upon emphasizing differential suscepti-bility to contagion. Such people may in effect ask themselves, "Why did I not succeed in warding off the disease, as I have on other occasions when I must have been exposed?" One per-son may answer this question by blaming himself for not getting enough exercise; another by blaming himself for not having taken his daily vitamins recently; still another by blaming others who have stirred up in him violent aggressive feelings which have kept him awake nights and brought him to a point of ex-haustion.

People may also differ widely in their preferred therapeutic techniques. One person places great reliance on laxatives, what-ever the ailment; another is greatly comforted by swallowing pills or sucking on cough drops. For some, rest and assurance of being well taken care of by others may seem essential; for still others, a resolution to quit smoking, to temper sexual indulgence, or to eat fewer fatty foods, may play an important part in en-abling them to feel they are getting well and will then be able to stay well.

The outcome of our study would of course suggest that such variations in reaction to illness, among different individuals in our society, are likely to be in considerable part a product of variations in general personality characteristics among them. It would also suggest, though less persuasively, that the personality characteristics determining these reactions to illness are in part a resultant of variations in the experience of different individuals in childhood, variations among individuals in our society which are parallel to those we have dealt with among societies in customary child training practices. We have no evidence to present on this question of the origins of individual differences in reactions to illness among members of our society. It seems likely, however, that clear awareness of such possibilities could be useful to physicians in dealing with their patients' emotional reactions to illness, attempts at self-medication, and attitudes toward treatment prescribed or recommended by physicians.

In the light of our general purpose in this study, the concentration of attention on reactions to illness was a matter of convenience. Other possible cultural indices of adult personality characteristics might well have been chosen instead for analysis. It seems likely that what we have found to be true for reactions to illness would also be true for a variety of other customs. The term "projective systems" as applied to a variety of customs implies an expectation that they will be in considerable part a reflection of personality characteristics. Thus our findings should be of some interest to students of art, mythology, and religion. Even within the framework of a well-established body of belief and practice, such as that of Christianity or Mohammedanism, there is room for considerable variation in emphasis and interpretation from one cultural group to another and from one period to another. Such variation may be influenced by differences in typical personality among various cultural groups, differences which in turn may be in part a function of variations in child training practices. Here again we have no evidence to offer, and merely wish to call attention to suggestions which emerge from our study and which may merit further exploration.[3]

Future Research

Our study, like any other single study of this sort, can by its very nature not give a definitive answer to the scientific ques-

3. In the case of mythology such an exploration has already been begun by McClelland and Friedman (1952) and by Wright (1952). Striking results have also been obtained by Barry (1952) in a study relating our

tions at which it is directed. Its ultimate significance depends upon its place in a larger body of accumulating knowledge. Our study should not be taken as establishing the validity of certain hypotheses beyond reasonable doubt. It should rather be taken as contributing some evidence of their validity, and as showing clearly that they are worthy of further investigation. Further cross-cultural study, and further systematic studies of the correlates of individual differences within our society and within other societies, are needed before we can feel a great deal of confidence one way or the other in a judgment about the validity of any of the hypotheses we have tested here. For this reason we hope that our study will serve to stimulate such work.

In the case of future cross-cultural research, the difficulties we have faced in our study highlight certain technical needs. Studies of this sort are handicapped by the small number of societies for which relevant information is available. We hope therefore that our study may help strengthen the interest of ethnographic fieldworkers in collecting the kinds of information that are needed for cross-cultural studies of culture and personality, so that better information may eventually be available for a larger number of societies. Studies of this sort are also handicapped (in relation to some of their aims) by the necessity of relying upon cultural indices of personality characteristics rather than upon more direct measures of the personality characteristics of the present members of a society. Hence there is great potential value for cross-cultural research in the use of projective techniques and other technical devices which can yield these direct measures. But for purposes of cross-cultural comparison it is important that these techniques be of such a nature and applied in such a way that real comparison between one society and another is justified. We hope that our study may stimulate further efforts toward the solution of these technical problems which have already begun to receive much attention in recent years.

---

measures of child training practices to formal aspects of decorative art in various primitive societies.

REFERENCES

REFERENCES are separated into two groups. The first group, GENERAL REFERENCES, consists of publications which have been referred to in the book for other purposes than that of citing ethnographic sources. These publications are arranged alphabetically by author.

The second group, ETHNOGRAPHIC REFERENCES, includes at least one major source for the ethnography of each of the 75 societies used in this study, with emphasis on sources most informative on child training and on customs relating to illness. It includes all sources cited in the book, but it does not include all sources which were consulted by our judges. These publications are arranged alphabetically by the name of the society. For societies marked with an asterisk the files of Human Relations Area Files, Inc. (now in part available at a number of American universities) were employed.

GENERAL REFERENCES

Abraham, K. 1927. *Selected papers.* London: Hogarth Press.

Alexander, F. 1948. *Fundamentals of psychoanalysis.* New York: Norton.

Allport, G. W. 1942. The use of personal documents in psychological science. *Soc. Sci. Res. Counc. Bull.,* no. 49.

Baldwin, A. L. 1942. Personal structure analysis: A statistical method for investigating the single personality. *J. abnorm. soc. Psychol.,* 37, 163–183.

Barry, H. III. 1952. Influences of socialization on the graphic arts. Unpublished honors thesis, Department of Social Relations, Harvard University.

Benedict, R. 1934. *Patterns of culture.* Boston: Houghton Mifflin.

——— 1938. Continuities and discontinuities in cultural conditioning. *Psychiatry,* 1, 161–167.

——— 1946. *The chrysanthemum and the sword: Patterns of Japanese culture.* Boston: Houghton Mifflin.

Brown, J. S. and Farber, I. E. 1951. Emotions conceptualized as intervening variables—with suggestions toward a theory of frustration. *Psychol. Bull.,* 48, 465–495.

Bush, R. R. and Whiting, J. W. M. 1952. On the theory of psycho-analytic displacement. (In press)

Carl, L. J. 1949. Experimental study of dependency in children. Unpublished Ph.D. dissertation, State Univ. of Iowa.

Cattell, R. B. 1950. The principal culture patterns discoverable in the syntal dimensions of existing nations. *J. soc. Psychol.*, 32, 215–253.

Cowles, J. T. 1937. Food-tokens as incentives for learning by chimpanzees. *Comp. Psychol. Monogr.*, 14, no. 5.

Davis, W. A. and Havighurst, R. J. 1946. Social class and color differences in child-rearing. *Amer. sociol. Rev.*, 11, 698–710.

——— — ——— 1947. *Father of the man.* Boston: Houghton Mifflin.

Dollard, J. 1938. Hostility and fear in social life. *Social Forces*, 17, 15–26.

Dollard, J., Doob, L. W., Miller, N. E., Mowrer, O. H. and Sears, R. R. 1939. *Frustration and aggression.* New Haven: Yale Univ. Press.

Dollard, J. and Miller, N. E. 1950. *Personality and psychotherapy.* New York: McGraw-Hill.

Driver, H. E. and Kroeber, A. L. 1932. Quantitative expression of cultural relationships. *Univ. Calif. Publ. Amer. Archaeol. Ethnol.*, 31, 211–256.

Dyk, Walter (ed.). 1938. *Son of Old Man Hat: A Navaho autobiography.* New York: Harcourt, Brace.

Edwards, A. L. 1946. *Statistical analysis for students in psychology and education.* New York: Rinehart.

Eggan, D. 1943. The general problem of Hopi adjustment. *Amer. Anthrop.*, 45, 357–373.

Erikson, E. H. 1950. *Childhood and society.* New York: Norton.

Faigin, H. and Hollenberg, E. 1953. Child rearing and the internalization of moral values. (In preparation)

Fenichel, O. 1945. *The psychoanalytic theory of neurosis.* New York: Norton.

Feshbach, S. 1951. The drive reducing function of fantasy behavior. Unpublished Ph.D. dissertation, Yale Univ.

Ford, C. S. 1941. *Smoke from their fires: The life of a Kwakiutl chief.* New Haven: Yale Univ. Press.

——— 1945. A comparative study of human reproduction. *Yale Univ. Publ. Anthrop.*, no. 32.

Ford, C. S. and Beach, F. A. 1951. *Patterns of sexual behavior.* New York: Harper.

Freud, S. 1911. Psycho-analytic notes upon an autobiographical account of a case of paranoia. In Freud, S., *Collected papers.* London: Hogarth, 1924, v. 3, 387–470.

——— 1915. A case of paranoia running counter to the psychoanalytical theory of the disease. In Freud, S., *Collected papers*. London: Hogarth, 1924, v. 2, 150–161.

———— 1933. *New introductory lectures on psycho-analysis*. New York: Norton.

Garrett, H. E. 1947. *Statistics in psychology and education*, 3d ed. New York: Longmans, Green.

Gesell, A. and Ilg, F. L. 1943. *Infant and child in the culture of today*. New York: Harper.

Gillin, J. P. 1948. *The ways of men*. New York: Appleton-Century.

Gorer, G. 1943. Themes in Japanese culture. *Trans. N.Y. Acad. Sci.*, Series II, v. 5, no. 5, 106–124.

———— 1948. *The American people*. New York: Norton.

Gorer, G. and Rickman, J. 1950. *People of Great Russia: A psychological study*. New York: Chanticleer.

Guthrie, E. R. 1935. *The psychology of learning*. New York: Harper.

Hallowell, A. I. 1945. The Rorschach technique in the study of personality and culture. *Amer. Anthrop.*, 47, 195–210.

Henry, W. E. 1947. The thematic apperception technique in the study of culture-personality relations. *Genet. Psychol. Monogr.*, 35, 3–135.

Hobhouse, L. T., Wheeler, G. C., and Ginsberg, M. 1915. *The material culture and social institutions of the simpler peoples: An essay in correlation*. London: Chapman & Hall.

Hollenberg, E. and Sperry, M. 1951. Some antecedents of aggression and effects of frustration in doll play. *Personality: topical symposia*, 1, 32–43.

Horney, K. 1939. *New ways in psychoanalysis*. New York: Norton.

Horton, D. 1943. The functions of alcohol in primitive societies: A cross-cultural study. *Quart. J. Stud. Alcohol*, 4, 199–320.

Hull, C. L. 1943. *Principles of behavior*. New York: Appleton-Century.

———— 1951. *Essentials of behavior*. New Haven: Yale Univ. Press.

Kardiner, A. 1939. *The individual and his society*. New York: Columbia Univ. Press.

———— 1945. *The psychological frontiers of society*. New York: Columbia Univ. Press.

Kardiner, A. and Ovesey, L. 1951. *The mark of oppression: A psychosocial study of the American Negro*. New York: Norton.

Kluckhohn, C. 1943. Covert culture and administrative problems. *Amer. Anthrop.*, 45, 213–227.

———— 1944. Navaho witchcraft. *Pap. Peabody Mus. Amer. Archaeol. Ethnol., Harvard Univ.*, 22, no. 2.

Kroeber, A. L. 1948. *Anthropology: race, language, culture, psychology, prehistory*. New York: Harcourt, Brace.

LaBarre, W. 1945. Some observations on character structure in the Orient: The Japanese. *Psychiatry,* 8, 319–342.

Levin, H. 1952. Permissive child-rearing and adult role behavior in children. (Paper read at annual meeting of Eastern Psychological Association, March 28.)

Lewin, K. 1935. *A dynamic theory of personality.* New York: McGraw-Hill.

Lindemann, E. 1944. Symptomatology and management of acute grief. *Amer. J. Psychiatry,* 101, 141–148.

Linton, R. 1936. *The study of man.* New York: Appleton-Century.

Lowell, E. 1952. The effect of conflict on motivation. Unpublished Ph.D. dissertation, Harvard Univ.

McClelland, D. C. and Friedman, G. A. 1952. A cross-cultural study of the relationship between child-training practices and achievement motivation appearing in folk tales. In Swanson, G. E., Newcomb, T. M., and Hartley, E. L., *Readings in social psychology* (rev. ed.). New York: Holt. Pp. 243–249.

MacKinnon, D. W. 1938. Violation of prohibitions. In Murray, H. A., *et al., Explorations in personality.* New York: Oxford Univ. Press. Pp. 491–501.

McNemar, Q. 1949. *Psychological statistics.* New York: Wiley.

Maier, N. R. F. 1949. *Frustration: The study of behavior without a goal.* New York: McGraw-Hill.

Malinowski, B. 1927. *The father in primitive psychology.* New York: Norton.

Mead, M. 1928. *Coming of age in Samoa.* New York: Morrow.

———— 1942. *And keep your powder dry.* New York: Morrow.

Merton, R. K. 1940. Bureaucratic structure and personality. *Social Forces,* 18, 560–568.

Miller, N. E. 1944. Experimental studies of conflict. In Hunt, J. McV. (ed.), *Personality and the behavior disorders.* New York: Ronald. v. 1, 431–465.

———— 1948. Theory and experiment relating psychoanalytic displacement to stimulus-response generalization. *J. abn. soc. Psychol.,* 43, 155–178.

———— 1951. Learnable drives and rewards. In Stevens, S. S. (ed.), *Handbook of experimental psychology.* New York: Wiley. Pp. 435–472.

Miller, N. E. and Dollard, J. 1941. *Social learning and imitation.* New Haven: Yale Univ. Press.

Miller, N. E. and Kraeling, D. 1952. Displacement: greater generalization of approach than avoidance in a generalized approach-avoidance conflict. *J. exp. Psychol.,* 43, 217–221.

Mowrer, O. H. 1950. *Learning theory and personality dynamics.* New York: Ronald.

Murdock, G. P. 1937. Correlations of matrilineal and patrilineal institutions. In Murdock, G. P. (ed.), *Studies in the science of society*. New Haven: Yale Univ. Press. Pp. 445–470.

——— 1945. The common denominator of cultures. In Linton, R. (ed.), *The science of man in the world crisis*. New York: Columbia Univ. Press. Pp. 123–142.

——— 1949. *Social structure*. New York: Macmillan.

Murdock, G. P. and Whiting, J. W. M. 1951. Cultural determination of parental attitudes: The relationship between the social structure, particularly family structure and parental behavior. In Senn, M. J. E. (ed.), *Problems of infancy and childhood: Transactions of the Fourth Conference, March 6–7, 1950*. New York: Josiah Macy, Jr. Foundation. Pp. 13–34.

Murdock, G. P., et al. 1950. *Outline of cultural materials: 3rd revised edition*. New Haven: Human Relations Area Files, Inc.

Murray, E. J. and Miller, N. E. 1952. Displacement: steeper gradient of generalization of avoidance than of approach with age of habit controlled. *J. exp. Psychol.*, 43, 222–226.

Nash, P. 1937. The place of religious revivalism in the formation of the intercultural community on Klamath Reservation. In Eggan, F. (ed.), *Social anthropology of North American tribes*. Chicago: Univ. of Chicago Press. Pp. 375–442.

Ogburn, W. F. 1922. *Social change with respect to culture and original nature*. New York: Huebsch.

Orlansky, H. 1949. Infant care and personality. *Psychol. Bull.*, 46, 1–48.

Riesman, D. 1950. *The lonely crowd: A study of the changing American character*. New Haven: Yale Univ. Press.

Sears, R. R. 1943. Survey of objective studies of psychoanalytic concepts. *Soc. Sci. Res. Counc. Bull.*, no. 51.

——— 1951. A theoretical framework for personality and social behavior. *Amer. Psychol.*, 6, 476–483.

Sears, R. R. and Wise, G. W. 1950. Relation of cup feeding in infancy to thumb-sucking and the oral drive. *Amer. J. Orthopsychiat.*, 20, 123–138.

Simmons, L. W. 1937. Statistical correlations in the science of society. In Murdock, G. P. (ed.), *Studies in the science of society*. New Haven: Yale Univ. Press. Pp. 495–517.

——— (ed.). 1942. *Sun Chief: The autobiography of a Hopi Indian*. New Haven: Yale Univ. Press.

Skinner, B. F. 1938. *The behavior of organisms*. New York: Appleton-Century.

Spier, L. 1927. The ghost dance of 1870 among the Klamath of Oregon. *Univ. Wash. Publ. Anthropol.*, 2, 39–56.

Tolman, E. C. 1932. *Purposive behavior in animals and men.* New York: Century.

—— 1935. Psychology vs. immediate experience. *Philos. Sci.,* 2, 356–380.

Walker, H. M. 1943. *Elementary statistical methods.* New York: Holt.

White, L. A. 1949. *The science of culture.* New York: Farrar, Straus.

Whiting, B. B. 1950. Paiute sorcery. *Viking Fund Publ. Anthrop.,* no. 15.

Whiting, J. W. M. 1941. *Becoming a Kwoma.* New Haven: Yale Univ. Press.

Wolfe, J. B. 1936. Effectiveness of token-rewards for chimpanzees. *Compar. Psychol. Monogr.,* 12, no. 5.

Wright, G. O. 1952. Projection and displacement: a cross-cultural study of the expression of aggression in myths. Unpublished Ph.D. dissertation. Graduate School of Education, Harvard Univ.

ETHNOGRAPHIC REFERENCES

°ABIPONE

Dobrizhoffer, M. 1822. *An account of the Abipones, an equestrian people of Paraguay.* London: Murray.

°AINU

Batchelor, J. 1895. *The Ainu of Japan.* New York.

—— 1901. *The Ainu and their folk-lore.* London: The Religious Tract Society.

—— 1927. *Ainu life and lore.* Tokyo: Kyobunkwan.

Howard, B. D. 1893. *Life with Trans-Siberian savages.* London: Longmans, Green.

ALORESE

DuBois, C. 1944. *The people of Alor.* Minneapolis: Univ. of Minnesota Press.

°ANDAMANESE

Man, E. H. 1883. *On the aboriginal inhabitants of the Andaman Islands.* London: Trübner.

Radcliffe-Brown, A. R. 1933. *The Andaman Islanders.* Cambridge: Cambridge Univ. Press.

ARAPESH

Mead, M. 1935. *Sex and temperament in three savage tribes.* New York: Morrow.

—— 1938–1947. The Mountain Arapesh. *Anthrop. Pap. Amer. Mus. Nat. Hist.,* 36, 139–349; 37, 317–451; 40, 159–420.

*ASHANTI

Rattray, R. S. 1927. *Religion and art in Ashanti.* Oxford: Clarendon.
———— 1929. *Ashanti law and constitution.* Oxford: Clarendon.

*AZANDE

DeGraer, A. M. 1929. L'art de guérir chez les Azande. *Congo,* 10, 220–254, 361–408.
Evans-Pritchard, E. E. 1937. *Witchcraft, oracles and magic among the Azande.* Oxford: Clarendon.
Lagae, C. R. 1926. *Les Azande ou Niam-Niam.* Bruxelles: Vromant.

BAIGA

Elwin, V. 1939. *The Baiga.* London: Murray.

*BALINESE

Bateson, G. and Mead, M. 1942. *Balinese character.* New York: New York Academy of Sciences.
Weck, W. 1937. *Heilkunde und Volkstum auf Bali.* Stuttgart: Enke.

*BENA

Culwick, A. T. and Culwick, G. M. 1935. *Ubena of the river.* London: Allen & Unwin.

*CHAGGA

Dundas, C. 1924. *Kilimanjaro and its people.* London: Witherby.
Gutmann, B. 1909. *Dichten und Denken der Dschagganeger.* Leipzig.
———— 1924–25. Der Beschwörer bei den Wadschagga. *Arch. Anthrop.,* 48, 46–57.
Raum, O. F. 1940. *Chaga childhood.* London: Oxford Univ. Press.

*CHAMORRO

Thompson, L. 1941. *Guam and its people.* San Francisco: American Council, Institute of Pacific Relations.

CHENCHU

Fürer-Haimendorf, C. von. 1943. *Aboriginal tribes of Hyderabad.* London: Macmillan.

*CHEWA

Steytler, J. G. 1934. Ethnographic report on the Achewa tribe of Nyasaland. Unpublished manuscript.

*CHIRICAHUA

Opler, M. E. 1941. *An Apache life way.* Chicago: Univ. of Chicago Press.

*COMANCHE

Linton, R. 1945. The Comanche. In Kardiner, A., *The psychological frontiers of society.* New York: Columbia Univ. Press. Pp. 47–80.

*COPPER ESKIMO

Jenness, D. 1922. *The life of the Copper Eskimos.* (Report of Canadian Arctic Expedition, 1913–18, vol. 12a.) Ottawa: Acland.

°DAHOMEANS

Herskovits, M. J. 1938. *Dahomey: An ancient West African kingdom.* New York: Augustin.

°DOBUANS

Fortune, R. F. 1932. *Sorcerers of Dobu.* New York: Dutton.

°DUSUN

Rutter, O. 1929. *The pagans of North Borneo.* London: Hutchinson.

Staal, J. 1923–25. The Dusuns of North Borneo. *Anthropos,* 18–19, 958–977; 20, 120–138.

°FLATHEAD

Turney-High, H. H. 1937. The Flathead Indians of Montana. *Mem. Amer. Anthrop. Assoc.,* no. 47.

°HOPI

Dennis, W. 1940. *The Hopi child.* New York: Appleton-Century.

Simmons, L. W. (ed.). 1942. *Sun Chief: The autobiography of a Hopi Indian.* New Haven: Yale Univ. Press.

Stephen, A. M. 1936. *Hopi journal of Alexander M. Stephen.* New York: Columbia Univ. Press.

°IFUGAO

Barton, R. F. 1930. *The half-way sun.* New York: Brewer and Warren.

———— 1938. *Philippine pagans: The autobiographies of three Ifugaos.* London: Routledge.

°JIVARO

Karsten, R. 1935. *The head-hunters of Western Amazonas.* Helsingfors.

Stirling, M. W. 1938. Historical and ethnographical material on the Jivaro Indians. *Bull. Bur. Amer. Ethnol.,* no. 117.

°KAZAK

Castagne, J. 1930. Magie et exorcisme chez les Kazak-Kirghizes et autres peuples Turcs orientaux. *Revue des Études Islamiques,* 4, 53–156.

Levchine, A. de. 1840. *Description des hordes et des steppes des Kirghiz-Kazaks ou Kirghiz-Kaissaks.* Paris: Imprimerie Royale.

Radloff, W. 1884. *Aus Sibirien.* Leipzig: Weigel.

°KIWAI

Landtman, G. 1927. *The Kiwai Papuans of British New Guinea.* London: Macmillan.

°KURTATCHI

Blackwood, B. 1935. *Both sides of Buka Passage.* Oxford: Clarendon.

°KUTENAI

Turney-High, H. H. 1941. Ethnography of the Kutenai. *Mem. Amer. Anthrop. Assoc.*, no. 36.

°KWAKIUTL

Boas, F. 1921. Ethnology of the Kwakiutl. *Ann. Rep. Bur. Amer. Ethnol.*, 35, 43–1481.

———— 1932. Current beliefs of the Kwakiutl Indians. *J. Amer. Folklore*, 45, 177–260.

Ford, C. S. 1941. *Smoke from their fires*. New Haven: Yale Univ. Press.

°KWOMA

Whiting, J. W. M. 1941. *Becoming a Kwoma*. New Haven: Yale Univ. Press.

°LAKHER

Parry, N. E. 1932. *The Lakhers*. London: Macmillan.

°LAMBA

Doke, C. M. 1931. *The Lambas of Northern Rhodesia*. London: Harrap.

°LAPP

Scheffer, J. 1704. *The history of Lapland*. London.

Turi, J. 1931. *Turi's book of Lappland*. London: Cape.

°LEPCHA

Gorer, G. 1938. *Himalayan village*. London: Michael Joseph.

Morris, J. 1938. *Living with Lepchas*. London: Heinemann.

°LESU

Powdermaker, H. 1933. *Life in Lesu*. New York: Norton.

°MALEKULA

Deacon, A. B. 1934. *Malekula*. London: Routledge.

Leggatt, T. W. 1893. Malekula, New Hebrides. *Rep. Australas. Assoc. Adv. Sci.*, 4, 697–708.

°MANUS

Fortune, R. 1931. Manus religion. *Oceania*, 2, 74–108.

Mead, M. 1930. *Growing up in New Guinea*. New York: Morrow.

°MAORI

Best, E. 1924a. *The Maori*. Wellington: Tombs.

———— 1924b. *The Maori as he was*. Wellington: Dominion Museum.

MARQUESANS

Handy, E. S. C. 1923. The native culture in the Marquesas. *Bull. Bernice P. Bishop Mus.*, no. 9.

Linton, R. 1939. Marquesan culture. In Kardiner, A., *The individual and his society*. New York: Columbia Univ. Press. Pp. 137–196.

°MARSHALLESE

Erdland, A. 1914. *Die Marshall-Insulaner*. Münster: Aschendorff.

Finsch, O. 1898. *Ethnologische Erfahrungen und Belegstücke aus der Südsee*. Wien: Holder.

Krämer, A. and Nevermann, H. 1938. *Ralik-Ratak (Marshall-Inseln)*. Hamburg: Friederichsen, DeGruyter and Co.

°MASAI

Hollis, A. C. 1905. *The Masai: Their language and folklore*. Oxford: Clarendon.

Merker, M. 1904. *Die Masai*. Berlin: Reimer.

°MURNGIN

Warner, W. L. 1937. *A black civilization*. New York: Harper.

Webb, T. T. 1933. Aboriginal medical practice in East Arnhem Land. *Oceania*, 4, 91–98.

°NAURU

Hambruch, P. 1914. *Nauru*. Hamburg: Friederichsen.

Stephen, E. 1936. Notes on Nauru. *Oceania*, 7, 34–63.

°NAVAHO

Kluckhohn, C. 1944. Navaho witchcraft. *Pap. Peabody Mus. Amer. Archaeol. Ethnol., Harvard Univ.*, 22, no. 2.

——— 1947. Some aspects of Navaho infancy and early childhood. *Psychoanalysis and the Social Sciences*, 1, 37–86.

Kluckhohn, C. and Leighton, D. 1947. *The Navaho*. Cambridge: Harvard Univ. Press.

Leighton, D. and Kluckhohn, C. 1947. *Children of the people*. Cambridge: Harvard Univ. Press.

°OMAHA

Fletcher, A. C. and LaFlesche, F. 1911. The Omaha Tribe. *Ann. Rep. Bur. Amer. Ethnol.*, 27, 17–654.

Fortune, R. F. 1932. Omaha secret societies. *Columbia Univ. Contrib. Anthrop.*, v. 14.

°ONTONG-JAVANESE

Hogbin, H. I. 1930. Spirits and the healing of the sick in Ontong Java. *Oceania*, 1, 146–166.

——— 1931. Education at Ontong Java. *Amer. Anthrop.*, 33, 601–614.

PAIUTE (Harney Valley)

Whiting, B. B. 1950. Paiute sorcery. *Viking Fund Publ. Anthrop.*, no. 15.

——— Unpublished field notes.

°PALAUNG

Milne, L. 1924. *The home of an Eastern clan*. Oxford: Clarendon.

*PAPAGO

Densmore, F. 1929. Papago music. *Bull. Bur. Amer. Ethnol.*, no. 9.

Joseph, A., Spicer, R. B. and Chesky, J. 1949. *The desert people.* Chicago: Univ. of Chicago Press.

Underhill, R. M. 1939. Social organization of the Papago Indians. *Columbia Univ. Contrib. Anthrop.*, v. 30.

*PUKAPUKANS

Beaglehole, E. and Beaglehole, P. 1938. Ethnology of Pukapuka. *Bull. Bernice P. Bishop Mus.*, no. 150.

———— — ———— 1941. Personality development in Pukapukan children. In Spier, L., Hallowell, A. I., and Newman, S. S. (eds.), *Language, culture, and personality.* Menasha, Wis.: Sapir Memorial Publication Fund. Pp. 282–298.

*RIFFIANS

Coon, C. S. 1931. Tribes of the Rif. *Harvard African Studies*, v. 9.

Westermarck, E. 1926. *Ritual and belief in Morocco.* London: Macmillan.

*RWALA

Musil, A. 1928. *The manners and customs of the Rwala Bedouins.* New York: Czech Academy of Sciences and Arts and Charles R. Crane.

SAMOANS

Mead, M. 1928. *Coming of age in Samoa.* New York: Morrow.

———— 1930. Social organization of Manua. *Bull. Bernice P. Bishop Mus.*, no. 76.

*SANPOIL

Ray, V. F. 1933. *The Sanpoil and Nespelem.* Seattle: Univ. of Washington Press.

*SIRIONO

Holmberg, A. R. 1946. The Siriono. Unpublished Ph.D. thesis, Yale University.

———— 1950. *Nomads of the long bow.* Washington: U.S. Gov't. Print. Off.

SLAVE

Honigmann, J. J. 1946. Ethnography and acculturation of the Fort Nelson Slave. *Yale Univ. Publ. Anthrop.*, no. 33.

*TANALA

Linton, R. 1933. The Tanala. *Anthrop. Ser. Field Mus. Nat. Hist.*, v. 22.

———— 1939. The Tanala of Madagascar. In Kardiner, A., *The individual and his society.* New York: Columbia Univ. Press. Pp. 251–290.

*TAOS

Parsons, E. C. 1936. Taos Pueblo. *Gen. Ser. Anthrop.*, no. 2.

*TENINO

Murdock, G. P. and Whiting, J. W. M. Unpublished field notes.

*TETON

Erikson, E. 1939. Observations on Sioux education. *J. Psychol.*, 7, 101–156.

MacGregor, G. 1946. *Warriors without weapons.* Chicago: Univ. of Chicago Press.

*THONGA

Junod, H. A. 1927. *The Life of a South African tribe* (2d ed.). London: Macmillan.

*TIKOPIA

Firth, R. 1936. *We, the Tikopia.* London: Allen & Unwin.

*TIV

Akiga. 1939. *Akiga's story: The Tiv tribe as seen by one of its members.* London: Oxford Univ. Press.

*TROBRIANDERS

Malinowski, B. 1927. *Sex and repression in savage society.* New York: Harcourt, Brace.

———— 1929. *The sexual life of savages in northwestern Melanesia.* New York: Liveright.

*VENDA

Stayt, H. A. 1931. *The BaVenda.* London: Oxford Univ. Press.

*WAPISIANA

Farabee, W. C. 1918. The Central Arawaks. *Anthrop. Publ. Univ. Penna. Mus.*, 9, 13–131.

*WARRAU

Schomburgk, R. 1922. *Travels in British Guiana, 1840–44, vol. 1.* Georgetown, British Guiana: Daily Chronicle Office.

WESTERN APACHE

Goodwin, G. 1942. *The social organization of the Western Apache.* Chicago: Univ. of Chicago Press.

*WITOTO

Whiffen, T. 1915. *The North-West Amazons.* London: Constable.

*WOGEO

Hogbin, H. I. 1935. Sorcery and administration. *Oceania*, 6, 1–32.

———— 1943. A New Guinea infancy: From conception to weaning in Wogeo. *Oceania*, 13, 285–309.

———— 1946. A New Guinea childhood: From weaning till the eighth year in Wogeo. *Oceania*, 16, 275–296.

YAGUA

Fejos, P. 1943. Ethnography of the Yagua. *Viking Fund Publ. Anthrop.*, no. 1.

*YAKUT

Jochelson, W. 1934. The Yakut. *Anthrop. Pap. Amer. Mus. Nat. Hist.*, 33, 35–225.

Seroshevskii, V. L. 1896. *Yakuty.* St. Petersburg.

*YUKAGHIR

Jochelson, W. 1926. The Yukaghir and the Yukaghirized Tungus. *Mem. Amer. Mus. Nat. Hist.*, v. 13.

*YUNGAR

Grey, G. 1841. *Journals of two expeditions of discovery in Northwest and Western Australia.* London.

Nind, S. 1832. Description of the natives of King George's Sound (Swan River Colony) and adjoining country. *J. Roy. Geograph. Soc.*, 1, 21–51.

*ZUNI

Benedict, R. 1934. *Patterns of culture.* Boston: Houghton Mifflin.

Goldfrank, E. S. 1945. Socialization, personality, and the structure of Pueblo society (with particular reference to Hopi and Zuni). *Amer. Anthrop.*, 47, 516–539.

Parsons, E. C. 1917. Notes on Zuni. *Mem. Amer. Anthrop. Assoc.*, no. 4, 151–327.

Stevenson, M. C. 1901–02. The Zuni Indians: Their mythology, esoteric fraternities and ceremonies. *Ann. Rep. Bur. Amer. Ethnol.*, 23, 13–608.

APPENDIX

IN THIS APPENDIX are presented the major data, as analyzed by our judges, which were utilized in our study. Listed here are all the ratings or judgments used for the tests of our main hypotheses, with the following exceptions:

1. Ratings of child training practices which did not meet our intermediate criterion of confidence (cf. p. 59) are omitted. Such ratings were used only to illustrate the effect of including judgments of low reliability (in Chapter 9); we feel they probably have no other use to justify their inclusion here.

2. Where ratings and rankings are both available, we present here only the ratings. We will be glad to supply the rankings to any reader who may wish them.

3. Most of the variables used only in Chapter 11 are not included here, as they are presented in the tables in that chapter for the societies for which the index of guilt is available. Ages at beginning of socialization are not presented in tables, however, and are included here.

The appendix is for convenience broken into two halves, one dealing with child training practices and one dealing with customs relating to illness.

CHILD TRAINING PRACTICES

The variables of child training practices are designated by capital letters, as follows.

Ratings of initial satisfaction potential (*described on pp. 50–52*)

    A. Oral satisfaction potential

    B. Anal satisfaction potential

    C. Sexual satisfaction potential

    D. Dependence satisfaction potential

    E. Aggression satisfaction potential

        (For variables A through E the plain type means that all three judges were confident of their ratings; italics mean that the ratings reached our intermediate criterion of confidence; and a dash means that ratings were not made or did not reach our intermediate criterion of confidence.)

F. Average satisfaction potential (i.e., average of variables A through E)

(For variable F the plain type means that the value is based on confident judgments for all 5 variables; italics mean that it is based on judgments of at least intermediate confidence for all 5 variables.)

Ratings of socialization anxiety (described on pp. 52–55)

G. Oral socialization anxiety
H. Anal socialization anxiety
I. Sexual socialization anxiety
J. Dependence socialization anxiety
K. Aggression socialization anxiety

(For code for these variables see note above under variable E.)

L. Average socialization anxiety

(For code for this variable see note above under variable F.)

Estimated age at beginning of serious socialization (described on pp. 55–56)

M. Age at weaning
N. Age at toilet training
Q. Age at beginning of modesty training
P. Age at beginning of training in heterosexual play inhibition
Q. Age at beginning of independence training

(For variables M through Q no distinction is made between the few confident judgments and the greater number which meet only the intermediate criterion of confidence.)

CUSTOMS RELATING TO ILLNESS

Customs relating to illness are designated by small letters, as follows.

Explanations of illness (defined on pp. 150–153)

a. Oral explanations
b. Anal explanations
c. Sexual explanations
d. Dependence explanations
e. Aggression explanations

(For variables a through e, + means presence and 0 means absence, as defined on p. 154.)

Performance therapies (defined on pp. 194–197)

f. Oral performance therapy
g. Anal performance therapy

h. Sexual performance therapy
i. Dependence performance therapy
j. Aggression performance therapy
(For variables f through j, + means presence and 0 means absence, as defined on pp. 193–197. A dash means that the culture failed to be rated at all by one judge on therapy.)

Avoidance therapies (defined on pp. 209–210)

k. Oral avoidance therapies
l. Anal avoidance therapies
m. Sexual avoidance therapies
n. Dependence avoidance therapies
o. Aggression avoidance therapies
(For variables k through o, + means presence and 0 means absence, as defined on p. 210. A dash means that the culture failed to be rated at all by one judge on therapy.)

Fear of others (defined on pp. 263–265 and 286)

p. Fear of human beings
q. Fear of spirits
r. Over-all fear of others
s. Fear of ghosts
t. Fear of animal spirits
(For variables p through t the entry is the sum of ratings by two judges, each on a scale from 0 to 6.)

RATINGS OF CHILD TRAINING PRACTICES

	A	B	C	D	E	F	G	H	I	J	K	L	M	N	O	P	Q
Abipone	—	—	6	14	—	—	—	—	14	14	7	11	4.0	—	—	—	—
Ainu	13	16	17	9	6	12	10	9	7	14	16	13	2.3	—	7.0	—	4.0
Alorese	9	16	13	12	14	13	14	9	13	15	16	13	—	1.8	5.3	6.5	2.1
Andamanese	16	—	12	17	9	—	8	—	10	11	9	12	—	—	—	—	—
Arapesh	16	9	12	18	9	13	10	13	16	7	15	15	3.3	—	4.3	6.3	4.3
Ashanti	13	10	10	12	9	11	12	18	14	14	16	13	—	—	—	—	—
Azande	16	10	8	18	11	13	11	11	13	16	16	12	3.5	—	—	—	5.3
Baiga	14	13	18	13	11	14	15	12	8	14	11	11	2.3	3.0	—	10.0	—
Balinese	13	12	17	13	15	14	10	11	7	15	11	9	2.7	4.7	—	10.7	2.5
Bena	13	16	11	15	11	13	8	6	9	10	12	13	1.8	0.8	—	—	4.0
Chagga	14	6	14	16	11	12	14	15	14	10	12	14	2.7	—	—	11.7	4.0
Chamorro	11	9	11	17	8	11	12	15	15	9	18	9	0.9	—	—	—	3.7
Chenchu	18	13	12	15	12	14	8	8	10	12	9	—	5.7	—	—	—	3.0
Chewa	—	—	17	—	—	—	—	—	9	—	—	—	—	—	8.0	—	—
Chiricahua	14	12	9	13	7	11	10	12	17	14	18	14	2.0	—	3.7	6.7	4.0
Comanche	16	14	16	16	16	16	10	10	6	11	7	9	1.5	1.2	—	—	2.7
Copper Eskimo	16	—	—	15	14	—	9	—	—	12	9	13	3.0	—	—	—	—
Dahomeans	11	8	11	15	10	11	13	17	13	10	13	13	2.5	2.0	6.0	8.3	5.0
Dobuans	10	9	10	11	9	10	16	15	15	17	15	16	—	—	3.2	—	4.0
Dusun	11	—	—	16	16	—	—	—	—	14	5	—	—	—	11.0	—	4.5
Flathead	16	12	10	17	—	—	7	12	12	9	—	12	3.2	—	—	—	—
Hopi	14	12	11	14	5	11	10	11	12	10	18	—	2.0	1.5	—	7.7	2.7
Ifugao	16	—	14	14	12	—	9	—	6	13	12	—	—	—	—	—	5.0
Jivaro	12	—	—	—	9	—	10	—	—	—	17	—	2.5	—	—	—	—

RATINGS OF CHILD TRAINING PRACTICES (continued)

	A	B	C	D	E	F	G	H	I	J	K	L	M	N	O	P	Q
Kazak	12										17						
Kiwai	18	11		10	10		11				10	11	3.5			9.0	6.0
Kurtatchi	15	14	12	16	13	14	6	10	18	10	14	14	1.8				3.3
Kutenai	13	14	9	11	12	12	15	11	13	16	16	12	2.0	1.5			2.8
Kwakiutl	16	14	11	14	9	12	11	6	12	17	11	13	2.5	3.0			2.8
Kwoma	15	14	11	19	13	15	15	8	15	16	12	11	2.0				
Lakher	14	12	12	14	14	13	10	13	9	13	12		2.0				
Lamba	15		15		12		13		8				2.0				
Lapp	15			16			13				17	11	2.0				4.0
Lepcha	15	10	17	14	7	13	12	9	6	11	10	12	2.8	2.2	6.7	10.7	4.5
Lesu	12	13	18	16	10	14	13	15	9	15			2.2	2.0		11.0	2.5
Malekula	16		10	14			7			14	7		2.0				2.7
Manus	16	9	10	12	17	13	11	15	16	11	14	12	2.5	1.2		6.5	3.0
Maori	11	14	9	16	13	13	12	10	8	15	8	12	1.3	2.2			4.3
Marquesans	6	13	19	12	11	12	17	10	4	12	9	10	0.5	1.0	10.0		
Marshallese	13		15	13	14				6	11	8		3.0				
Masai	11		15		13		13		8		7						
Murngin	15		16	15	16				7	12							
Nauru	12			14	8		10		11	15							2.2
Navaho	16	14	10	16	10	13	14	11	14	15	11	13	2.0	2.2	3.0		
Omaha	13				7		13				13	12	2.5				4.0
Ontong-Javanese	15	10	8	16	12	12	6	16	14	11	12	13	3.0				
Paiute	16	15	15	16	6	14	9	10	14	10	21			1.2	8.5		
Palaung	12			16			9			11	17						

	A	B	C	D	E	F	G	H	I	J	K	L	M	N	O	P	Q
Papago	16	13	9	18	9	13	7	9	13	9	15	11	2.3	1.9	3.7	—	3.7
Pukapukans	15	12	18	15	13	15	12	13	5	14	12	11	1.5	1.7	—	—	2.1
Riffians	10	—	—	13	11	—	—	—	15	—	—	14	—	—	—	—	—
Rwala	14	13	9	12	11	11	12	11	16	16	14	14	2.5	—	6.5	8.0	2.8
Samoans	15	12	11	15	13	12	12	9	13	13	14	12	—	—	—	—	3.3
Sanpoil	17	7	12	17	8	11	11	14	15	13	14	13	2.3	2.8	—	7.0	—
Siriono	16	16	20	15	17	17	10	6	5	14	8	9	2.0	1.7	—	—	3.7
Slave	16	13	12	16	10	13	8	12	11	8	14	11	1.7	0.3	4.5	—	—
Tanala	16	3	7	14	9	10	10	18	13	11	13	13	—	—	—	—	3.7
Taos	10	—	—	15	—	—	15	—	—	—	17	—	—	—	—	—	—
Tenino	15	14	11	15	12	13	10	11	14	15	13	13	2.0	2.2	6.0	7.5	6.0
Teton	16	14	11	17	14	14	8	8	12	12	14	11	2.7	2.2	—	6.3	3.5
Thonga	16	11	10	14	15	13	15	13	11	15	12	13	2.6	—	—	—	3.3
Tikopia	12	13	14	12	11	12	6	8	6	9	10	8	—	—	5.0	—	2.7
Tiv	—	—	13	—	15	—	—	—	14	—	12	—	—	—	—	—	—
Trobrianders	15	11	18	15	12	14	12	13	9	13	8	11	2.0	—	—	10.0	2.7
Venda	16	12	9	15	11	13	7	10	12	11	15	11	3.0	—	—	—	—
Wapisiana	16	—	7	16	—	—	—	17	17	—	—	—	3.2	—	—	—	—
Warrau	16	—	—	—	—	—	7	—	—	—	—	—	3.0	—	—	—	—
Western Apache	12	12	9	16	11	12	13	8	16	13	13	13	1.3	2.7	1.3	—	4.3
Witoto	17	—	11	14	—	—	8	—	11	12	—	—	—	—	—	—	—
Wogeo	15	13	12	17	12	14	7	10	16	9	11	11	2.8	2.0	7.3	—	3.8
Yagua	13	16	13	15	13	14	8	8	10	10	11	9	1.8	—	—	—	—
Yakut	13	13	14	11	10	12	11	8	8	12	13	10	3.3	—	—	—	2.0
Yukaghir	17	11	—	—	—	—	8	10	—	—	—	—	—	—	—	—	—
Yungar	18	—	—	—	16	—	7	—	—	—	11	—	3.5	—	—	—	—
Zuni	—	—	—	—	9	—	—	—	—	—	15	—	—	—	—	—	—

RATINGS OF CUSTOMS RELATED TO ILLNESS

	a	b	c	d	e	f	g	h	i	j	k	l	m	n	o	p	q	r	s	t
Abipone	o	o	o	o	o	+	+	o	o	o	+	+	o	o	o	9	3	12	3	0
Ainu	+	+	o	+	o	+	+	o	+	+	+	+	o	o	o	6	10	16	5	9
Alorese	+	+	+	+	+	o	o	o	o	o	+	+	o	o	+	5	9	14	9	0
Andamanese	+	o	o	o	o	+	+	o	o	+	+	+	o	+	+	4	10	14	10	0
Arapesh	o	+	+	o	o	o	o	o	o	o	+	+	o	o	o	10	8	18	8	3
Ashanti	o	+	o	o	o	o	o	o	o	o	+	o	o	o	o	5	8	13	5	0
Azande	|	|	|	|	|	|	|	|	|	|	|	|	|	|	|	10	5	15	0	3
Baiga	o	o	+	+	+	+	+	o	o	+	+	+	o	+	o	10	8	18	7	3
Balinese	+	+	+	o	+	+	o	+	+	+	o	+	o	o	+	4	9	13	3	3
Bena	o	o	o	+	o	+	o	o	+	o	o	+	o	+	+	7	8	15	7	0
Chagga	+	+	o	o	o	+	o	o	o	+	+	o	o	+	o	9	9	18	9	0
Chamorro	+	+	o	o	o	+	o	o	+	+	+	+	o	o	+	6	10	16	4	0
Chenchu	o	+	o	+	+	+	+	o	+	o	+	+	o	o	+	2	8	10	8	3
Chewa	o	o	o	+	o	+	o	o	o	o	+	o	o	o	+	8	9	17	8	10
Chiricahua	|	|	|	|	|	|	|	|	|	|	|	|	|	|	|	9	10	19	8	8
Comanche	+	o	+	+	o	+	o	o	+	+	+	o	o	o	o	5	8	13	2	0
Copper Eskimo	+	o	+	o	+	o	o	o	o	+	o	o	o	o	o	7	8	15	8	5
Dahomeans	+	+	o	+	o	+	o	o	o	+	+	o	o	+	+	6	7	13	7	9
Dobuans	o	o	o	o	o	+	o	o	+	o	+	+	+	o	+	8	9	17	0	0
Dusun	o	o	+	o	o	o	o	o	o	+	o	+	o	o	o	0	9	9	8	0
Flathead	o	o	o	+	+	+	o	o	+	o	o	+	o	+	+	0	4	4	0	0
Hopi	o	+	o	+	+	+	+	o	o	o	+	+	+	o	o	8	9	17	0	8
Ifugao	+	o	o	o	+	o	o	o	+	o	+	o	+	o	o	8	10	18	8	0
Jivaro	+	o	o	o	+	+	+	o	o	+	o	+	+	+	+	10	9	19	4	7

	a	b	c	d	e	f	g	h	i	j	k	l	m	n	o	p	q	r	s	t
Kazak	o	o	o	o	o	+	o	o	+	+	o	+	o	o	+	0	8	8	0	3
Kiwai	o	+	+	o	o	o	o	+	o	o	+	+	+	+	o	9	9	18	4	6
Kurtatchi	+	+	+	o	o	+	o	o	+	o	+	o	o	o	o	9	6	15	4	0
Kutenai	o	o	o	o	o																					6	0	6	0	0
Kwakiutl	+	+	+	o	o	+	+	o	+	+	+	+	o	+	+	10	8	18	8	3
Kwoma	+	+	+	+	+	+	o	o	o	+	+	+	+	o	o	10	4	14	4	2
Lakher	o	o	o	o	+	+	o	o	o	o	+	o	o	+	+	7	9	16	0	8
Lamba	+	+	+	+	+	+	o	o	o	+	+	+	o	+	+	4	10	14	9	0
Lapp	o	o	o	+	+	+	+	o	+	+	+	+	o	o	+	10	9	19	8	4
Lepcha	+	+	+	+	+	+	o	o	+	+	+	+	o	o	o	7	5	12	3	2
Lesu	+	+	o	+	o	o	+	o	+	+	+	+	+	+	o	9	3	12	3	0
Malekula	+	+	+	o	+	o	o	o	+	o	o	o	+	o	+	10	7	17	7	0
Manus	+	+	+	o	o	+	o	o	+	o	+	+	+	o	o	4	11	15	11	0
Maori	+	o	o	+	+	o	+	o	+	+	o	+	o	+	o	9	10	19	9	7
Marquesans	+	o	o	+	o	+	o	+	o	o	+	o	o	o	o	7	10	17	8	0
Marshallese	o	o	o	+	o	o	+	o	+	+	+	+	+	+	o	7	9	16	9	0
Masai	+	+	o	+	o	+	+	o	o	o	+	+	o	+	o	6	3	9	1	0
Murngin	o	+	+	+	+	+	+	o	o	+	o	+	o	o	o	10	7	17	7	0
Nauru	o	o	o	o	o	o	o	o	o	o	+	+	o	o	o	9	8	17	8	3
Navaho	+	+	+	o	+	+	+	o	o	+	+	+	+	+	+	7	10	17	9	0
Omaha	+	o	o	o	+	o	+	o	+	o	+	+	o	+	+	10	7	17	7	0
Ontong-Javanese	o	o	o	o	o	o	o	o	o	+	o	+	o	+	o	6	10	16	10	10
Paiute	o	o	o	o	+	+	o	o	+	+	o	+	o	+	o	11	10	21	8	4
Palaung	o	+	+	+	+																					8	10	18	0	9
Papago	o	o	+	o	+	+	+	o	o	o	+	o	o	o	+	4	9	13	8	0
Pukapukans	+	o	+	+	+	+	+	o	+	+	+	+	o	o	o	6	8	14	8	0

345

	a	b	c	d	e	f	g	h	i	j	k	l	m	n	o	p	q	r	s	t
Riffians	+	+	+	+	+	+	0	+	0	+	0	0	+	0	0	9	10	19	0	4
Rwala	0	+	+	+	0	+	+	0	+	+	0	0	+	+	0	7	8	15	0	0
Samoans	0	0	0	0	+	−	−	−	−	−	−	−	−	−	+	5	8	13	8	0
Sanpoil	0	0	0	+	+	+	+	0	0	+	+	+	0	0	−	9	9	18	3	7
Siriono	+	0	0	+	0	+	0	0	0	+	0	0	0	+	0	2	10	12	3	3
Slave	0	0	0	0	+	+	0	0	0	0	+	0	0	+	0	8	4	12	0	4
Tanala	0	0	0	+	0	+	0	0	0	+	0	0	0	+	0	7	9	16	9	0
Taos	0	+	0	0	+	+	0	0	+	+	0	+	0	0	+	10	8	18	0	4
Tenino	0	0	0	+	0	+	0	0	0	0	+	0	0	0	+	8	8	16	0	4
Teton	0	0	0	0	+	+	0	0	+	0	0	0	0	0	0	0	10	10	3	0
Thonga	0	0	+	+	0	+	+	0	0	+	+	+	+	0	+	7	7	14	6	0
Tikopia	0	0	0	+	0	0	0	0	+	+	+	+	0	0	0	5	8	13	0	4
Tiv	+	0	0	0	0	−	−	−	−	−	0	−	−	−	+	9	10	19	0	4
Trobrianders	0	+	+	+	0	0	0	0	0	0	0	0	0	0	−	10	9	19	7	4
Venda	0	+	0	+	0	−	−	−	−	−	−	−	−	−	0	9	7	16	0	4
Wapisiana	0	0	0	+	0	0	0	0	+	0	0	0	0	−	−	10	9	19	0	0
Warrau	0	0	0	0	0	−	0	0	+	0	+	0	+	+	−	3	8	11	4	0
Western Apache	0	0	+	0	0	0	+	0	+	+	0	0	+	+	+	8	9	17	7	5
Witoto	+	0	0	+	+	+	0	0	0	0	+	0	0	+	0	10	9	19	6	3
Wogeo	0	0	0	0	0	0	0	0	0	0	0	0	0	0	0	10	6	16	0	0
Yagua	0	0	0	0	0	0	0	0	+	+	0	0	0	0	0	11	1	12	5	0
Yakut	0	0	0	+	+	0	−	0	−	−	−	−	−	0	0	6	10	16	3	3
Yukaghir	+	0	0	+	+	−	0	−	−	−	−	−	−	−	+	4	10	14	0	0
Yungar	0	0	0	0	0	−	0	0	0	0	0	0	0	0	−	10	8	18	4	4
Zuni	+	0	0	0	+	+	0	0	+	0	+	+	0	+	0	10	4	14	4	0

346

NAME INDEX

Abraham, K., 142
Alexander, F., 219
Allport, G. W., 9

Baldwin, A. L., 9
Barry, H., III., 323
Beach, F. A., 223
Beaglehole, E., 80, 93
Beaglehole, P., 80, 93
Benedict, R., 2, 6, 198
Blackwood, B., 72, 88
Brown, J. S., 147, 284, 294
Bush, R. R., 292
Butler, S., 227

Carl, L. J., 240
Cattell, R. B., 11
Cowles, J. T., 136

Davis, W. A., 66, 67, 70, 77, 84, 102–104, 141
Dennis, W., 83, 84
Dollard, J., v, 15, 20, 135, 225, 235, 255, 274, 277, 292
Doob, L. W., v, 235, 274, 292
Driver, H. E., 39
DuBois, C., 79, 88, 90, 91
Dyk, W., 4

Edwards, A. L., 126, 165
Eggan, D., 13
Elwin, V., 81
Erikson, E. H., 13

Faigin, H., 238, 246
Farabee, W. C., 81
Farber, I. E., 147, 284, 294
Fenichel, O., 131–135, 219
Feshbach, S., 275
Firth, R., 81
Ford, C. S., vi, 4, 40, 72, 223
Freud, S., 28, 224–227, 269–271
Friedman, G. A., 323

Gesell, A., 55
Gillin, J. P., 17, 31
Ginsberg, M., 39
Glenn, H., vi
Goodwin, G., 85
Gorer, G., 5, 6, 96, 97, 229
Guthrie, E. R., 20

Hallowell, A. I., 4
Havighurst, R. J., 66, 67, 70, 77, 84, 102–104, 141
Henry, W. E., 4
Herskovits, M. J., 75
Hobhouse, L. T., 39
Hollenberg, E., 238, 246, 294
Holmberg, A. R., 73, 75, 101, 157
Horney, K., 219
Horton, D., 11, 40
Howard, B. D., 93
Hull, C. L., v, 18, 20, 30, 137, 141, 266, 289–293, 295

Ilg, F. L., 55

SUBJECT INDEX

Aggression
  anxiety: fixation of, 144, 161–168, 178, 186–189, 202–205, 209, 210; relation to fear of others, 273–304; relation to guilt, 235–237
  explanations of illness, 153
  satisfaction: fixation of, 144, 167, 168, 197, 198, 200, 202–204, 209, 210; relation to fear of others, 282, 283
  therapeutic practices, 197, 198, 209, 210
  training: examples of, 98–105; relation to other systems, 107–118
Ainu, 91, 93, 234, 239, 245, 251
Alorese, 79, 88, 90, 156, 158–161, 234, 239, 245, 249, 251
American, middle-class, 66, 67, 70, 71, 73, 74, 77, 79, 80, 84–86, 88, 91, 93, 94, 97, 99, 102–104, 114, 115, 320; Negro, 219
Anal
  anxiety: fixation of, 143, 158, 159, 162–168, 178, 186–189, 202–204, 209, 210; relation to fear of others, 281; relation to guilt, 236
  explanations of illness, 150, 151
  satisfaction: fixation of, 143, 167, 168, 195, 200, 202–204, 209, 210; relation to fear of others, 282, 283

therapeutic practices, 195, 209
training: age of, related to guilt, 256; examples of, 73–77; relation to other systems, 107–118
Anxiety: initial, 169, 282, 283; socialization, 47, 52–55, 68, 169, 170, 209–211, 213–215, 233–237, 265–269, 281; see also Aggression anxiety, Anal anxiety, Dependence anxiety, Oral anxiety, Sex anxiety
Arapesh, 82, 95, 96, 156, 159–161, 234, 239, 245, 249, 251
Ashanti, 104
Azande, 160, 234, 239, 245, 249, 251

Baiga, 41, 72, 81, 156, 159, 196
Balinese, 156, 158, 160
Behavior systems, definition of, 45, 46; interrelations of, 107–118; see Aggression, Anal, Dependence, Oral, Sex
Behavior theory, 14, 15, 50–53, 135–139, 213–216, 224–227
Belief, 28, 193, 206, 207
Bena, 40, 41, 74, 156, 160, 234, 239, 245, 249, 251

Cause and effect, direction of, 187–190, 309, 318, 319
Chagga, 74, 82, 156, 158–161, 234, 239, 245, 249, 251

THE YALE PAPERBOUNDS